INTRODUCTION TO SOCIOLOGY

INTRODUCTION TO SOCIOLOGY

Dr. S.S. Ralhan
Dr. S.R. Lambat

Commonwealth

Introduction to Sociology

Edition : 2015

ISBN 81-311-0037-5

Published by :
COMMONWEALTH PUBLISHERS PVT. LTD.
4831/24, Prahlad Street,
Ansari Road, Darya Ganj,
New Delhi - 110002
Ph. : 23272541, 23257835
Fax : 91- 011- 23257835
e-mail : commonwealthbooks@gmail.com

Laser Typesetting by :
Arjun Computers
Delhi - 110051

Printed at :
Roshan Offset Printers
Delhi

PREFACE

A sociologist looking at the same college classroom would analyse it some what differently, focusing on social relationships, rather than on individual behaviour or the specific course content. Some of the things a sociologist might focus on would be power relations, rules of conduct, and class characteristics.

The purpose of this book is to present the material in a very lucid and clear way. The book is equally good and of interest to the general reader who are more conscious about the healthy change in social life instead of to much coverage of the subject.

It is hoped the book will be found to be of interest to beginners and the general public alike.

Dr. S.S. Ralhan
Dr. S.R. Lambat

CONTENTS

	Preface	*v*
Chapter		Pages
1.	The Sociological Eye	1
2.	Science and Methods in Sociology	19
3.	The Structure of Society	44
4.	Culture	69
5.	Socialisation	98
6.	Sex Roles	132
7.	Social Groups	168
8.	Social Stratification	195
9.	Racial and Ethnic Minorities	237
10.	Organisation and Bureaucracy	281
11.	Collective Behaviour	308
	Bibliography	344

1

THE SOCIOLOGICAL EYE

USING THE SOCIOLOGICAL PERSPECTIVE

Before starting a new course, students may know who is teaching it and what other students have said about the instructor and the subject. During the first class they will be interested in learning who else is in the class, what the professor looks and sounds like, what is on the reading list, how many papers are required, and whether and when exams are given. Throughout the course, students will assess the lecturer's knowledge, personality, and skill as an instructor. In short, a student's evaluation of a class is based on a *personal* reaction to a particular professor and subject.

A sociologist looking at the same college classroom would analyse it somewhat differently, focusing on social relationships, rather than on individual behaviour or the specific course content. Some of the things a sociologist might focus on would be power relations, rules of conduct, and class characteristics.

There is an unequal distribution of power in the classroom: the teacher has control over the topics of conversation and directs the flow of class discussion by determining who will talk when. The teacher also has the ultimate power to determine grades. There are many social supports for this unequal distribution of power. The instructor gets paid for being in the classroom, while the students must pay. The teacher stands at the front of the group and can fully observe each of the students, while the students line up in rows and can only make direct contact with a limited number of other students. The instructor has access to each student's work and thereby has the full power of comparison and judgment, while each student sees only his or her own work.

Teachers have a variety of institutional supports at their command: they can delay returning reserve books to the library without paying a fine; they can examine each student's academic record; and they can have any student physically expelled from the classroom. All of these factors contribute to a teacher's power. On the other hand, the teacher's power is not absolute. If the students refuse to come to class, refuse to pay attention in class, refuse to do the work, or complain to the administration about the quality of teaching, the teacher's power will be curtailed. These power relations in the classroom operate without regard to any particular student or any particular teacher. The classroom has a sociological power structure all its own, which can be analysed in its own right without consideration for individual habits, histories, personality traits, or desires.

The sociologist will also analyse the rules of conduct in a classroom. These are the unspoken rules and expectations that every one more or less follows. For example, people rarely rip off their clothes during class time; everyone shows up pretty much on time; the teacher talks about the intended course material and not about his or her hobbies or sports interests; people take turns when they speak and do not speak all at once; everyone (except perhaps the teacher) sits down during the class time; the class period has a designated beginning and ending which are observed. These rules, again, be long to the accepted order of things in the classroom and can be discussed without any reference whatsoever to particular students or particular teachers.

As a unit the class has characteristics of its own, which are not properties of any individual in the class. For example, the class meets in a certain room; is of a certain size; has a specific average age of students; has a specific number of men and women in it; has a specific number of science majors, upper and lower classmen; and so on. Each of these characteristics belongs to the *class* as a whole; they are not the characteristics of each individual in that class.

All of these observations about the college classroom are sociological observations. They concern patterns and regularities that will occur regardless of the individuals who occupy that classroom. The sociological perspective clearly differs from other perspectives one might use to observe a classroom. An architect, for example, might pay attention to the size of the space, the comfort of the furniture, the arrangement of the desks in relation to the space, the quality of the acoustics. A doctor might look at the physical condition of class members, including skin tone, eye brightness, manifestations of fever or disability. And a painter or photographer might notice the quality of the light in the room and how it affects shadows and contours, the variety of poses assumed by class members, the differences in anatomy, the colours of students' clothing.

Whenever we attempt to make sense of the world around us we must make choices about what details we will attend to in constructing our meanings. The *sociological perspective* trains us to pay attention to those details that are regular and patterned, details that are not unique to a particular situation or to particular people in those situations.

Social Facts

For those of us brought up to believe in our individual worth and uniqueness it is sometimes difficult, if not infuriating, to hear ourselves talked about as if our individual histories, biographies, and feelings were of no consequence at all. Since all of us feel ourselves to be unique and special, we may resent being chucked into categories for the convenience of a sociologist. But the truth of the matter is we all use categories and abstractions all the time. How often have you used or heard the terms "the older generation," "hippies," "dope addicts" "feminists," "blacks," "jocks," "wasps"? These are all categories of people who have something in common, but who as individuals have a great deal that is unique. And yet, the terms are useful for explaining and giving meaning to the things in the world which we try to understand.

Despite our resistances to categorisation, there are certain things about human social life that simply cannot be explained by reference to individual feelings or behaviour. Emile Durkheim, a pioneering French sociologist of the nineteenth century, pinned down this truth when he posited the existence of something called a *social fact,* which is an entity in its own right, different from the elements (or individuals) of which it is composed (Durkheim, 1938) Durkheim compared the uniqueness of the social fact to the uniqueness of the human body: although the human body is made up of cells, there would be no way of discovering the properties or capacities of the human body by examining only its separate cells. In short, the whole is greater than the sum of its parts. "It is very certain that there are in the living cell only molecules of crude matter. But those molecules are in contact with one another, and this association is the cause of the new phenomena which characterise life, the very germ of which cannot possibly be found in any of the separate elements" (Durkheim, 1938).

The same part-whole relationship is true for individuals and social facts. There are properties of social life that simply cannot be explained by reference to the activities, sensibilities, or characteristics of any individual. We need only look at our own lives to realise how inescapable this conclusion is. For example, consider a few social facts that make modern urban life less than pleasant - crime rates and bureaucratic red tape.

Crime Rates - When we walk down a big city street late at night most of us are, to say the least, wary. Is this wariness purely a psychological trait of ours? Can we explain it by exploring our childhood experiences? Not likely. Our wariness stems from the social fact of crime rates. We know that, statistically, street crimes occur most often at night in urban areas. Our private fears as we hasten down the street are attributable not to psychological quirks but to social facts. Even the crime rates themselves, although composed of the sum of individual acts, are social realities that surpass the activities of any one criminal. If we compare the rates of crime in different localities at different hours of the day, we find that crime rates are highest in urban areas at night. Thus, our fear as we walk down a deserted city street after dark is not prompted by our knowledge of individual criminals nor by our own psychological obsessions, but rather by our knowledge of a social fact - a crime rate - which surpasses both us as individuals and criminals as individuals.

Red Tape - When we find ourselves entangled with large bureaucratic organisations, such as government agencies, and we encounter the frustrations of "red tape run-around," are those frustrations attributable to our own inabilities to get things done quickly? Are they the fault of the receptionists and secretaries who shuttle us around with triplicate forms? The frustrations are, of course, the fault of neither. Large organisations require complicated record-keep ing procedures, ordered hierarchies, and separate departments simply by virtue of their size. The unpleasantness of bureaucratic procedures can be explained only by a social fact - the size of the organisation. Since it is true that the larger an organisation the more division of labour there will be, the more clear-cut the hierarchy will be, and the more divisions and departments there will be (Blau and Meyer, 1971), we can understand our private experiences of frustration only in terms of a nonpersonal reality. The size of an organisation is a property of that organisation and not of any of the individuals involved in it, and therefore we must look to a social reality to explain a very individual experience. These two examples suggest that Durkheim was right: "Society is not a mere sum of individuals. Rather, the system formed by their association represents a specific reality which has its own characteristics" (Durkheim, 1938).

But the existence of social facts that have characteristics and properties of their own is not the only reason for adopting the sociological perspective. There is another even more compelling reason. Every experience that a human being undergoes, no matter how private it may seem, is somehow touched and shaped by social forces that are not of that person's making. While this statement may seem exaggerated and overly dramatic, by examining a few of our most private experiences we can see just how important social conditions are in determining the course of our inner lives.

Being Sick - Surely, it would seem, being sick is an entirely private experience. When we are lying in bed with fever, aches, and pains, absorbed in our own personal miseries, how can there be any social forces at work on us? There can be and there are. In the first place, how do we know that what we are feeling is sickness? In some societies fever, aches, and pain are symptoms of visitations from spirits. The individual plagued with these discomforts is not treated as a sick person but as a person "possessed". In our society, however, we treat these symptoms as manifestations of treatable diseases, When we experience these symptoms we have learned from our culture to call ourselves sick. There are some maladies which may be just as uncomfortable as flu symptoms - such as a pulled muscle, a broken finger, a poison ivy rash - but we do not call them sicknesses. Thus, the very definition of what is "sick" is something we have learned from our social world; it is not a property of the physical discomfort itself.

The society we live in also has a set of widely understood rules about how we behave when we are sick. For certain illnesses we are entitled to malinger in bed, free from all obligations that might sap our strength. For others, we are expected to continue our daily round of activities. Thus, if your sociology lecturer did not show up for a scheduled class one day and sent word that he or she was absent because of a painful stubbed toe or an infected hangnail, class members would be rightfully indignant at the lecturer's irresponsibility ("rightfully" because we have all learned that these are not debilitating illnesses). On the other hand, if the lecturer showed up for class despite a raging fever and headache, he or she would have been responsible beyond the call of duty, that is, beyond the expectations of our society about sickness behaviour (Jaco, 1972).

Rules about behaviour during illness govern not only how much activity the sick person is excused from, but also how the sick person is to conduct his or her recovery In our society a sick person who is not terminally ill has an obligation to behave in a way that will lead to full recovery. He or she is expected to follow medical instructions concerning medication, rest, exercise, and interaction with others. An individual who does not follow these instructions, and thereby prolongs the illness, is termed "a malingerer," "an attention seeker," "a self-destructive person," or a downright "burden". When we are sick we take on a very specific role, that of a "sick person," and thereby incur a set of obligations and rights that have been carefully defined for us by our society's "sickness rules".

The sickness rules also tell us who is qualified to heal us. In American society we are expected to be healed by a qualified medical doctor. We do not go to medicine men, to witch doctors, to spiritual exorcists, or to mediums for cures (as is done in other societies) but we go to a man or woman who has had a certain amount of certified education and training and who the society says is qualified to perform healing practices.

Thus, being sick is far from a purely private experience. While, again, there is a great deal of room within the confines of the sick role for individual performances, the general outline of the role is *socially* and not individually defined.

Suicide One **-** One final example, involving the seemingly most private act of all, should convince us that no crevice of our inner lives is unaffected by social forces. From studies of rates of suicide among different groups in the population and among populations in different nations, it has been discovered that certain social factors influence an individual's chances for self-destruction (Durkheim, 1951). Suicide rates are higher for single people than for married people, higher during periods of economic inflation or depression than during periods of economic stability, higher among urbanites than rural citizens. In fact, certain social conditions that have nothing to do with the individuals who are the subjects of their results operate to create "suicide currents" within a population, and these currents "are just as real and just as much external to the individual as are the physical and biological forces that produce death by disease" (Barnes, 1948, p. 510). Thus, even those lonely moments of self-obliteration may have their roots in the larger context of the social order.

If, then, we recognise that individual experiences can only be understood with reference to larger social forces, how are we to go about understanding those forces? How, in short, are we to *do* sociology?

THE DEVELOPMENT OF SOCIOLOGY

The history of doing sociology in a systematic, recognisable manner is a very short one. Although attempts to develop patterned social codes to enhance the social order date back to 2000 B.C., it was not until the end of the eighteenth century that social philosophy (Philosophical *ideas* about how the world does or might run) gave way to social science (systematic *studies* of how the world does, in fact, run). The roots of the scientific approach to the study of society were established early in the seventeenth century with the arrival of the Age of Reason, when men like Bacon and Descartes argued that observation, experimentation, and reason must replace philosophy, religion, and moral musings. But it was not until the French philosopher Henri de Saint-Simon (1760 - 1825) imagined a "political science" that the discipline as we now know it achieved a recognisable form (Saint-Simon, 1964). When Saint-Simon's student and colleague Auguste Comte changed the name of the new approach to *sociology,* the sociological enterprise was officially underway. Comte theorised that human intellectual development was an evolutionary process based on scientific progress. He believed that positivism - the use of experimentation and observation - was crucial for encouraging and continuing the natural process of progress. If human beings were to create a more satisfying social world, they would have to encourage the natural process of progress toward that goal through the exercise of scientific discipline (Comte, 1915).

Once sociology had been given an official baptism by Saint-Simon and Comte, the science of society became a tool for those who were wrestling with the vast social problems that were arising everywhere in Europe as a result of the changes brought by the Industrial Revolution. Social thinkers all over Europe began turning to sociology or to the sociological perspective for solutions to the misery and confusion left in the wake of urbanisation, industrialisation, and bureaucratisation. But the solutions these thinkers arrived at were not always the same or even compatible.

Herbert Spencer, for instance, an Englishman who wrote in the late nineteenth century and was extremely influential in his time in both Europe and America, believed that society developed through natural processes. It was he (and not Darwin) who coined the phrase "survival of the fittest". By this he meant that through natural selection societies would work out the optimum social arrangements. Spencer believed, for example, that national governments should not make legislation concerning social progress because such legislation would interfere with the natural order of societal development. Thus, such public policies as public education, public health care, and work laws should not be undertaken by social legislation because those who were fittest would be able to fend for themselves. Furthermore, to interfere with their successes would be to interfere with the progress of natural societal growth. For Spencer, what *was* in the universe was synonymous with what *ought* to be (Spencer, 1898).

This view was vehemently opposed by Karl Marx, who believed that revolution and not evolution was the key to Europe's ills. Marx felt that differentiation in society comes about not through natural selection of the fittest but through the consolidation of groups of people who have similar economic interests and experiences. The structure of society, for Marx, was based on economic foundations: people's relationship to the means of production determines their position in the society, and this position fully influences values, attitudes, and behaviour. Since the different groups, or classes, had different economic interests, they would, inevitably, be antagonists. For Marx, the only means by which the economically oppressed classes could convince the economically advantaged classes to relinquish some of their supremacy was through revolution. After the revolution, it would be possible to create a classless society in which everyone laboured according to ability and everyone received according to need. Thus, Marx believed that social change would come about by planned social action (Marx, 1955, 1967). This, of course, is a very different view from Spencer's, which suggested that if you leave the world alone it will eventually cure its own ills.

Although both these theorists believed that they were describing the world as it really was, neither of them drew upon strictly scientific methods to document their observations convincingly. What was needed now were innovative research techniques that would be suitable to the. scientific study of society. The first major step toward this needed innovation was taken by Emile Durkheim. He collected international statistics on the incidence and preconditions of suicide and organised these statistics in such a way that they empirically documented his theories about social organisation.

Durkheim's empirical approach, the giant step between social philosophy and social science, has been pursued particularly vigorously by American sociologists. As in Europe, American sociology first focused on the formidable social problems of the day, including crime and poverty, social disorder and deviance. But early in its development, American sociology began to adopt the scientific perspective, placing heavy emphasis on observation and scientific measurement. However, the total acceptance of the scientific approach has always been tempered by the realisation, first fully elaborated by Max Weber, that human beings are not inanimate objects that can be manipulated and studied like rocks, minerals, or cells. Human beings have feelings, thoughts, consciousness, attitudes, and values which are best reckoned with and accounted for by empathy, or *Verstehen,* as Weber called it (1964). The scientific study of human beings must include elements of insight and empathy if it is to stay true to the actual conditions of human life.

Today, sociology reflects the change from social philosophy to social science (tempered with insight and empathy), and "schools" of sociology have come to emphasise one or the other of the approaches put forth by the founders of the field.

THEORETICAL ORIENTATIONS

The first and most crucial step in the exploration of any unknown phenomenon is the formulation of questions about that phenomenon. The questions we ask strongly influence the explanations we arrive at. An old joke about a pessimist and an optimist perfectly illustrates this axiom of scientific pursuit. The pessimist, pointing to a glass with some water will say, "That glass is half empty." The optimist will answer, "No, it's not; it's half full." Although both pessimist and optimist have observed the same phenomenon, their explanations of what they saw differ because they are concerned with different questions. So it is when sociologists try to explain human social behaviour. Depending on how they formulate their questions, they often come up with different explanations for the same phenomena. The different types of questions that a sociologist is likely to ask reflect his or her theoretical orientation. In sociology, as in all scientific disciplines, there are several different theoretical orientations, each of which has its ardent admirers and detractors. In America the most prevalent theoretical orientation is the structural functional approach.

Structural-Functionalism

Sociologists with a *structural-functional* approach study the way each part of a society contributes to the functioning of the society as a whole. Social balance is emphasised. Since sociologists with the structural-functional orientation view society as a system of interrelated parts, they are mainly interested in the contributions or "purposes" these parts serve for on-going social life. For example, in trying to explain why all human societies have a family system, the structural-functionalists will ask: What function (need) does the family system fulfil for the larger society? The answers to this question will all highlight the contributions that family systems make to the on-going life of societies. For example, families ensure that someone will be responsible for the care of dependent infants. Or take the case of political machines, which continue to flourish in American cities despite periodic condemnations by important members of American society (Merton, 1968). Structural-functionalists would say that these machines serve positive {though unrecognised) functions for some members of society. For example, they provide a political voice for new immigrants and minority groups.

By looking at the social world through a structural-functionalist perspective, sociologists often develop convincing explanations for the existence of social phenomena that would otherwise be puzzling or incomprehensible. For example, one of the most influential functionalists. Kingsley Davis, once asked these questions: "What is there about the nature of human society that causes it to give rise to, and maintain [prostitution] while at the same time it condemns the practice? What functions does prostitution serve that are not served by other institutions in the society?" (Davis, 1937). As a result of this line of questioning, Davis came up with some innovative and convincing answers. For example:

1. Prostitution provides a sexual outlet for those who cannot at the moment find permanent or stable partners (for example, travelling salesmen, sailors, businessmen at conventions).
2. Prostitution provides a sexual outlet for those who do not have the energy or will to pursue more elaborate forms of courtship.
3. Prostitution provides a source of sexual satisfaction during times when more stable relationships are

temporarily out of kilter (for example, during separation, divorce, widowerhood).

4. Prostitution provides an outlet for sexual perversions that cannot be expressed in long-term enduring relationships, helping to preserve those relationships.
5. Prostitution provides partners for those men who are, for whatever reason, unable to compete in the ordinary sexual marketplace (for example, the disfigured, handicapped, impotent).

While Davis's analysis makes sense, it provides only a limited explanation for the existence of prostitution, and this limitation is imposed by the very questions he asks in the beginning: "What functions does prostitution serve that are not served by other institutions in the society?" (Note that Davis is viewing society from the male perspective alone.) There are more questions to ask about prostitution, but they would probably come out of a different theoretical orientation.

Conflict Orientation

One of the orientations standing in opposition to the functional approach focuses on conflict and opposition rather than on social balance. This approach has several contemporary proponents, whose objections to the functionalists are echoed in the statement: "[In functionalism] there is much concern with social order and norms, little with social discord and power, opposition and oppression. The functional orientation introduces a conservative bias into sociological analysis ... in the specific sense that it directs attention to system maintenance and stability and diverts attention from conflict and change" (Blau, 1972).

A sociologist with the *conflict* approach would ask questions about who benefits and who is systematically deprived by certain social patterns. They would ask about the overall conditions of society that even allow certain phenomena to be functional at all. For example, a sociologist with a conflict orientation would ask these questions about prostitution:

1. If prostitution has arisen and flourished to accommodate the restless male, why has it not also arisen to accommodate the restless female?
2. What are the costs of prostitution to society? These include the costs of creating an out-caste group, the prostitutes themselves, and the costs for men, in hypocrisy, deception, and *self*-deception.
3. What are the contradictions in the laws of society that create legal institutions (monogamous marriage) and at the same time condone the violation of these institutions?
4. How can changes in the practice of prostitution be brought about?

These questions will clearly give rise to different answers about the nature of prostitution - its causes and consequences - than resulted from the functionalist approach. While neither approach is "right" or "wrong," each provides a distinctive explanation for the same social phenomenon, and sociologists of one orientation must be aware of the questions that might arise from a different perspective.

Symbolic Interaction

A third and increasingly popular orientation to studying social phenomena is the *symbolic interactionist* approach. Sociologists who follow this perspective focus their attention not on large social structures and institutions, but on the day-to-day communication that occurs when people interact in face-to-face situations. The emphasis is on the meaning of social life as it is interpreted by individuals going about their daily business. Regarding prostitution, an interactionist would want to know not so much why it exists or why it generally is practiced by women, but *how*-people actually go about contracting for sexual services. The interactionist would ask questions like these:

1. What kinds of interactions take place between purchaser and purchased?
2. How are the signals arranged between a prostitute and her "John" so that each knows the other as a potential temporary partner.
3. What do the prostitute and her customer make of their interaction; what meaning does it have for each?
4. How are the rules of the interaction established, and what are the codes of understood behaviour?

These types of questions would tell us more about the process of prostitution and its meaning for the participants than about its consequences for the larger social system.

Using any one of these perspectives we would come to understand something about the ubiquitous social phenomenon, prostitution, but we would learn different things from each orientation. In doing or studying sociology we must always remain aware of the underlying orientation so that we will be alert to the questions that have not been asked and to the biases of those that have been.

THE USES OF SOCIOLOGY

Whatever a sociologist's orientation, his or her task will always be the same: to understand and interpret events and patterns that transcend particular individuals, particular cultures, and particular historical moments. Unlike the psychologist, who is concerned with specific individuals in specific situations, the sociologist tries to uncover basic truths about human social behaviour in general. "Know thyself" becomes, for the sociologist, "Know thy social being." But what good does it do to know the social being? Have sociologists simply devised a new vocabulary for personal introspection? Not really.

Sociological concepts and findings have been adopted for many purposes beyond self-revelation. For example, historians have begun to focus on issues like the daily workings of family life - just how many people actually did live together under one roof and who was in charge?

Questions are now being asked about the prestige of specific historical occupations - was it considered better in a certain period and place to be a shipbuilder or a tradesman? Historians have recently begun to use sociological techniques in their research, and their findings will give us better information about the quality as well as the chronology of the historical past.

Political scientists, too, have incorporated the sociological perspective. They have begun to focus on such sociological issues as: How do different people acquire political views? What is the relationship between political attitudes of parents and children? How does the process of formal education contribute to political opinions? These are sociological questions which, until the last few decades, have been overlooked by most political scientists.

But sociology has been useful not only in enriching its fellow disciplines, it has also had its own unique impact on public programmes and policy. For example, sociologists and psychologists have informed us of the effects of public school segregation for both white and black children over the past several years (Coleman, 1966; Mosteller and Moynihan, 1972; Averch, 1972). The findings of sociological studies have been applied to such thorny problems as how to provide better health care for low-income families (Rainwater, 1968; Dreitzel, 1971), and how to demobilise soldiers without provoking anger and resentment in those left behind (Shils, 1961).

Sociology has also been useful in exploding unexamined popular myths. For example, it is the work of sociologists that has led to the realisation that most of the people who are incarcerated in state mental hospitals are not psychotic or dangerous (Scheff, 1966). On the basis of this work the laws permitting involuntary commitment to mental hospitals have been made stricter, and civil rights are gradually being restored to mental patients. The mental hospital was also the site of the remarkable finding by sociologists that when mental patients become psychotic on the ward, they are sometimes responding not so much to inner erratic impulses as to tension generated by the staff when it is in conflict over patient care (Stanton and Schwartz, 1954).

Recently, in response to the increasing interest in a negative income tax (which would provide extra income to those who earn less than a certain minimum), sociologists studied the ways in which poor people spend additional income. They demonstrated with hard evidence that poor people, like people everywhere, spend the money to free themselves from menial tasks and to provide their children with niceties (Mathematica, 1974). If and when Congress does consider a proposal for a negative income tax, sociologists will be ready with data on how such extra income would be spent, allaying the fears of cautious Congresspersons that the poor will "squander" the extra funds.

One of the newest, and perhaps most ambitious, undertakings of sociologists concerned with applied rather than theoretical work has been the attempt to develop *social indicators.* Every January the Council of Economic Advisors issues detailed reports on the nation's economy, as measured by statistics on growth, employment, inflation, and the gross national product. But until quite recently there has been no parallel attempt to monitor the *quality* of life in this country. As Harvard professor Raymond Bauer told a Senate subcommittee on social planning in 1971, "While we could reduce hunger, we do not know just who is hungry. While we could reduce crime, our knowledge of even how many crimes of what type are committed is highly imperfect. While we could improve the quality of life, we do not know what our citizens value in their lives" (Bauer, in Melville, 1973, p. 13).

In the last five to ten years sociologists, alongwith other social scientists, have begun to develop a system of social indicators comparable to our existing system of economic indicators. These social indicators are designed to measure such seeming intangibles as aspirations and satisfactions in health, work, friendship, family, marriage and community. Other quality-of-life issues that are being studied and measured include prejudice, political alienation, changing roles (particularly for women), and fear of crime.

The goal of all these studies is to develop a set of social indicators that will give policy-makers a sense of what it is like to live in America during a certain year or period. If the quality of life at any particular moment can be accurately assessed and compared with the quality at another time policy-makers will have a factual and realistic foundation on which to base their decisions about social programmes. The social-indicators movement is one of the first large-scale attempts to put sociologist knowledge to practical work. As the public begins to gain more confidence in sociological approaches and methods surely there will be others.

2

SCIENCE AND METHODS IN SOCIOLOGY

THE NATURE OF SCIENCE

Essentially, science is a *method* for collecting and explaining facts. Scientists confine their investigations to phenomena that can be observed and measured, and to statements about the relationships among phenomena that can be verified by independent observers. Empirical proof is the basis of all science. Researchers are expected to approach their work in a detached way and to report their findings accurately. Other scientists then retest these findings to make sure they contain no false statements. In the words of one of the characters in C.P. Snow's novel *The Search,* "Now if false statements are to be allowed, if they are not to be discouraged by every means we have, science will lose its one virtue, truth. The only ethical principle which has made science possible is that the truth shall be told at all times" (p. 281). Scientists seek the truth and attempt to eliminate, or at least minimise, personal bias and error by applying the scientific method to their research.

The Scientific Method: Emile Durkheim's Study of Suicide

The publication of Emile Durkheim's *Suicide* in 1897 marked the beginning of a revolution in thinking about social behaviour. In Durkheim's time suicide was explained as an individual act caused by either mental illness or inherited suicidal tendencies, or as the effect of climate on reasoning. If these really *were* the causes, then why did suicide rates vary from period to period? If suicide is caused by forces within individuals, why should more people kill themselves in one country than in another? Durkheim decided to find out why by conducting one of the first scientific studies of social behaviour.

He began by checking existing theories against the facts. A preliminary review of official records revealed that suicide rates were highest in countries that had the lowest rates of mental illness, suggesting that insanity alone did not explain suicide. And while more women than men were confined to mental asylums, more men than women committed suicide. This observation suggested that suicide is not related to heredity for if it were, men and women would be affected equally. Nor did the facts support the climatic theories of suicide. All that remained was the fact that suicide rates varied from one social group to another. Durkheim concluded, "We have shown in fact that for each social group there is a specific tendency to suicide explained neither by the organic-psychic construction of the individuals nor the nature of the physical environment. Consequently, by elimination, it must necessarily depend upon social causes and be itself a collective phenomenon. . . ." (1951, p. 145).

At this point Durkheim had done nothing more than formulate a proposition: suicide has some relationship to social causes. A philosopher might stop here, having shown by the logical process of elimination that suicide is related to social causes. But logical deduction is not enough; scientists demand empirical proof. The first step toward obtaining such proof is to translate the problem into terms that can be tested.

Defining the Problem - Defining terms and concepts in a precise way is often more difficult than it would seem. For example, what is suicide? If a person dies because he or she miscalculates danger or fails to take necessary precautions, is that suicide? Examining the different implications of this word, Durkheim concluded that the term *suicide* refers to "all cases of death resulting directly or indirectly from a positive or negative act of the victim himself, which he knows will produce this result" (p. 44). Durkheim decided to use official records for his study even though he realised that many suicides went unreported.

The next problem was to define *social causes* in some concrete way. When scientists study abstract concepts such as prejudice, religiosity, or economic stability, for example, they must define these ideas in terms of variables that can be measured. This is called an *operational definition.* For purposes of study the scientist may define religious beliefs in terms of membership in religious organisations; economic stability in terms of fluctuations on the stock market. In *Suicide,* Durkheim decided to use statistics on religious affiliation, marital status, military involvement, and economic and political stability as measures of the social causes of suicide.

Durkheim hypothesised that suicide rates would vary: for Catholics, Protestants and Jews; for married and unmarried people; for soldiers and civilians; in times of economic and political stability and unrest. An *hypothesis* is a statement about the relationship between two or more variables, phrased in such a way that it can be proved *or disproved* empirically. For example, the statement; "God exists," is simply an assertion; it can be neither proved nor disproved. The statement, "People who attend church regularly believe in God," can be tested (by interviewing people who attend church and people who do not), and is therefore an hypothesis. A *variable* is some fact or condition that is subject to change. In Durkheim's study religious affiliation, marital status, and so on were the independent variables, the factors thought to affect the suicide rate; the suicide rate was the dependent variable, the actor expected to change in relation to the independent variables.

In any scientific study the *independent variable* is a quality or factor that influences the dependent variable. The *dependent variable* is a quality or factor that is affected by one or more independent variables.

Collecting and Interpreting Data - Once his terms were defined and his hypotheses formulated, Durkheim had to decide how to collect data that would prove or disprove the hypotheses. This involved selecting the group or groups to be studied, evaluating various sources of information, and deciding how to measure the variables. Depending on the problem being investigated, a researcher might design an experiment, conduct interviews, spend time observing the way people interact in certain settings, or examine records. (A researcher may actually use several of these data-collection methods.) Durkheim chose to use official records on suicide from a number of European nations.

Examining these records, he found that more Protestants than Catholics, and more Catholics than Jews committed suicide. Suicide rates varied inversely with marital status (single people committed suicide most often, married people with children least often), and and soldiers were more prone to suicide than civilians. Durkheim also discovered that suicide rates rose during periods of sharp economic reversals (inflations or depressions), but fell during periods of political instability. These findings had to be interpreted. Why, for example, do suicide rates vary with religious affiliation?

The answer was not obvious. Certainly religious beliefs did not explain the variations Durkheim found. The Catholic church teaches that suicide is a sin, while Jewish doctrine is vague on the subject. Yet Jews had the lowest suicide rates. Durkheim resolved this paradox by looking beyond specific religious beliefs to the *social impact* of different faiths. Protestantism emphasises skepticism and individualism; Catholicism and Judaism stress tradition and authority while at the same time demanding that a person become involved in the religious community. Similarly, married people (particularly parents) are involved with other people in a way that single people are not. Durkheim reasoned that the stronger the social groups to which people belong, the more they depend on these groups and the more likely they are to take other people into account when making decisions. People who have few ties to their community are more likely to take their own lives than people who are deeply involved with their families and religious groups.

Forming a Theory - Building on this interpretation of the available data on suicide, Durkheim formulated a general theory about the individual's relationship to society. In everyday conversation we use the word theory to distinguish abstract ideas from fact: we say, "That may be true in theory, but not in fact." In science, a *theory* is an explanation of something. Durkheim's theory may be summarised as follows: Society is not simply a collection of people; it has an existence of its own and exercises a determining influence on the way people think and act. In other words, the individual is a product of the groups to which he or she belongs.

The function of theory in science is to summarise and order information in a meaningful way, to suggest new ways of looking at phenomena, and to stimulate new research. The test of a theory is whether or not it can predict what will happen, given certain conditions.

Critical Assessment - Like other communities, the scientific community is governed by certain values and norms, which in turn distinguish it from most other communities. These norms include making results available to everyone and analysing each other's work according to preestablished impersonal criteria. The norms of science have been applied to Durkheim's work on suicide. Some sociologists have questioned his data by asking whether official records are an accurate measure of suicide rates. Not only do people cover up suicides, but they may do so in systematic ways that would distort the patterns that Durkheim analysed. For example, records revealed that Protestants had a higher suicide rate than Catholics. But what if Catholics simply concealed more suicides than Protestants did?

Still other researchers have built on Durkheim's work, either replicating the study in another place and time or extending his ideas to other forms of social life. For example, some sociologists have asked whether a lack of social involvement is related to other forms of deviant behaviour, such as crime.

The value of a scientific study lies partly in the information the researcher collects and partly in the newinvestigations it stimulates. The accuracy of scientific findings is assessed by testing their validity and reliability. *Validity* is the degree to which a scientific study measures what it attempts to measure. *Reliability* is the degree to which a study yields the same results when repeated by the original researcher or by other scientists.

SCIENCE AND SOCIOLOGY

> There can never be, and has never been, "disinterested" research in the social field, as there can be in the natural sciences. Valuations are, in fact, determining our work even if we manage to be unaware of it. And this is true, however much the researcher is subjectively convinced that he is simply observing and recording the facts. (Myrdal, 1973, p. 9)

The question of whether sociology is a science comparable to physics, biology and astronomy has never been completely resolved. Auguste Comte, the French philosopher and founder of positivism believed that all aspects of social life could be measured, analysed and explained with the tools of natural science. He also believed that sociologists would ultimately be able to solve social ills, just as medical scientists have learned to cure many physiological ills. In contrast, Max Weber, the German sociologist and political economist, emphasised the *subjective* elements of social behaviour. He argued that empathy and insight are as valuable to the sociologist as hard facts are; that to understand social phenomena; the researcher must "get inside" them.

This debate continues today, with some sociologists emphasising the need to replace insight with hard facts and others arguing that sociology cannot and should not imitate the natural sciences because they are fundamentally different. Quite simply, people are not atoms. They do not always march obediently through experiments: they change their minds, they talk back, they elude precise quantitative analysis - sometimes deliberately. Nor do social variables remain constant over time and place. The law of gravity and the composition of water are the same in America and Europe, the same today as they were yesterday. But no two families are exactly alike, and even ideas about what the family *should be* vary enormously from one culture to another, from one generation to the next. In the words of economist Gunnar Myrdal:

> The really important difference between [social scientists] and our natural science colleagues is that we never reach down to constants-like the speed of light or sound in a particular medium, or the specific weights of atoms or molecules. We have nothing corresponding to the universally valid measurements of energy, voltage, ampere, etc. The regularities we find do not have the firm general validity of "laws of nature." (1973).

Perhaps most significant, the sociologist's relationship to his or her subject is quite different from the astronomer's relationship to the stars or the physicist's relationship to energy. Objectivity is a major problem for all social scientists. As Herbert Spencer wrote nearly a hundred years ago:

> To cul himself off in thought from all his relationships of race, and country, and citizenship - to get rid of all those interests, prejudices, likings, superstitions, generated in him by the life of his own society and his own time - to look on all the changes societies have undergone and are undergoing, without reference to nationality or creed, or personal welfare; is what the average man cannot do at all, and what the exceptional man can do very imperfectly. (1877, p. 74).

Does this mean that sociology is merely masquerading as a science, or does it mean that sociologists should confine themselves to collecting hard facts, to conducting surveys, and to other forms of information-getting in which personal bias can be minimised? Not necessarily. It means, first, that it is essential for sociologists to recognise their biases and assumptions and to state them explicitly, and second, that they should combine the quantitative (or hard) and qualitative (or soft) approaches to the study of social behaviour. Durkheim's study of suicide illustrates this last point. By collecting data he was able to prove that suicide rates varied with religious affiliation, marital status, military involvement, and economic and political stability. But it was *insight* that enables Durkheim to perceive the underlying variable - the degree of involvement in social groups. The uniqueness of social behaviour enables sociologists to contribute to the natural sciences by examining the social forces that influence physicists, biologists and astronomers (see, for example, Kuhn, 1970).

The Methods of Sociology

Having described how Durkheim used scientific methods to analyse suicide rates, we now examine the specific procedures and techniques that sociologists use to study social behaviour. They include both objective and subjective measures.

Survey Research - *Surveys* composed of questionnaires, interviews, or a combination of the two, enable sociologists to gather information about large numbers of people. Surveys may be used to make predictions about how people will behave (for example, election polls), to test hypotheses, and to measure public opinion.

The validity of a survey depends on the care with which the researcher constructs interviews or questionnaires and on the selection of a representative sample. Theoretically, a sociologist who is interested in the attitudes of American college students toward politics or sex or any other issue could hire an army of interviewers to contact every student in the country. However, the cost and time involved in such a venture would be prohibitive. For these very practical reasons, sociologists generally question only a sample of the population. In this context, *population* refers to all the people with the characteristics the researcher wants to study - all American college students, for example. A *sample* is a limited number of people selected from the population.

There are several ways to choose a sample, and the method used depends on what the researcher is studying. One form is the *random sample.* In effect, the researcher puts the names of all people in the population in a barrel, blindfolds himself, and picks as many names as he needs, leaving the selection to chance. The more sophisticated and more usual technique is to assign each person in the population a number and to pick a sample from a table of random numbers, which is designed so that there is no pattern reading across, down, or diagonally. With a random sample each person in the population has an equal chance of being selected; researcher bias is eliminated.

Box 2.1

Surveying Public Opinion

The questions given below have been selected from a public opinion survey conducted by the National Opinion Research Center. NORC is a general research institute designed to measure public opinion, to conduct surveys for government agencies and nonprofit organisations, and to train graduate students.

1. Think of how your life is going now. Do you want it to *continue in much the same way as it's going now;* do you wish you could *change some parts of it;* or do you wish you could *change many parts of it.*
   —— Continue much the same way
   —— Change some parts
   —— Change many parts
2. In Chicago recently a family had to decide between letting its newborn baby die, or have an operation that would leave the baby blind for life. Which course would you have chosen?
   —— Let die
   —— Operate
   —— Don't know
3. Do you think it will be best for the future of this country if we take an active part in world affairs, or if we stay out of world affairs?
   —— Active part
   —— Stay out
   —— Don't know
4. Suppose there is a revolution in one of the countries of South America, and it looks as though a Communist government will take over. Do you think the United States should or should not send in American troops to prevent this?
   —— Should send American troops
   —— Should not send American troops
   —— Don't know

Source : Survey Research Service, NORC, University of Chicago, SRS-857; June 1965.

Most people think a big sample is more accurate than a smaller one, but this is not necessarily true. Not size, but polling a true cross section of the population being studied is the key to accuracy. A famous example of this was the attempt to predict the winner of the 1936 presidential election. A popular magazine, *Literary Digest,* sent post card ballots to 10 million people chosen from telephone directories and auto registration lists. The *Digest* predicted, on the basis of 2 million returns, that Landon would beat Roosevelt by a landslide. Meanwhile, a young man named George Gallup sampled 312,551 people and correctly predicted that FDR would win. The editors of the *Literary Digest* were stunned by the election results. How could their giant survey have been so wrong? The key to accuracy was not the *number* of people polled, but their characteristics. During the depression, only middle- and upper-class people could afford telephones and automobiles, and a disproportionate number of middle-and upper-class people were Republicans. As it turned out, the less well-off, who voted heavily for Democrat Franklin Roosevelt, decided the election (Labovitz and Hagedorn, 1971, p. 33; Hennessy, 1970, pp. 79 - 81). The *Literary Digest* had incorrectly assumed that the more people they contacted, the better their chances of accurately predicting the election.

Gallup's success was not a matter of luck - he had polled a scientific cross section that accurately represented the proportion of Republicans and Democrats in the *entire* population of voters. Selecting a sample that accurately reflects the proportion of different groups in the population being studied is called *stratified random sampling*.

The accuracy of a survey also depends on the way questions are worked. A survey will be meaningless if respondents do not understand the questions, if they do not answer truthfully, and if their answers can be interpreted in different ways. With mailed questionnaires, it is difficult to judge whether or not respondents take the survey seriously, and the information collected may be only a superficial measure of actual beliefs, habits and preferences.

There is also a danger of middle-class bias. It is generally easier to elicit responses from middle-class respondents than from welfare clients, who have reason to be suspicious of official-looking papers and of strangers who ask questions. Moreover, in face-to-face interviews, people tend to give the socially acceptable answer. For example, Richard Carter found that when he asked Bowery bums if they were married, a surprising number said no. However, when he asked instead, "Where is your wife?" many more gave truthful answers, without stopping to think about the implications of desertion (Carter, in Hennessy, 1970. p. 110).

In addition, researchers face the problem of translating responses into statistics. If a pollster asks a hundred different people what they think of an administration, he or she may get a hundred different answers. How, then, can the results be presented? Because of this problem, researchers use structured questions wherever possible - that is, questions that can be answered yes or no, true or false; multiple-choice questions; and rating questions, where a respondent indicates the extent to which he or she agrees or disagrees with a statement on a scale of one to five.

Experiments - Sociologists conduct experiments when they want to study cause-and-effect relationships. In simplest terms, sociological *experiments* consist of exposing subjects to a specially designed situation and systematically recording their reactions. The advantage of experiments over other methods is that they allow the researcher to study the impact of only one or two variables, which is hard to do in real-life situations.

For example, Philip Zimbardo wanted to study the impact of prison life on guards and inmates. He might have studied actual prisoners and guards in their natural setting, but he would have had to follow prison rules, and his findings would have been complicated by such variables as differences in individual background. Instead, he ran an experiment using student volunteers (Zimbardo, 1972). By using people who were neither guards nor prisoners, Zimbardo was able to study the effects of social roles on behaviour. In actual prisons he would not have been able to separate the actors from their roles as easily.

Zimbardo began by constructing a prison in the basement of the psychology building at Stanford University. A group of twenty-four normal college students ("normal" according to accepted psychological tests) were divided into two subgroups - half were guards, half were prisoners. The two groups were matched for socioeconomic background, education and race. One night, without warning, the prisoners were collected in a simulated arrest. All were given uniforms and numbers and confined in the basement jail. The guards were dressed appropriately and instructed on their responsibility for maintaining order. Two days after the experiment began, rumors of a prisoner rebellion began to spread. The "guards" reacted with surprising brutality, to which the "prisoners" submitted with little resistance. This brief experiment dramatised how even ordinary students could succumb to prison roles in just a few days. Zimbardo concluded that the institutional structure of prisons has much more to do with how real guards and prisoners behave than do their personalities.

Stanley Milgram's experiments on obedience were equally controversial (1965; 1973). Milgram recruited subjects by placing ads in a local paper, calling for volunteers for an experiment on learning. Over a period of several years, over a thousand people from all walks of life participated. When a subject arrived at the lab, he or she was introduced to two other people. One, dressed in a lab coat, was the experimenter; the other, dressed in street clothes, was supposed to be a second volunteer. In reality, however, this second person was part of the experimental team. Milgram explained that he was conducting a test of the effects of punishment on learning, and asked the subject to play the role of "teacher". The second person, or "student," was strapped to a chair and wired with electrodes. The "teacher" was given a seat at an impressive-looking shock machine and was told to ask the "student" a series of questions and to administer increasing doses of electric shock for each wrong answer. The shock board was labelled from 15 volts (SLIGHT SHOCK) to 450 volts (DANGER - SEVERE SHOCK).

As the experiment proceeded, the "student" gave a number of wrong answers. He began to complain when the shocks reached 175 volts, and by 285 volts was emitting what Milgram describes as agonised screams. Eventually, the "student" demanded to be released. Nearly all of the "teachers" became troubled when the "student" complained, and turned to the experimenter for advice. They were told to continue. In reality, the shock machine was a fake and the "students" were acting, but the "teachers" did not know this. Nevertheless, two-thirds of the subjects continued to press the shock button, right up to 450 volts.

The chief drawback with experiments is that a laboratory is one step removed from real life, and the setting itself may influence the way people behave. For example, Milgram's subjects may have obeyed the experimenter because they believed he was a doctor and, presumably, doctors do not harm people. For this reason, researchers may run two tests with two matched groups. One group, the *experimental group,* actually undergoes the experiment. The other, the *control group,* is brought to the lab and exposed to everything *but* the independent variable. The experimenter then compares the responses of the two groups.

Still, the question of whether observations made in a laboratory apply to real-life situations remains. Some researchers avoid this problem by conducting experiments in the field. One of the most famous field experiments in sociology was conducted by Elton Mayo at Western Electric Company's Hawthorne plant in Chicago (Roethlisberger and Dickson, 1939). Mayo wanted to learn how variations in lighting, coffee breaks, pay plans (salary vs. piece rate), and the like affected worker output in a factory. The management felt sure that employees would work harder if they were paid in proportion to what they produced; they also thought that coffee breaks would improve morale. To their dismay however, Mayo and his colleagues found that *every* change they made increased output. Employees worked faster when management increased coffee breaks as well as when they *decreased* them. Mayo concluded that it wasn't lighting or coffee breaks or even salary incentives that raised productivity, but rather the attention the employees were getting. The positive impact that an experiment has just because the researchers are giving people extra attention is known as the *Hawthorne effect*. Sociologists may try to eliminate the Hawthorne effect by using hidden tape recorders and other "unobtrusive measures" (Webb, *el al.*, 1966), but there is some question as to whether it is ethical to experiment on people without their knowledge.

Participant Observation - One of the oldest yet most controversial research methods in sociology is *participant observation*. Participant observers deliberately involve themselves in the activity, group, or community they are investigating in order to gain an insider's view. William Foote Whyte (1955), for example, moved into a low-income Italian-American community that was uncharted territory in the late 1940s. Before Whyte's study, street corner residents were known to the outside world primarily as clients of social workers, as defendants in criminal trials, or simply as the masses (p. xvii). Whyte met Doc, the leader of the Norton gang, through a social worker. Doc then introduced him to the other residents, and for eighteen months Whyte shot pool, played cards, bowled, dated, "chewed the fat," and most important, watched his subjects. In time he became a fixture on the street corner, a trusted friend who was able to learn how these people conducted their daily lives. Like Herbert Gans, author of a similar study *(The Urban Villagers,* 1962), Whyte "tried to describe the way of life of [these] people as they might describe it themselves if they were sociologists" (p. x). This is the primary goal of participant observation: to obtain intimate, firsthand knowledge of a way of life. In effect, the investigator uses himself as a research instrument. He knows how the people he is studying feel because he feels the same way. Other studies in this genre include Festinger's report on a doomsday group *(When Prophecy Fails,* 1956); Becker's investigation of medical students *(Boys in White,*

1961), and his studies of dance musicians and marijuana smokers *(The Outsiders,* 1963).

Participant observation requires exceptional self-discipline. The first problem for field workers is gaining access to the group he or she wants to study and establishing rapport with its members. If researchers reveal their intentions, they risk putting their subjects on guard; if they conceal their motives, they must live with pretense and duplicity for the duration of the study. Participant observers must develop techniques for recording their observations faithfully and systematically without influencing the way people act. They must become involved in the group life without letting their own emotions blind them.

An important advantage of participant observation is that it is extremely flexible. Whyte found, for example, that "as I sat and listened, I learned the answers to questions that I would not even have had the sense to ask" (p. 303). Skilled field workers observe behaviour in its natural setting; they can see behind individuals' public selves and discern the relationships between what people say and what they do. However, even good participant-observational studies have problems. The observations of the researcher may or may not reflect the group as a whole. There is always some danger that the field worker will rely on information gained from the more articulate and outgoing members of the group; that he or she will misinterpret the significance of certain events. Moreover, in participant observation the sample is necessarily small.

For these reasons, observational studies are generally used to uncover relationships that can then be tested more systematically. But despite the limitations of participant studies, many of the classics of sociology rest on observational research that uncovered significant aspects of social life. For example, Whyte found that low-income neighbourhoods are highly structured communities - not the chaotic places they appear to be to outsiders; Gans argued that residents of Boston's West End were not "frustrated seekers after middle-class values" (p. x), but had a culture of their own. Both of these findings were radical ideas in their time.

A *case study* is an intensive observational study, supplemented by formal interviews, surveys, data gathered from official records, and whatever other information may seem relevant. The researcher attempts to learn everything there is to know about a particular group, community, or incident. Examples are the Lynds profiles of Middletown, U.S.A. (1929; 1937); Clifford Shaw's life history of a juvenile delinquent (1966), and Hadley Cantril's anatomy of a lynching in Leeville, Texas (1963).

The Time Variable - An important variable in much of sociological research is *time.* People and institutions often change more slowly than can be easily observed. Sociologists solve this problem in two ways. One is the *cross-sectional study,* which simultaneously looks at different groups of people at different stages of change. For example, a survey may sample the political opinions of adolescents, parents and grandparents in order to see how aging affects political ideology. This is a quick and economical method, but it has its dangers. It assumes, for example, that the adolescents it samples today will become like their parents in twenty years and like their grandparents in forty years, when in fact young people today may not adopt their parents' attitudes twenty years from now; they may think very differently.

The second solution, a *longitudinal study,* is a more accurate research tool because it follows the same people over a number of years. No assumptions about people becoming like other people are necessary. In one well-known longitudinal study. T.M. Newcomb analysed the effect of Bennington College on students' political attitudes. Newcomb questioned the same group of graduates over twenty years, and found that, years after they had left college, Bennington alumni were still unusually liberal for people of their socioeconomic class {1943; 1963). One problem with longitudinal studies is that they are expensive and slow. We are often so eager for quick results that they are rare in American sociology, though more common in Europe.

Sometimes the problem is not slow change but change so rapid that an event is over before we can begin to study it. Then the sociologist has no choice but to do an *ex post facto study.* In such studies, variables that could not be measured while an event was happening, can be controlled statistically after the fact. The numerous government studies of civil disorders, initiated after the riots of the late 1960s, are *ex post facto* studies.

Interpreting Data

Politicians, advertisers and journalists are so fond of quoting statistics that it sometimes seems as if they believe there is magic in numbers. Many people take statistics as gospel: "You can't argue with the facts," they say. Others believe you can use numbers to prove or disprove almost anything, and automatically stop listening when they hear the phrase, "Statistics indicate . . ." The truth lies somewhere in between these two points of view.

Box 2.2

Classifying Data: Mean, Median and Mode

Frequently researchers summarise data on a given population by calculating central tendencies, or averages. There are three ways to do this:

The *mode* is the figure that occurs most often in the data. For example, a researcher studies seven families and finds that their yearly incomes are:

$ 3,000	$ 11,000
$ 3,000	$ 15,000
$ 7,500	$ 90,000
$ 9,000	

The model income in this group of families is $ 3,000 a year. The mode does not give any indication of the range in data, and it is only useful when a researcher wants to show which statistic appears most often.

The *mean* is what we call the average in everyday conversation. To calculate the mean you simply divide the sum of all the figures by the number of items. The mean or average income for the families above is $ 19,786 ($ 138,500 ÷ 7). Researchers frequently calculate the mean because it includes and reflects all the available data. However, as the

Box 2.2 - *(Contd)*

example here illustrates, the mean can be misleading. The fact that one of the families in this group has an income of $ 90,000 a year obscures the fact that six of the seven families have incomes of less than $ 19,786 a year. The mean is most useful when the range of figures is narrow.

The *median* is the number that falls in the middle of a series of figures, in this case $ 9,000 a year. The median is useful because it does not allow extremes (here $ 3,000 and $ 90,000) to hide the central tendency. Frequently, researchers calculate both the mode and the median in order to present an accurate impression of their findings.

The data a researcher collects in a survey, experiment, or observational study does not speak for itself. Data must be classified, and trends and relationships identified for a study to be meaningful. For example, knowing the age of every American is useless, but knowing what per cent of the population is under twenty-five, between twenty-six and forty, forty-one and sixty-four, sixty-five and over is extremely valuable. The most common and useful methods of classifying statistics are explained in the accompanying boxes.

Box 2.3

How to Read A Table

The following steps for interpreting the accompanying table are general guides which can be applied to any chart or table.

1. Read the title to find out what kind of information is in the table and how it is presented. Per cent of the total responses is the measurement in this table, but not in all. Some tables present their data in thousands.
2. Look for headnotes and footnotes that may explain how the data were collected, why certain variables were studied, and whether data were collected differently for some of the categories. In the accompanying table, a slightly different category was used on two of the dates in the survey (see footnote 1). A footnote explaining how the data were collected provides one way of assessing their validity. This table has no such explanation and moreover does not tell how large the sample was. The source of the data, usually given at the bottom of a chart or table, is another measure of validity. For example, the organisation that did this survey (the Gallup polls) is well known for its quality. The source note is also a clue to whether the researchers were objective or biased.

Box 2.3 - *(Contd)*

3. Read the labels for each column and row to learn exactly what data appear in the table. Here, the column labels indicate that the authors broke the totals down by sex and community size. Four different-sized communities were surveyed, and people were asked to answer "Yes," "No," or "Can't say" when asked whether they are afraid to walk alone at night. The row labels at the left tell us that responses are being compared over a seven-year period, from 1965 to 1972.
4. Look at the data and find the highest, lowest and average rates. Then compare them with the other data in the table. Here the totals in the first three columns give you an idea of the overall response. The per cent saying they were afraid to walk at night varied slightly, around 30 per cent, until December 1972, when it rose sharply to 42 per cent.
5. Draw conclusions about the information in the table and consider what other questions it raises. Here, note how the totals break down by sex. They differ greatly, which shows how grand totals can hide important differences in the data. Not only are women two-and-a-half times as likely to say "Yes" to this question, but they account for most of the sharp increase in 1972. Also, note the difference community size makes. The percentage increases with community size. The sharpest increase comes between the second and third categories, and the last two sizes are nearly the same. It seems, then, that people in cities with populations from 50,000 to over 500,000 tend to fear the streets at night more than people in smaller towns. Further research might reveal the influence of other variables, such as age, income, race and education.

Once a researcher has organised his or her findings, a decision must be made about what the facts man. A few simple examples illustrate the hazards of interpreting data. Suppose a researcher who is interested in the relationship between literacy rates and income collects data on Spain, Israel and Kuwait. He or she discovers that per capita income is highest in Kuwait, where literacy rates are lowest, and concludes that the less literate people are, the more money they earn. This researcher has made the common error of relying on grand averages, which often conceal significant patterns. For although Kuwait is a rich *nation,* the vast majority of its *people* are extremely poor. If the researcher had

Table 2.1
Persons Afraid to Walk Alone at Night: 1965 – 1972
By Sex and Community Size (by per cent)

				Sex						Community size (Population)											
	Total			Male			Female			Under 2,500			2,500 To 49,999			50,000 To 499,999			500,000 and Over		
Year (Month)	Yes	No	Can't Say	Yes	No	Can't Say	Yes	No	Can't Say	Yes	No	Can't Say	Yes	No	Can't Say	Yes	No	Can't Say	Yes	No	Can't Say
1965 (April)[1]	34	63	3	17	80	3	49	47	4	21	77	2	29	67	4	41	54	5	48	49	3
1967 (August)[1]	31	67	2	16	82	2	44	53	3	21	78	1	22	77	1	38	57	5	40	57	3
1968 (September)	35	62	3	19	79	2	50	47	3	24	74	2	33	65	2	42	53	5	41	56	3
1972 (December)	42	57	1	22	77	1	61	39	-	28	71	1	40	59	1	51	49	-	48	51	1

– Represents zero.
[1]The category "Don't Know" was used instead of "Can't Say."
Source : American Institute of Public Opinion, Princeton, N.

examined literacy rates for different *income groups* in each country instead of literacy rates for entire nations, he or she would have discovered that there is a direct relationship between literacy and income.

Data on crime and deviance are notoriously misleading. Statistics on mental illness, drug use, and homosexuality are nothing more than a count of the people who happen to come to the attention of police, social workers, and other public officials. These data do not include drug users who escape detection, or those people who are wealthy enough to afford private treatment for mental illness. Most people assume that crime is a lower-class phenomenon, whereas in fact white-collar (or middle-class) crimes, such as fraud and embezzlement, account for far greater dollar losses than do muggings and burglaries. Similarly, most people believe the crime rate has risen sharply in the last decade. While the crime rate may indeed have risen, some of this increase is due simply to improved methods of reporting and recording crimes - how much, it is difficult to say. In short, the way in which researchers interpret and analyse their data is as important as the care they take in collecting it.

THE POLITICS OF SOCIOLOGY : VALUES, ETHICS AND USES

Sociology is founded on the belief that it is possible to apply the scientific method to the study of social behaviour. Yet if sociology has proven anything in its brief history, it is that people are cultural animals, and that separating them from their social moorings is impossible. Thus, sociologists find themselves in the awkward position of striving for objectivity on the one hand and recognising the importance of subjectivity on the other. Can this dilemma be resolved?

Value-free Sociology: A Myth or a Reality?

For generations sociologists have laboured under the eleventh commandment, "Thou shalt not commit a value judgment." Every textbook, every lecturer stresses this point. But what do they mean? Do they mean that sociologists should not express opinions about issues that lie outside their sphere of competence? Should they be indifferent to the moral implications of their work? Should they never speak out on the probable consequences of public policy? Should they never attempt to correct popular beliefs, such as the idea that certain races or ethnic groups are inferior? Should they never express values in their role as teachers?

In Alvin Gouldner's view, sociologists must stop pretending that their field can or should be value-free. Sociologists, like everyone else, are products of their times, and they cannot divorce themselves from their values and beliefs. In choosing an area for study, in deciding how to research a particular question, the sociologist inevitably makes certain assumptions about what is significant. For sociologists to deny their predispositions and biases, writes Gouldner, is absurd.

> If truth is a vital thing, as Weber is reputed to have said on his deathbed, then it must be all the truth we have to give, as best we know it, being painfully aware that even as we offer it we may be engaging in unwitting concealment rather than revelation. If we would teach students how science is made, really made rather than as publicly reported, we cannot fail to expose them to the whole scientist by whom it is made with all his gifts and blindnesses with all his methods and his *values* as well. (1962, p. 212).

Gouldner agrees with Gunnar Myrdal (1969) that sociologists can counteract bias only by explicity stating their theoretical assumptions and values.

Howard S. Becker carries this argument a step further. He contends that sociologists always take sides, not only because they have the sympathies and likes and dislikes of all people, but because investigating one point of view requires them to temporarily disregard another (1967). For example, the researcher who talks to inmates after a prison riot will arrive at one picture of the incident; the researcher who talks to guards and wardens will obviously come to another. Which is correct? For the sociologist both are true, both relevant. Even interviewing both guards and inmates does not solve the problem, because the researcher will still analyse the data according to her or his theoretical orientation. Social realities are always complex; there is always more than one side to a story. Only by including these different perspectives can sociologists gradually approach all the facts. Becker acknowledges that this is a long-term solution.

> What do we do in the meantime? .. . We take sides as our personal and political commitments dictate, use our theoretical and technical resources to avoid the distortions that we might introduce into our work, limit our conclusions carefully, recognise the hierarchy of credibility for what it is, and field as best we can the accusations and doubts that will surely be our fate. (1967 p. 247)

Becker cautions, however, that in giving some rein to their sympathies sociologists must resist the desire to suppress unpleasant findings and the temptation to disregard what they do not like seeing.

Professional Ethics

The debate over objectivity in sociology spills over into a number of complex ethical questions. Sociology is not a self-supporting enterprise. Like most researchers, sociologists depend on grants from public and private institutions for financial support. While these organisations do not dictate what researchers should find in their studies, they do exercise indirect control over the choice of topics by funding research in some areas but not in others. Intentionally or not a discipline may adjust its priorities to those funding agencies.

Often there is a fine line between obtaining funds from an agency and working for the government or private interest groups. This is why Project Camelot, for example, became so controversial. The project was conceived in the Special Operations Research Organisation (SORO) of the army. Its purpose, as described in a recruiting letter, was to devise procedures for "assessing the potential for internal war within national societies" and to "make it possible to predict and influence politically significant aspects of social change in the developing nations of the world" (Horowitz, 1965, p. 4). In other words, the army wanted to learn what circumstances sparked revolutions in underdeveloped nations, and what the governments of these nations could do to prevent them - hence the name "Camelot" which in the director's mind connoted "a stable society with peace and justice for all."

The army backed its interest with an allocation of $ 6 million and successfully recruited some of the most respected social scientists in this country. Enthusiasm was high; participants believed Project Camelot would be an opportunity to influence government policy directly and to "educate" the army. As far as they could tell, military officials has no intention of interfering with their work.

The project was abruptly terminated when Chilean officials protested to the State Department, and the Chilean press began to publish stories about academic spies. Neither the State Department nor the Senate was willing to jeopardise friendly relations with Latin American nations for the sake of gathering data, and there was some question as to the army's true motives.

Although Project Camelot never got off the ground, it did raise numerous questions during its brief history. Is it ethical for social scientists to work for the military? Many American sociologists thought not. But Project Camelot was an opportunity to study political order and disorder in depth. Would the project have become so controversial if it had been launched with private funds? After all, there is nothing to prevent military strategists from using (or misusing) research conducted with private money.

Equally problematic are questions about sociologists' responsibilities toward the people they study. Does a researcher have the right to deceive people about his or her intentions, to risk exposing and hurting them in the name of scientific inquiry? Milgram, for example, recruited subjects for his experiment by lying to them. It is difficult to estimate the impact participation had on the subjects: one man told Milgram his wife had said, "You can call yourself Eichmann" (1973). Zimbardo's techniques have also been questioned. The "prisoners" had not been told that they would actually be arrested, and they did not know where they were being taken. During the experiment, three became so hysterical or depressed that they were released after two days, and the entire study was cancelled after six days, although it was originally planned to run six weeks.

George Ritzer (1972) suggests that we ask the following questions in evaluating research:

1. Did the researcher harm the subjects he or she studied?
2. Did the researcher affect the subject's behaviour and thereby invalidate his or her conclusions?

   To which we add,

3. Could the researcher have obtained the same data without deceiving people and injuring their self-esteem?

The question of whether sociologists should actively participate in the political arena also involves ethical issues. Many believe sociologists should remain neutral; that taking a stand would contaminate the discipline. "But as Robert Lynd suggested in *Knowledge for What?*:

> Somebody is going to interpret what the situation, [the facts] means. . . . When the social scientist, after intensive study of a problem, avoids extrapolating his .data into the realm of wide meaning, however tentatively stated, he invites others presumably more biased than himself - e.g., the National Association of Manufacturers, the American Federation of Labour, the advertising man, the American Legion and so on - to thrust upon the culture their interpretations. (1939, pp, 185-86)

In short, Lynd and many other sociologists argue that social scientists should suggest social policies because if they don't, others, with their own special interests at heart, will.

3

THE STRUCTURE OF SOCIETY

LEVELS OF SOCIAL STRUCTURE

A pickup truck drives slowly down the street. The truck stops as it comes abreast of a man sitting on a cost-iron porch and the white driver calls out, asking if the man wants a day's work. The man shakes his head and the truck moves on up the block, stopping again whenever idling men come within calling distance of the driver. At the Carryout corner, five men debate the question briefly and shake their heads no to the truck. The truck turns the corner and repeats the same performance up the next street. In the distance, one can see one man, then another, climb into the back of the truck and sit down. In starts and stops, the truck finally disappears.

What is it we have witnessed here? A labour scavenger rebuffed by his would-be prey? Lazy, irresponsible men turning down an honest day's work for an honest day's pay? . . .

Let us look again at the driver of the truck. He has been able to recruit only two or three men from each twenty or fifty he contacts. To him, it is clear that the others simply do not choose to work. Singly or in groups, belly-empty or belly-full, sullen or gregarious, drunk or sober, they confirm what he has read, heard and knows from his own experience; these men wouldn't take a job if it were handed to them on a platter. (Liebow, 1967, pp. 29-30).

Why are these men hanging around on street-corners? And why are many others like them hanging around corners in urban ghettos across the country?

Sociologists answer these questions in two ways. One way is by examining the *micro level* of social structure, that is, the pattern of personal interactions that characterise everyday life. This would mean investigating interpersonal relationships on the streetcorner to learn how these men see themselves and relate to others in face-to-face situations; how they balance their values and aspirations with their experiences.

The second approach is to focus on the *macro-level* of social structure, that is, the large social patterns that shape an entire society. These patterns are beyond any one person's control, yet they play a powerful role in shaping our lives. For example, the hierarchy of jobs and rewards, national patterns of prejudice and discrimination, the expectations that each sex has for the other are macro forces, which strongly influence the lives not only of streetcorner men but of all of us.

The Micro-level

From all appearances the truck driver is correct. But appearances can be misleading, as Elliot Liebow demonstrates in *Tally's Corner* (1967). In fact, most of the men who refused the driver's offer already have jobs. Sweets, for example, works nights in office buildings, hotels, and other public places, "Cleaning up middle-class trash"; Tally, a labourer, has the day off because bad weather stopped construction where he was working. Irregular hours and irregular jobs such as these are the rule in the ghetto. Other men on the street refused work because they were disabled. (Accidents occur more often on construction sites and in factories where unskilled labourers work than they do in offices.) Some of the men are drawing nearly as much and in some cases more money from unemployment compensation than they could earn as labourers. A few are working quite hard at illegal activities - "buying and selling sex, liquor, narcotics, stolen goods, or anything else that turns up" (p. 33). And Tonk is on

Table 3.1
Work Orientations of Welfare and Nonwelfare Fathers[1]

	Welfare Fathers		Urban, Working Fathers	
Orientations	*Black*	*White*	*Black*	*White*
1. Life aspirations	3.61	3.63	3.71	3.66
2. Work ethic	3.40	3.36	3.53	3.41
3. Lack of Confidence in ability to succeed	2.76	2.55	3-22	2.44
4. Acceptability of welfare	2.40	2.21	1.97	1.61
5. Work beyond need for money	2.97	3.04	3.26	3.09
6. Train to improve earning ability if poor	3.74	3.58	3.60	3.63
Number of respondents	81	163	500	175

[1]Items were rated on four-point scales. The higher the rating, the stronger the orientation.
Source: Adapted from Leonard Goodwin, *Do the Poor Want to Work?* (Washington, D.C.: The Brookings Institution), 1972, p. 73.
A recent survey of welfare and working fathers, both black and white, found no significant differences in life aspirations, the desire to work, and several other orientations listed in Table 3.1. The orientations were rated on a four-point scale, with (4) being the highest possible rating. It is clear that fathers on welfare as well as those who work have a strong desire to work, to improve themselves, and to earn more than a minimal income. At the same time, they are not very confident that they will succeed (orientation 3). The one notable difference concerns the orientation toward welfare; those who are on it are more inclined to accept it than those whose taxes pay for it.

the corner because he is afraid that if he goes to work his wife will disgrace him by taking the opportunity to be unfaithful.

Actually, only a handful of the men lingering on the street fit the truck driver's image: Arthur has no intention of looking for a job; Leroy is playing pinball instead of reporting to work; Sea Cat quit a job last week without giving notice; and Richard drank away his entire paycheck on the weekend. Why aren't these men out working or looking for work? Many people think the poor don't want to work, that somehow they have escaped the work ethic. (See Table 3.1 for the results of a study that disputes this view.)

The streetcorner man, many believe, lives from moment to moment, indulging his whims "with no thought for the costs, the consequences, the future" (p. 64). Working regularly, saving, accepting responsibility for a wife and children, planning for the future are alien to him. He doesn't care about being respectable; in fact, he makes fun of those who are. He lives in a world of gambling, liquor and drugs, fancy cars and clothes (when he can get them), "fancy women," fast talk and fast money. Liebow rejects this characterisation entirely He argues that to understand these men's attitudes and why they hold the kinds of jobs they do or why they fail to look for work, we have to look beyond the streetcorner to the macro-level of social structure.

The Macro-level

Moving back from the close-up view, Liebow analyses the position of Tally and his neighbours in the American economic and class system, and shows that this position shapes not only their jobs, but also their feelings about themselves. First, Liebow calls attention to the kinds of jobs that are available to these men - unskilled labourer, janitor, dishwasher, elevator operator, *busboy,* delivery *boy.* Not one of these occupations pays enough to enable a man to support a family. Not one has any future. "The busboy or dishwasher who works hard becomes, simply, a haro-working busboy or dishwasher. Neither hard work nor perseverance can conceivably carry the janitor to a sit-down job in the office building he cleans up. . . . The job ... is a dead end" (p. 63). Perhaps more important, none of these jobs offers any kind of prestige or status.

> Neither the streetcorner man who performs these jobs nor the society which requires him to perform them assesses the job as one "worth doing and worth doing well." Both employee and employer are contemptuous of the job. The employee shows his contempt by his reluctance to accept it or to keep it, the employer by paying less than is required to support a family. Nor does the low-wage job offer prestige, respect, interesting work, opportunity for learning or advancement, or any other compensation, (p. 58).

There are several reasons why Tally and the other men Liebow observed find themselves in unstable and unrewarding jobs. Most obviously, they lack the education or training that would qualify them for better jobs. More subtly, they lack the contacts in the business world that middle-class people establish in the process of growing up. Also, they are black, which may explain all the rest.

Tally, like many of this contemporaries, was raised in the South some forty years ago, when schools were segregated and local boards of education did not consider educating blacks very important. Recent studies indicate that conditions for blacks in big cities as well as in rural southern districts have not changed as much as one might expect. For example, Owen (1972) found that expenditures per pupil in terms of teachers' salaries are significantly higher in predominantly white, middle-class schools than they are in predominantly black, inner-city schools. Typically, teaching posts in ghetto schools are considered hardship assignments; seniority brings transfers out. Thus, inner-city schools lose their most experienced and often most talented teachers. "The schools in the ghetto have lost faith in the ability of their students to learn, and the ghetto has lost faith in the ability of the schools to lead," wrote black psychologist Kenneth Clark (1965). Martin Deutsch (1960) found that teachers in urban schools spend as much as 80 per cent of their time in the classroom coping with nonacademic problems and trying to maintain control. In the meantime, the demand for higher education in the job market grows.

In addition, American society is structured in such a way that blacks and other minorities are seldom able to obtain training as apprentices in the lucrative trade unions. As recently as 1968, the justice Department was prosecuting sixteen trade unions and one building trades council of the AFL-CIO for racial discrimination (Hill, 1969, p. 201). Racial prejudice, manifest in many ways, set distinct boundaries around the opportunities available to Tally and his friends.

Box 3.1

In the News

Unanticipated Consequences: "A Health Problem on the Reservation"

In our discussion of poverty and unemployment among a group of black men, we uncovered one of the most basic principles of sociology -that the society in which we live affects our lives in ways that we may not always be aware of. Knowing the social structure clarifies these unanticipated consequences. Racial discrimination, for example, boomerangs back at society by contributing to the welfare rolls. Similarly, an action that has been carefully planned to effect a change in one institution or segment of society may have a totally unanticipated consequence in another, as the following excerpt suggests.

WHITESBURG, Ky - The elimination of the military draft is considered one of the good things of the Nixon years. But it has also meant the end of a fairly regular flow of draft detesting young medical students seeking to do their time in the Public Health Service.

This has hit the Indian Health Service's 51 Indian hospitals and 77 health centers hard. These critical facilities had been staffed to a large extent by medical personnel seeking to avoid the draft. This means that to a large extent these facilities are now facing difficulties in being staffed at all.

"We don't do anything really spectacular or medically unique," one overworked Indian Health Service doctor said in South Dakota. "What would be monumental is the mess if these services were cut."

Though by no intentional act of policy, this is precisely what is happening now. Even as health statistics continue to point to continuing unnecessary Indian health tragedies, the hospitals that are the base for whatever medical services do exist on reservations are facing an imminent shortage of personnel. ... In 1969, for example, over 3,000 medical students sought Public Health Service jobs, with many specifying reservation work as a first or second choice. In 1973, the number of applicants had plummeted to under 500.

Source: Phil Primack; "A Health Problem on the Reservation," *The New York Times,* January 7,1974.

In summary, attempting to explain poverty and unemployment by analysing only the micro-level of social structure - the way a group of men conduct their lives on a day-to-day basis - does not give us a complete picture. The larger aspects of social structure - including the educational system, the hierarchy of jobs and rewards, and racial discrimination - must all be taken into account.

ELEMENTS OF SOCIAL STRUCTURE: NORMS, STATUS AND ROLES

Our discussion so far has focused on the levels of social structure, on the way social forces affect our lives. In this section we will take a closer look at the elements of social structure through which society shapes our attitudes and actions - *norms, status* and *roles*.

Norms

In *Games People Play* (1964), Eric Berne describes the greeting ritual of the American:

> "Hi!" (Hello, good morning.)
> "Hi!" (Hello, good morning.)
> "Warm enough forya?" (How are you?)
> "Sure is. Looks like rain, though." (Fine. How are you?)
> "Well, take care yourself." (Okay.)
> "I'll be seeing you,"
> "So long."
> "So long." (p. 37)

This brief exchange is conspicuously lacking in content. If you were to measure the success of this conversation in terms of information conveyed, you would have to give it a flat zero. Nevertheless, both people leave the scene feeling quite satisfied. They have said no more and no less than the situation (a meeting of co-workers, neighbours, or acquaintances) required. Each behaved quite properly, in accord with accepted social norms.

Norms are the guidelines people follow in their relations with one another: they are shared standards of desirable behaviour. Norms not only indicate what people should or should not do in a given situation, but they also enable them to anticipate how others will interpret and respond to their words and actions. Norms vary from society to society, from group to group within societies, and from situation to situation. Behaviour which in one society is the height of propriety in another may be disgraceful. For example:

> Among the Ila-speaking peoples of Africa, girls are given houses of their own at harvest time where they may play at being man and wife with boys of their choice. It is said that among these people virginity does not exist beyond the age of ten. [In contrast] among the Tepoztlan Indians of Mexico, from the time of a girl's first menstruation, her life becomes "crabbed, cribbed, confined". No boy is to be spoken to or encouraged in the least way. To do so would be to court disgrace, to show oneself to be crazy or mad. (Ember and Ember, 1973, p. 318)

In this country a generation ago, virginity was highly prized; today, in marked contrast, virgins of twenty-two or twenty-three probably try to hide their inexperience, and may even wonder about there being something wrong with themselves.

Some norms are situational, that is, they apply to specific categories of people in specific circumstances. We consider it appropriate for a person to pray to God in church, or to speak to people who have long since "gone to the other side" during a seance (even if we think the seance is phony). But a person who addresses God or invokes spirits during a dinner party or in a subway train will probably be considered insane. (See Goffman, 1959, pp. 75 - 79 on occult involvement.)

Norms also vary in intensity, that is, some are more important to people than others. The days when people stare at men who wear their hair long are over. Nobody bothers very much if students lie about having been sick when they hand in papers late, or if a woman violates custom by retaining her maiden name after she is married. But other norms (called mores) are held more intensely. Incest taboos, for example, are nearly universal. The degree to which norms are enforced - through social pressure or legal action -depends on both the intensity of the norm and on the number of people who consider it important. The fact that the penalty for rape in some states is the death sentence tells a great deal about the intensity of norms concerning sexual relations, womanhood and male aggression. The more serious the crime, the more intense the norm (or norms) behind it.

Social norms even govern our emotions and perceptions. For example, people are *supposed* to feel sad and act depressed when a member of their family dies. The jury in Camus's novel *The Stranger* condemns Meursalt to death primarily because he went to a movie (even worse, a comedy) on the day his mother died - certain proof that he was "inhuman" (Henry, 1965, p. 15). Similarly people are supposed to pay attention to some things but not to others. For example, we consider it bad taste to gawk at a couple who are quarrelling bitterly or to eavesdrop on an intimate conversation (particularly if the conversation is about the eavesdropper). We expect a male doctor to ignore the beauty of a female patient who disrobes in his office, but we would consider it odd for him to do so under other circumstances.

What is so interesting about social norms is how most people follow them automatically; alternatives never occur to them. This is particularly true of unspoken norms that seem self-evident, such as answering a person who addresses you. People conform because it seems right; because to violate norms would damage their self-image (or "hurt their conscience"); because they want approval and fear ridicule, ostracism, and in some cases, punishment. As a result, social relations are relatively predictable and orderly - at least on the surface.

Status and Roles

A *status* is a position in the social structure that determines where a person fits in the community and how he or she should relate to other people. Status may be ascribed or achieved. An *ascribed status* is one that is assigned to a person at birth or at different stages in the life cycle - for example, being male or female, a Mexican-American, a Kennedy, a teenager, a senior citizen. Each of these characteristics (sex, ethnic background, age) influences how a person is expected to act and how he or she will be treated. For example, to be born a Rockefeller guarantees a high social position; to be born poor and black still guarantees obstacles and restrictions. An *achieved status* is a position a person attains through personal effort. Physician, politician, artist, teacher, the town drunk, or the Boston Strangler - each of these is an achieved status. (Once a person attains a deviant status, he may be marked for life.

One of a person's ascribed or achieved statuses may largely determine his or her social identity). This may be an occupation that demands most of a person's time and energy (such as the presidency), or it may be position of particular symbolic significance. For example, impressionist Jean Renoir was not just a man who happened to earn a living by painting; he *was* an artist. When Renoir was so crippled by arthritis that he could no longer use his hands, he had brushes strapped to his wrists so that he could continue with his life's work. For children in our society, age and sex are most salient: they identify themselves as five- or seven-year-olds, as boys or girls. These are important facts they know about themselves. For adults, occupation is usually most significant. However, race, sex, or age may come first; for example, Kenneth Clark is a *black* psychologist, Bella Abzug is the *female* Representative from New York, and Eubie Blake is a ninety-year-old pianist.

Statuses have considerable impact on how people act, and on how others act toward them. Every status carries with it a socially, prescribed *role* - that is, expected behaviour patterns, obligations and privileges. From the age of five, for example, American children begin to learn the role behaviours that are associated with their status as students. Raising hands, doing homework, studying for tests are all aspects of the role that students are expected to perform.

One status may carry several roles. For example, a medical student fills one role in relation to his or her teachers and others in relation to fellow students, nurses and patients. Similarly, an actor or actress fills different roles with other actors, the director, stagehands, the audience, the press. The complex of roles that accrues to a single status is a *role set* (Merton, 1968, pp. 422-23).

Of course, there is a great deal more room for role interpretation in real life than there is in the theater. No two people who occupy the same status perform their roles identically. Individuals differ in what they believe is expected of them. For example, one professor perceives her role to be that of challenging students, making them doubt and question established theories; another sees his role as dispensing knowledge. Whether or not individuals live up to their roles is still another question. A father who perceives his role as being a pal to his children may actually relate to them in a formal and rather distant way; a president who perceives his role as upholding the Constitution may actually violate that document in his day-to-day decisions.

Although in the beginning, playing a new social role may involve acting and pretense, people tend to *become* what they play at being:

> One feels more ardent by kissing, more humble by kneeling and more angry by shaking one's fist. That is, the kiss not only expresses ardor but manufactures it. Roles carry with them both certain actions and emotions and attitudes that belong .to these actions. The professor putting on an act that pretends to wisdom comes to feel wise. The preacher finds himself believing what he preaches. The soldier discovers martial stirrings in his breast as he puts on his uniform. In each case, while the emotion,or attitude may have been present before the role was taken on, the latter inevitably strengthens what was there before. In many instances there is every reason to suppose that nothing at all anteceded the playing of the role in the actor's consciousness, in other words, one becomes wise by being appointed a professor, believing by engaging in activities that presuppose belief, and ready for battle by marching in formation. (Berger, 1963, p. 96).

Roles, then, transform both the action and the actor.

Role Strain and Role Conflict - "People generally want to do what they are supposed to do" (Goode, 1969, p. 485), but it isn't always easy or even possible. Sometimes people experience difficulty in meeting the demands of a role, *Role strain* may occur when conflicting demands are built into a role. For example, one part of a foreman's role is to maintain good relations with the people working under him. At the same time, he is expected to act as a representative of management, enforcing decisions from above. Often these two demands are in direct conflict.

Role strain also occurs when people cannot meet the demands of their role. Liebow found, for example, that most street-corner men had married early, with high hopes of becoming good husbands and fathers. But most failed, financially at first, then emotionally. "Where the father lives with his own children, his occasional touch or other tender gesture is dwarfed by his unmet obligations. No matter how much he does, it is not enough" (p. 87).

Role conflict describes situations where fulfilment of one role automatically results in the violation of another. The classic example is the black policeman. As a black man he knows the system is weighted against black people; as a policeman, however, he acts as an agent of that very same system. Soldiers may experience intense role conflict. Young men who have been brought up to feel that killing is wrong are expected to fire guns and drop bombs. Many try to resolve this conflict by not using their weapons. Writing after World War II, S.L.A., Marshall estimated that even when being fired upon, only 25 per cent of the soldiers fired back (1947, p. 50).

THE IMPACT OF SOCIAL STRUCTURE: PRISONERS OF SOCIETY?

Having said that norms structure emotions and perception as well as overt behaviour, that people tend to become what they play at being, and that role strain and conflict create intense personal anguish, we run head on into the question of whether people are prisoners of society. Are we mere puppets, blindly following society's rules, obediently acting out our parts? To deny the impact of norms, statuses, and roles on our attitudes and behaviour would be foolish. At the same time, however, people *feel* that they are free, that they make decisions, that they are the authors of their lives. Is this feeling of self-determination a delusion? Sociologists would agree that to some extent it is. People tend to lose their awareness of the impact of social pressure (if they were ever conscious of it at all). There is much debate within sociology as to how free we really are. In this section we present that debate.

Society in People: The Structuralist Position

Peter L. Berger has few, if any qualms about unmasking our most cherished beliefs, including our ideas about love.

> In Western countries, and especially in America, it is assumed that men and women marry because they are in love. There is a broadly based popular mythology about the character of love as a violent, irresistible emotion that strikes where it will, a mystery that is the goal of most young people and often of the not-so-young as well. As soon as one investigates, however, which people actually marry each other, one finds that the lightning-shaft of Cupid seems to be guided rather strongly within very definite channels of class, income, education, racial and religious background. (1963, p. 35).

Berger goes on to describe the courtship ritual as a couple proceeds from movie dates to meeting the family, from holding hands to "what they originally planned to save for afterwards," from planning evenings to planning a future, and to the decisive scene in the car, under the moon, when one or the other proposes. He writes, "Neither of them have invented this game or any part of it. They have only decided that it is with each other, rather than with other possible partners, that they will play it." While there is room for innovation and improvication, "too much adlibbing is likely to risk the success of the whole operation" (p. 86).

Is Berger just being cynical? No, he is expressing a view shared by many students of human behaviour. One of America's great social theorists, Robert K. Merton, has explained how people acquire the attitudes of society and come to think of them as their own (1938). In Merton's view, conforming and nonconforming behaviour alike are the result of social pressure. Individuals construct a self-image by comparing themselves to members of groups to which they belong, groups with which they want to be affiliated, and those from which they want to disassociate themselves. In the process, individuals assimilate norms and values that direct their behaviour. For example, in the 1950s and 1960s. American society taught that it is right and legitimate -perhaps even mandatory - to seek love and marriage by courting a member of the opposite sex in prescribed ways.

The feelings of free choice, of spontaneity and passion that accompany the chase only indicate the extent to which these goals and means have been internalised.

> Society ... is not only something "out there," . . . but it is also something "in here," part of our innermost being. . . . Society not only controls our movements, but shapes our identity, our thoughts and our emotions. The structures of society become the structures of our own consciousness. (Berger, 1963, p. 121).

It seems then that we are not only prisoners of society, we are prisoners who busily mend and strengthen the walls of our jail.

Innovation and Improvisation: The Symbolic Interactionist Position

The idea that people act out the roles society prescribes, unthinking and unreflecting, strikes many sociologists as an exaggeration. In attempting to describe and fix the patterns of everyday life, there is a danger of slipping into the notion that the patterns create the behaviour, rather than *vice versa*. This is roughly equivalent to saying the game plays the person. Moreover, critics of the structuralist view argue that it underplays the ambiguity in face-to-face encounters. Only on stage is the outcome of two people meeting predetermined.

Symbolic interactionists stress the situational character of social behaviour. They argue that people do not interact according to a blueprint of social instructions. Instead they constantly evaluate each other's behaviour and react accordingly (Blumer, 1966). Social interaction is seen by the symbolic interactionists to be a very delicate and complex process. Even the statement "I love you" may evoke several reactions.

> If a man says "I love you," to a woman, she may wonder whether he means it, whether he loves her only, how much he loves her, whether he will love her next week or next year, or whether this love only means that he wants her to love him. She may even wonder

> whether his love includes respect and care, or whether his love is merely physical. "I love you" is surely an ambiguous message. The woman may come to the conclusion that his idea of love is not hers and therefore the kind of love he has to give would not make her happy. So in spite oi his caresses and in spite of the fact that she enjoys the man, the woman . . . breaks off. . . . Everything depends on who says what to whom and how he says it, and human beings scan each others' utterances to see what lies behind the words. {Henry, 1965, p. 191).

W.I. Thomas also pointed to the subjective quality of reality in his famous statement, "If men define situations as real they are real in their consequences" (1928, p. 572). Thomas meant that reality, like beauty, lies in the eye of the beholder. By itself, a symbol or a gesture - for example, hitting one's hands together - is meaningless. It becomes significant only when people invest it with meaning - in this case, applause. When two people meet they bring their own meanings, their own definition of the situation. Social order exists to the extent that people approach one another with similar understandings and expectations and share a common definition of the situation.

Discovering the Rules: Ethnontethodology - Some sociologists have become interested in uncovering the implicit understandings and expectations that guide social behaviour. *Ethnomethodology* refers to the study of the rules that underlie ordinary, everyday activities. (*Ethnos* is Greek for people; *meth* is a way of doing things.)

One ethnomethodologist, Harold Garfmkel, has devised a technique for uncovering these rules. His method is to discover the rules by *breaking* them (1967). For example, Garfinkel asked some of his students to pretend to be strangers on their next visit to their families. For fifteen minutes to an hour, the students maintained the polite distance of guests - speaking only when spoken to, using formal modes of address (Mr. Jones Instead of Dad), avoiding personal exchanges. Two of the forty-nine families thought the students were joking; one ignored the student's behaviour; the remainder were upset and annoyed. "Family members demanded explanations: What's the matter? What's gotten into you? Did you get fired? Are you sick? What are you being so superior about? Why are you mad? Are you out of your mind or just being stupid?" (pp. 47-48). In one way or another, the students' families tried to restore normal relations.

In other experiments, Garfinkel's students "made trouble" by attempting to bargain for items in a store (something Americans generally do not do); by breaking the rules in a game of tic-tac-toe (erasing the opponent's first move); and by closing in during a conversation so that they were nose-to-nose with the unsuspecting subject. Each of these violations of the rules of interaction produced confusion and often anxiety (in the students as well as in the "victim") and anger.

Garfinkel and the symbolic interactionists, then, do not deny that there are patterns in the way people relate to one another. Rather, they emphasise the point that "the established patterns of group life do not carry on *by themselves*" (Blumer, in Wallace, 1969, p. 237, italics added). Patterns exist because people bring similar meanings to situations, because they repeat behaviour that has "worked" in the past, because it is generally easier to live within norms than to violate them. Social guidelines and habits free people from the impossible task of reviewing alternatives and making decisions every minute of their lives. The micro interpersonal structure of society emerges from this process of defining situations, interpreting the acts of other people and adjusting one's own behaviour accordingly.

"The Presentation of Self" - For sociologist Erving Goffman, many of our daily activities can be explained as the self-conscious effort to manage (that is, control) the impression we make on others. In part to keep up appearances and save face, in part to get what we want from situations. Examples of this abound. College athletes wear practice shirts with their team number to class and social gatherings: girls living in dormitories often wait to answer the phone until they've been paged several times, so that everyone within earshot knows they received a call (Waller, in Coffman, 1959, p. 4). Practically no one answers the phone on the first ring-it would appear overanxious. At the beginning of a semester students generally try to impress professors with how bright they are. After exams, during the grading period, they may try to appear harried, even sick to evoke sympathy. In short, the way people act in public has an "on-stage" quality to it.

In the beginning of a romance, when man and woman are both a little unsure of how the other person perceives them, impressions becomes very important. In the following passage from Sylvia Plath's. *The Bell Jar.* (1971), Esther Greenwood, a shy studious freshman, receives her first kiss from Buddy Willard. Ecstatic, she strives to appear nonchalant.

> I stood pretending to admire the lights behind the chemistry lab while Buddy got a good footing on the rough soil. While he kissed me I kept my eyes open and tried to memorize the spacing of the house lights so I would never forget them.
>
> Finally, Buddy stepped back ... "Wow it makes me feel terrific to kiss you."
>
> I modestly didn't say anything.
>
> "I guess you go out with a lot of boys," Buddy said then.
>
> "Well, I guess I do." I thought I must have gone out with a different boy every week for a year.
>
> "Well, 1 have to study a lot."
>
> "So do I," I put in hastily. "I have to keep my scholarship after all."
>
> "Still, I think I could manage to see you every third weekend."
>
> "That's nice," I was almost fainting and dying to get back to college and tell everybody, (pp. 67-68).

In most cases, the person or persons one tries to impress -the audience - will act as if the performance were real. There is an unspoken pact: you support my act and I will support yours. Violations, by actor or audience, lead to hostility and ostracism. Occasionally a person will work to create a negative or antisocial, eccentric impression. More often, however, people strive to live up to socially accepted ideals of behaviour.

THE PATTERNS OF SOCIAL RELATIONSHIPS

Although most people think a lot about their relations with other people, few are aware of the structural regularities tha underlie social interaction. Yet the same patterns emerge again and again. In the following pages, we will discuss four basic patterns of social relationships, common to individuals as well as to whole societies: *exchange, cooperation, competition* and *conflict*.

Exchange

> Gratitude is like mercantile credit. The latter is the mainstay of business; and we repay our debts, not because it is right that we should discharge them, but in order more easily to borrow again. (La Rochefoucauld, *The Maxims)*

When a person or a group assists another for the express purpose of obtaining some material or emotional reward -and both parties understand this - they are engaged in an exchange, not in exploitation, *Social exchange* is based on the principle of reciprocity; that people should both help and not injure people who have helped them. By extension, giving a gift or performing a service creates an obligation on the part of the recipient - one that may be repaid in kind, or simply with gratitude. As George Simmel wrote, "Often the subtlest as well as the firmest bonds among [people] develop from this feeling" in Nisbet, 1970, p. 65).

Exchange is the most basic form of social interaction,

> Social exchange can be observed everywhere once we are sensitised. . . to it, not only in market relations but also in friendship and even in love ... as well as in many social relations between these extremes in intimacy. Neighbours exchange favours; children, toys; colleagues, assistance; acquaintances, courtesies; politicians, concessions; discussants, ideas; housewives, recipes. (Blau, 1964, p. 88).

These reciprocal transactions serve the important function of binding individuals and groups together with on-going networks of mutual obligations and gratitude.

Of course, social exchange is not always equal; love or respect may be one-sided. If one group in a society controls most of that society's resources, it may exercise unlimited power. Similarly, a person who extends assistance to someone who cannot reciprocate (but who does not refuse aid) places himself or herself in a superior position (Blau, in Nisbet, 1970, p. 66). But equal or unequal, exchange creates social bonds - between king and peasant, man and wife, the Senator from Maine and the Senator from Texas, officer and enlisted man, nation and nation. These links are crucial for the simple reason that many (if not most) of the things people need and value are scarce. And perhaps even more importantly, many are beyond the reach of individual effort.

Cooperation and Competition

Cooperation is one of several solutions to the problem of scarcity: people who recognise a common objective join forces to achieve their goal and share in the rewards. This is well illustrated by the net hunting once practiced by the Ik and neighbouring East African tribes. As many as a hundred people would move out onto the plains together. Some would set up a wide arc of nets attached to poles. From an advance position, women and small children would begin beating the grass to force the game toward the trap. Men and boys would wait with spears and bows and arrows - some within the net arc, some behind to catch the animals that escaped. Each member of the hunt shared equally in the day's catch [Turnbull, 1972, pp. 24-25). Net hunts were a tradition among the Ik; they had hunted this way for as long as anyone could remember.

Nisbet distinguishes this kind of *traditional cooperation,* which carries the weight of custom, from directed, contractual, and spontaneous cooperation. By *directed cooperation* he means the kind of joint activity people in authority force on those beneath them (1970, pp. 68-69). For example, an officer commands enlisted men to take a hill; a teacher insists that children share the baseball diamond; the federal government directs American citizens to pay taxes. Deutsch (1949) directed cooperation when he divided a class of psychology students into five-member teams for a six-week course in problem solving. He informed half the teams that individual grades would depend on what the *team* accomplished as a whole. Members of the other team were graded for individual achievement, the more common practice in American education. Deutsch found that students were more productive when they cooperated than when they competed with one another - at least on the tasks he assigned. But to generalise from this to the idea that cooperation is better than competition would be simplistic.

Contractual cooperation is a limited preplanned agreement to join forces in specific ways, for a specific period of time, to achieve specific goals. Unlike traditional cooperation, which is woven into a group's entire way of life, contractual cooperation is strictly utilitarian. According to exchange theorists, *all* cooperation is implicitly contractual, because the underlying question is, "What am I getting out of this? What am I giving?"

Of course, "the oldest, most natural, and widespread" form of cooperation is neither directed nor preplanned: it arises *spontaneously* when a situation seems to call for joint action. For example, during the northeast power blackout of 1965, New Yorkers helped to direct traffic; storeowners by and large resisted the temptation to raise the price of candles to meet the demand; and hotels opened their lobbies to stranded commuters.

This is not to say that crises always inspire cooperation. During the 1960s, for example, the Ik were forced off their game-rich plains (which were designated national parks and reserves) into the arid mountains above. Threatened with starvation they became extremely individualistic. No one shared food anymore; children were left to forage on their own; people literally took food from the mouths of the old and the sick. In his somewhat controversial analysis of "the sociology of survival" among the Ik, Colin Turnbull suggests that cooperation, brotherhood, and even love can only exist where people enjoy at least a minimal standard of living. Whether or not this is true, spontaneous cooperation does depend on the norms of reciprocity, on the capacity to imagine oneself in another's role, and on communication (a shared definition of the situation) (Nisbet, 1970, p. 67).

Competition, two or more parties striving individually for an objective that only one can achieve, is a second solution to the problem of scarcity. In competition only one person or group wins; only one person can be elected president; only one team can win the World Series; in our society a man may marry only one woman at a time.

On the surface competition appears to be the opposite of cooperation, but this is not really the case. Competition rests on a foundation of cooperation: rivals seek to *out do* not *undo,* one another. In other words, competition, like cooperation, has its rules and limits. For example, oil companies compete for buyers by advertising how many services they provide at local stations. But, with rare exceptions, they avoid so-called price wars; when one company raises prices, the others do so also. Only when environmentalist groups began to exercise pressure did the oil and auto companies begin to run ads about their concern for ecology - and, again, they acted together. In other words, they compete only within narrow, well-defined limits.

Conflict

The difference between competition and conflict is the difference between a prize fight and a brawl. *Conflict* develops when two parties conclude (rightly or wrongly) that the only way to obtain a contested goal is to thwart overpower, injure, eliminate, or otherwise neutralise the opposition. Conflict is unlimited: destroying the enemy becomes both the means and the end. The attempt to injure may be physical, as in wars, or symbolic, as when combatants wage a war of threats and insults (Turner, 1969, p. 823).

Common sense suggests that conflict is inherently disruptive and should be avoided at almost any cost. Alogical assumption to be sure, but sociologically inaccurate. In fact, one of the primary functions of conflict is the stimulation of *cooperation* within opposing groups (Simmel, 1955). Struggles with outsiders invariably bring insiders closer together. As Georg Simmel notes- France owes its unity to the wars with England; Spain, to its battles against Moorish invaders; this country, originally to the War of Independence (p. 101). Similarly, students begin to think and act as a group when the administration suddenly raises tuition, families tend to draw together when one member is attacked.

Conflict may also define problems and revitalise norms and values that have fallen into disuse. For example, in the early 1950s relatively few white Americans were conscious of the extent to which blacks were being denied even the most basic civil rights: "The shock of recognition, the jolt of conscience, occurred only when the Negroes, through by-and-large nonviolent action in the South and through increasingly violent demonstrations in the North, brought the problem forcibly to the attention of white public opinion and the white power structure" (Coser, 1967, p. 86). Similarly, the shooting of student protestors at Kent State and Jackson State in 1970 exposed the more sinister implications of an all-out drive for law and order. Yes, a great many people saw student demonstrators as unwashed, ungrateful, un-American riffraff and supported politicians who said as much, but shooting and killing unarmed young people was another matter.

On a more personal level, conflict may revitalise relationships. "It has been said . . . that intimate relations, such as love and friendship, need occasional quarrels in order to be reminded of the happiness by the contrast with the discord they suffered; or in order to interrupt the closeness of the relationship - which, after all, has something coercive and enclosing for the individual - by an alienation which removes this pressure" (Simmel, 1955, pp. 110-11).

Conflict may also act as a catalyst for needed social change. After the race riots of the late 1960s both the McCone Commission appointed in California and the Kerner Commission appointed by president Johnson described the riots as more or less justified expressions of black outrage, and went on to recommend a "reordering of priorities" in America. In this sense, conflict can serve as a safety valve, bringing issues to the surface before they explode on a massive scale.

How are conflicts ended? When one party defeats the other; when one concedes; when both calculate that the costs of continued antagonism exceed the possible benefits of success and agree to a compromise; or when a sudden change in circumstances gives the two parties reason to forget their differences and join ranks. Surrender is always based on the assumption that the victors will discontinue their attacks (Turner, 1969, p. 823). The Biafrans, for example, did not surrender for so long, even though they were threatened with extinction, because they did not believe the federal government of Nigeria would (or could) stop its troops from killing them.

Achieving a compromise is even more complex. By definition, conflicts involve irreconcilable goals and/or groups. As Ralph Turner writes, "agreement on [the] issues does not erase the injury that each has done to the other in the course of the conflict" (p. 823). In essence, compromise depends on the willingness of each antagonist to act as if "the other did not fully mean what he said, that his threats were not really meant to be carried out, and that his insults did not express his most enduring feelings and views" (p. 824). There is an element of irrationality in compromise and accommodation, "something like a denial of what existed a moment before" (Simmel, 1955, p. 117). Soon after World War 11, for example, the people we had been killing - the Germans and the Japanese - became our close allies.

Surrender or compromise will be unnecessary, if, by chance or design, irreconcilable parties suddenly find they have an enemy or a problem in common. Muzafer Sherif (1958) demonstrated this in a famous experiment at a summer camp for boys. He divided the campers into two teams, and by setting up competitions where only the winning team got prizes, by tricking one team into thinking the other had spoiled its food, and by other means, Sherif created an extremely volatile situation. (In fact, he and his colleagues found it difficult to prevent as real a war as ten-year-olds are capable of waging!) However, when the camp's water supply was cut off and when a group of boys from another camp were brought in for a day of sports, the teams forgot how much they hated each other and joined forces. Thus, larger goals may turn enemies into collaborators, who then direct their energies against a new enemy.

Social Institutions

Much of social life and social controversy centers around certain basic needs that confront all societies: (1) organising activities so that people obtain the goods and services they need to live, while the society maintains a balanced relationship with the environment; (2) protecting people from external threats, such as military invasions, and from internal threats, such as crime; (3) replacing people who die or migrate; (4) transmitting norms and values to new members (children and immigrants); and (5) motivating people to fulfil their roles, to support the norms and values that define the meaning and purpose of life in a society. To some extent, solving these problems is a prerequisite for survival - survival of the people who make up a society and of their way of life.

Sociologists use the term *institution* to describe the relatively stable, widely accepted clusters of norms and values that develop around basic needs of a society. An example is the family, which is the center of a complex web of shoulds and should nots, ranging from the proper ways to feel and express sexual desire to norms defining responsibility for old people. The family is one solution to the problems of regulating sexual activity replenishing the population, assigning responsibility for children and initiating them into the ways of a society, defining relationships between people in a community (the kinship system), and settling economic questions (such as inheritance). Religion and law sanctify and protect the family. It is one of the natural facts of life that people take for granted. To be sure, not everyone in our society grows up in the traditional nuclear family (a mother, a father, and their children all living together), and not everyone grows up wanting to marry and have children of their own. Still, the traditional idea of a family carries considerable moral weight. In the discussion of *Tally's Corner,* for example, that fathers may desert their families because they cannot fulfil the traditional role of provider, and that relations between fathers and children are often tense for just this reason. Young and old couples living together without getting married, women demanding freedom from the home, easy divorce, easy sex, abortion, and the like would not be so controversial if the family were not a major social institution.

Institutions such as the family, religion, political, educational and economic systems channel human experience and activity in much the same way that instincts channel animal behaviour (Berger, 1963, p. 87). They are the basic social structures, the ideas and customs around which life in a society is organised.

4
CULTURE

THE ELEMENTS OF CULTURE

Much of what is known about culture comes from anthropological field studies of people whose ways are quite different from our own. In the field, anthropologists confront a dazzling array of unfamiliar objects and customs. They observe the way people design their villages and build their homes; they study their arts, the tools they make and how they use them. They analyse the family structure, economic transactions and political organisation. They listen to the villagers' tales, and watch children at play. Where possible they attend religious and other ceremonies. Gradually they begin to understand how the people think, what they expect from one another and what they value.

One lesson of anthropology is that a people's material culture, the things they produce *(artifacts),* reflects the nonmaterial elements of their culture (their *norms, values* and *beliefs).* It is no accident, for example, that the Oglala Sioux traditionally arrange their camp in a circle.

> The Oglala believe the circle to be sacred because the great spirit caused everything in nature to be round except stone. Stone is the implement of destruction. The sun and the sky, the earth and the moon are round like a shield, though the sky is deep like a bowl. Everything that breathes is round like the stem of the plant. Since the great spirit has caused everything to be round mankind should look upon the circle as sacred, for it is the symbol of all things in nature except stone. It is also the symbol of the circle that makes the edge of

> the world and therefore of the four winds that travel there. Consequently it is also the symbol of the year. The day, the night and the moon go in a circle above the sky. Therefore, the circle is a symbol of these divisions of time and hence the symbol of all time.
>
> For these reasons the Oglala make their *tipis* circular, their camp-circle circular, and sit in a circle at ceremonies. (Walker, in Dundes, 1968, p. 304).

Similarly, in modern America the automobile reflects a whole complex of core values: freedom, physical and social mobility, individuality *and* "keeping up with the Joneses," prosperity, and the supremacy of technology. Most teenagers look forward to becoming sixteen because they will be able to drive. (How the gasoline shortage will affect this aspect of American culture is an intriguing question.)

Norms, values, beliefs, art and technology all play a part in that complex we call culture. The study of culture is the study of the meanings people attach to the things they do and the things they make. These meanings are stored in such symbols as the circle of the Oglala, the cross of Christians, the automobile, the flag, the handshake, and even the kiss.

Symbols

A *symbol* is an object, gesture, sound, colour, or design that represents something *other than itself.* For example, a circle is really nothing more than a closed curve, all points of which are at an equal distance from a point at the center. But for the Oglala Sioux, the circle represents all that they know and feel and believe about the universe. Symbols are arbitrary - they do not necessarily lock, sound, or otherwise resemble what they stand for. In some cultures black is the colour of mourning; in others, white or red suggests grief. These colours, like all symbols, derive their meanings from tradition and consensus, not from any inherent qualities. Symbols are collective creations - people in a society must agree on their meanings if they are to be understood. A gold band worn on the third finger of someone's left hand tells us that he or she is married *only* because in our culture it is a commonly recognised symbol for marriage. Of course, even though a wedding band is commonly understood to mean the wearer is married, the way the wearer and each of us interprets that condition has become quite flexible. For some, it means a lifelong partnership and absolute fidelity; for others, a greater measure of sexual and emotional freedom may be implied. Symbolic interactionists argue that the heart of social life is the sharing, conflict and manipulation of symbols.

Much human behaviour and nearly all human communication is symbolic. You may recall how witness after witness at the Senate hearings on Watergate told of the inner certainty that any order coming from the White House was legal and in the national interest; of the awe they said they felt in the presence of "the leader of the free world," "the most powerful man on earth." The presidency, they claimed, overwhelmed them. And Lyndon Johnson, the story goes, used to become enraged when he had invited antiwar spokesmen to the White House, talked with them, and as far as he could tell reached an understanding, only to find the very same people renewing their attack the next day. Why? Because they had not dared in his presence to disagree with the President.

Because symbols are arbitrary, they are highly flexible: the meaning of words and gestures can and does change. For example, the two fingers held in a V, once a very rude gesture, came to stand for victory when Churchill used it (palm forward) during World War II. In the 1960s antiwar activists revived the gesture as a symbol for peace, and this in turn became a standard greeting among members of the counterculture. (Although it seems to have died from overexposure, the V gesture will probably reappear with some new meaning in the future.)

Language

A *language* is a system of verbal and, in many cases, written symbols, with rules for putting them together. It is impossible to overestimate the importance of language in the development, elaboration and transmission of culture. Language enables people to store meanings and experiences and to pass this heritage on to new generations. Through words, we are able to learn from the experiences of others and from events at which we were not present. In addition, language enables us to transcend the here-and-now, preserving the past and imagining the future; to communicate with others and formulate complex plans; to integrate different kinds of experiences; and to develop abstract ideas.

The study of different languages has yielded numerous insights into culture. For example, the number of words available to describe an object, event, or concept in a language indicates how important it is to a people. Arabs, for example, have hundreds of words of describe camels and camel trappings, and almost as many to describe different kinds of horses. Eskimos have not one, but many words for snow. Water, a precious commodity in the arid Southwest, has numerous names in the Hopi language, as do yams in the Trobriand Islands (located north of New Guinea), where they are a staple. Similarly, Americans distinguish between sedans, station wagons, fastbacks, sports cars, convertibles, and compacts, suggesting the importance of automobiles in our culture. These words sensitise the individual Arab or Eskimo or Hopi or American to subtle variations that a person from a different culture might not even notice.

Language and Reality: The Sapir-Whorf Hypothesis - Cross-cultural studies led Edward Sapir and his student Benjamin Lee Whorf to theorise that language doesn't simply reflect culture, it actually *shapes* our thoughts and directs our interpretation of the world.)

> Language is not merely a reproducing instrument for voicing ideas but rather is itself the shaper of ideas, the programme and guide for the individual's mental activity, for his analysis of impressions, for his synthesis of his mental stock in trade. . . . We dissect nature along lines laid down by our native languages. The categories and types that we isolate from the world of phenomena we do not find there because they stare every observer in the face on the contrary, the world is presented in a kaleidoscopic flux of impressions which has to be organised by our minds - and this means largely by the linguistic systems in our minds. (Whorf, in Carroll, 1956, pp, 212-13).

Whorf based this theory on his comparison of the way Hopi Indians and English-speaking people think and speak about time. There are no tenses in the Hopi language, as there are in English, and no nouns for times, days, or years. As a result, the Hopi tend to think in terms of continuous movement, of becoming. In contrast, the English language provides numerous ways of marking or counting time, as if hours and days were things or objects. The necessity to choose one of several tenses makes English-speaking people acutely conscious of time and of time passing. English-speaking people think in terms of linear progressions.

> In our own culture, the line is so basic, that we take it for granted, as given in reality. . . . The line is found or presupposed in most of our scientific work. Our statistical facts are presented lineally as a *graph* or reduced to a normal *curve*. And all of us, I think, would be lost without our *diagrams*. We *trace* a historical development; *we follow the course* of history and evolution, *down* to the present and *up from* the ape.... And we ... follow a *line* of thought, a *course* of action or the *direction* of an argument... we *bridge* a gap in the conversation, or speak of the *span* of life or of teaching a *course,* or lament our *interrupted career.* (Lee in Dundes, 1968, pp. 334-35).

Such a linear conception of reality is alien to people in the Trobriand Islands. Dorothy Lee offers this approximation of how a Trobriand Islander would describe the planting of a coconut:

> Thou-approach-there coconut thou-bring-here-we-plant-coconut thou-go thou-plant our coconut. This-here it emerge sprout. We-push-away this we-push-away this-other coconut-husk-fiber together sprout it-sit together root. (Lee in Dundes, 1968, p. 336).

To an English-speaking person, accustomed to thinking of events as having beginnings, middles, and ends, such an account is confusing. But to a Trobriand Islander, whose only connecting word is one meaning *jump,* the description is very realistic and clear. Trobrianders do not think about beginnings and ends; the present is all. They do not see pleasurable sensual experiences as having a climax, but as an aggregate of good sensations. When talking about the pleasures of sex, Trobrianders attach no particular significance of orgasm. At

Box 4.1

The Power of Language

Does the generic use of the word *man* to denote human beings, male and female, perpetuate sexism? Writers use Man, with a capital M, when they want to sound grand, dignified, elegant. We speak of the average person as "the *man* in the street," and without thinking about it, link *he* to such high-prestige occupations as doctor and vice-president while using *she* with secretary and nurse. Men roar, bellow and growl, whereas women squeal, shriek, and purr. Textbooks for young children paint a valiant picture of *man's* accomplishments; more often than not women are treated as luggage: "the pioneers crossed the Plains with their wives, children and belongings" (Farb, 1973, pp. 141 - 44).

Joseph W. Schneider and Sally H. Hacker's study (1973) of the effects of the generic usage of *man* is particularly relevant here because they have focused on sociology textbooks. Over three hundred students in introductory sociology courses were asked to select photographs from newspapers and magazines to help illustrate topics in a proposed text. Students were given one of two lists. One of the list included Society, Urban Life, Political Behaviour, Industrial Life and Economic Behaviour; the other substituted Social Man, Urban Man, Political Man, etc. Schneider and Hacker wanted to know if there would be any difference in the pictures students submitted for these topics.

The results? Approximately 64 per cent of the pictures illustrating titles with the word *man* showed men only, compared to 50 per cent of the pictures submitted for Society, Urban Life, and other sexless titles. Where women did appear, they were usually on the periphery of action (for example, sitting in an audience) - except in pictures for the topics labelled the Family, Population and Social Man (which students apparently interpreted as Sociable Man). There were only a handful of women in the pictures for Crime and Delinquency. The researchers concluded that the generic use of man *does* perpetuate stereotyped images of men running the world.

Source: Peter Farb, *Word Play,* New York-Knopf, 1973, Joseph W. Schneider and Sally H. Hacker "Sex-Role Imagery and Use of the Generic 'Man' in Introductory Texts: A Case in the Sociology of Sociology." *The American Sociologist,* vol. 8 (1973): 12 -18.

Trobriand feasts the dessert is not saved for the end but eaten alongwith the other dishes in a meal. Pregnancy is welcomed, not as a time of waiting, but as a beautiful thing in itself. The essence of Trobriand culture is the celebration of life as a state of being. Their language, which does not permit them to arrange events in a linear or chronological way, shapes that reality.

Silent Communication - Anthropologist Edward T. Hall has extended Sapir and Whorf s theories about the role language plays in shaping thought to the study of *silent communication.* In his books *The Silent Language* (1959) and *The Hidden Dimension* (1966), Hall cites numerous examples of cultural differences in perception of time and space **and** sensory experience. For example, in public places Americans act as if they were alone. If an American is in a position to overhear a private conversation, he or she pretends to be deaf (often feigning involvement in a newspaper). Germans, in contrast, would never think of carrying on a private conversation in a public place; they wait until they are behind closed doors (1966, chaps. 11 and 12). When Arabs talk they like to be right up close to the other person; Americans tend to maintain a social distance of a foot or more, except for very intimate exchanges. Hall concludes that people from different cultures not only speak different languages, they inhabit different sensory worlds, and their experience of life can, as a result, very considerably.

Values and Norms

The Tangu, who live in a remote part of New Guinea, play a game called *taketak,* which in many ways resembles bowling. The game is played with a top that has been fashioned from a dried fruit and with two groups of coconut stakes that are driven into the ground (more or less like bowling pins). The players divide into two teams. Members of the first team take turns throwing the top into the batch of stakes; every stake the top hits is removed. Then the second team stops to the line and tosses the top into their batch of stakes. The object of the game, surprisingly, is not to knock over as many stakes as possible. Rather, the game continues until both teams have removed the *same* number of stakes. Winning is completely irrelevant (Burridge, 1957, pp. 88-89).

In a sense games are practice for "real life"; they reflect the values of the culture in which they are played. *Values* are the criteria people use in assessing their daily lives, arranging their priorities, measuring their pleasures and pains, choosing between alternative courses of action. The Tangu value equivalence: the idea of one individual or group winning and another losing bothers them, for they believe winning generates ill-will. In fact, when Europeans brought soccer to the Tangu, they altered the rules so that the object of the game was for two teams to score the same number of goals. Sometimes their soccer games went on for days! American games, in contrast, are highly competitive; there are *always* winners and losers. Many rule books include provisions for overtime and "sudden death" to prevent ties, which leave Americans dissatisfied. World Series, Superbowls, championships in basketball and hockey, Olympic Gold Medals are front page news in this country. In the words of the late football coach Vince Lombardi, "Winning isn't everything, it's the only thing."

Norms, the rules that guide behaviour in everyday situations, are derived from values, but norms and values can conflict. You may recall a news item that appeared in American newspapers in December 1972, describing the discovery of survivors of a plane crash 12,000 feet in the Andes. The crash had occurred on October 13; sixteen of the passengers (a rugby team and their supporters) managed to survive for sixty-nine days in near-zero temperatures. The story made headlines because, to stay alive, the survivors had eaten parts of their dead companions. Officials, speaking for the group, stressed how valiantly the survivors had tried to save the lives of the injured people and how they had held religious services regularly. The survivors' explanations are quite interesting, for they reveal how important it is to people to justify their actions, to resolve conflicts in norms and values (here, the positive value of survival vs, the taboo against cannibalism). Some of the survivors compared their action to a heart transplant, using parts of a dead person's body to save another person's life. Others equated their act with the sacrament of communion. In the words of one religious survivor, "If we would have died, it would have been suicide, which is condemned by the Roman Catholic faith" (Read, 1974).

Similar conflicts in norms and values are bound to occur as we gain the ability to alter genes. The ability to modify unborn children's genes so that they grow up taller or darker or even smarter than their parents lies in the not very distant future. Already scientists have made genetic copies of carrots and frogs. This is done by cloning, a process that creates a duplicate organism from a single cell. What is there to prevent people from seeking immortality through one or more facsimiles of themselves? And if artificial wombs are perfected, will parents decide to reject their offspring on delivery if the child does not live up to their expectations? Tampering with life may go against our cultural grain, but self-improvement, on the other hand, is very strongly favoured. The conflict between the two could create serious dilemmas.

These questions bring us to a crucial point about the elements of culture. A people's technology, art, language, norms and values are closely intertwined. Culture influences all areas of life. The things people take for granted as right and good and as valuable and possible, the way they respond emotionally and intellectually to their lives ultimately depends on the culture in which they live.

UNITY IN DIVERSITY

What is more basic, more "natural" than love between a man and woman? Eskimo men offer their wives to guests and friends as a gesture of hospitality; both husband and wife feel extremely offended if the guest declines (Ruesch, 1951, pp. 87 - 88). The Banaro of New Guinea believe it would be disastrous for a woman to conceive her first child by her husband and not by one of her father's close friends, as is their custom.

> The real father is a close friend of the bride's father.... Nevertheless the first born child inherits the name and possessions of the husband. An American would deem such a custom immoral, but the Banaro tribesmen would be equally shocked to discover that the first born child of an American couple is the offspring of the husband. (Haring, 1949, p. 33).

The Yanomamö of northern Brazil, whom anthropologist Napoleon A. Chagnon (1968) named "the fierce people," encourage what we would consider extreme disrespect. Small boys are applauded for striking their mothers and fathers in the face. Yanomamö parents would laugh at our efforts to curb aggression in children, much as they laughed at Chagnon's naivete when he first came to live with them.

The variations among cultures are startling, yet all peoples have customs and beliefs about marriage, and bearing and raising of children, sex and hospitality - to name just a few of the universals anthropologists have discovered in their cross-cultural explorations. But the *details* of cultures do indeed vary: in this country, not so many years ago, when a girl was serious about a boy and he about her, she wore his fraternity pin over her heart; in the Fiji Islands, girls put hibiscus flowers behind their ears when they are in love. The specific gestures are different but the impulse to symbolise feelings, to dress courtship in ceremonies, is the same. How do we explain this unity in diversity?

Cultural Universals

Cultural universals are all of the behaviour patterns and institutions that have been found in all known cultures. Anthropologist George Peter Murdock identified over sixty-cultural universals, including a system of social status, marriage, body adornments, dancing, myths and legends, cooking, incest taboos, inheritance rules, puberty customs, and religious rituals (Murdock, 1945, p. 124).

The universals of culture may derive from the fact that all societies must perform the same essential functions if they are to survive - including organisation, motivation, communication, protection, the socialisation of new members, and the replacement of those who die. In meeting these prerequisites for group life, people inevitably design similar-though not identical - patterns for living. As Clyde Kluckhohn wrote, "All cultures constitute somewhat distinct answers to essentially the same questions posed by human biology and by the generalities of the human situation" (1962, p. 317).

The way in which a people articulate cultural universals depends in large part on their physical and social environment - that is, on the climate in which they live, the materials they have at hand, and the peoples with whom they establish contact. For example, the wheel has long been considered one of humankind's greatest inventions, and anthropologists were baffled for a long time by the fact that the great civilisations of South America never discovered it. Then researchers uncovered a number of toys with wheels. Apparently the Aztecs and their neighbours did know about wheels; they simply didn't find them useful in their mountainous environment.

Adaptation, Relativity and Ethnocentrism

Taken out of context, almost any custom will seem bizarre, perhaps cruel, or just plain ridiculous. To understand why the Yanomamö encourage aggressive behaviour in their sons, for example, you have to try to see things through their eyes. The Yanomamö live in a state of chronic warfare; they spend much of their time planning for and defending against raids with neighbouring tribes. If Yanomamö parents did *not* encourage aggression in a boy, he would be ill equipped for life in their society. Socialising boys to be aggressive is *adaptive* for the Yanomamö because it enhances their capacity for survival. "In general, culture is ... adaptive because it often provides people with a means of adjusting to the physiological needs of their own bodies, to their physical geographical environment and to their social environments as well" (Ember and Ember, 1973, p. 30).

In many tropical societies, there are strong taboos against a mother having sexual intercourse with a man until her child is at least two years old. As a Hausa woman explains,

> A mother should not go to her husband while she has a child she is sucking ... if she only sleeps with her husband and does not become pregnant, it will not hurt her child, it will not spoil her milk. But if another child enters in, her milk will make the first one ill. (Smith, in Whiting, 1969, p. 518).

Undoubtedly, people would smirk at a woman who nursed a two-year-old child in our society and abstained from having sex with her husband. Why do Hausa women behave in a way that seems so overprotective and overindulgent to us? In tropical climates protein is scarce. If a mother were to nurse more than one child at a time, or if she were to wean a child before it reached the age of two, the youngster would be prone to *kwashiorkor,* an often fatal disease resulting from protein deficiency. Thus, long postpartum sex taboos are adaptive. In a tropical environment a postpartum sex taboo and a long period of breast-feeding solve a serious problem (Whiting, in Goodenough, 1969, pp. 511 - 24).

No custom is good or bad, right or wrong in itself; each one must be examined in light of the culture as a whole and evaluated in terms of how it works in the context of the entire culture. Anthropologists and sociologists call this *cultural relativity.* Although this way of thinking about culture may seem self-evident today, it is a lesson that anthropologists and the missionaries who often preceded them to remote areas learned the hard way, by observing the effects their best intentions had on peoples whose way of life was quite different from their own. In an article on the pitfalls of trying to "uplift" peoples whose ways seem backward and inefficient. Don Adams quotes an old Oriental story;

> Once upon a time there was a great flood, and involved in this flood were two creatures, a monkey and a fish. The monkey, being agile and experienced, was lucky enough to scramble up a tree and escape the raging waters. As he looked down from his safe perch, he saw the poor fish struggling against the swift current. With the very best

> intentions, he reached down and lifted the fish from the water. The result was inevitable. (1960, p. 22).

Enthnocentrism is the tendency to see one's own way of life, including behaviours, beliefs, values and norms as the only right way of living. Robin Fox points out that "any human group is ever ready to consign another recognisably different human group to the other side of the boundary. It is not enough to possess culture to be fully human, you have to possess *our* culture" (1970, p. 31).

Accounts of the first European contacts with Africa are a study in enthnocentrism. The Greeks and Romans were acquainted with the Egyptians and the Carthaginians, the Libyans and the Ethiopians, but not until the fifteenth century did Europeans venture south of the Sahara. The letters and journals of fifteenth and sixteenth-century explorers, merchants, and missionaries were popular reading in their day, and no wonder. Their tales overflowed with luria descriptions of cannibalism, incest, and "unbridled lust." Deep in the interior of the dark continent father "knew" daughter, sexuality ran rampant, people feasted on their friends and relatives (as well as their enemies). Religion, law, and government, reported the Europeans, were unknown. Any evidence of the great Sonniki dynasty in Ghana, founded in the second century A.D. (to name just one of the empires that flourished in African history) was overlooked. The following description is typical:

> The majority of them are entirely savage and display the nature of the wild beast.. . and are as far removed as possible from human kindness to one another; and speaking as they do with a shrill voice and cultivating none of the practices of civilised life as there are found among the rest of mankind, they present a striking contrast when considered in light of our own customs, (quoted by George, in Dundes, 1968, p. 25).

These accounts tell us a great deal more about what Europeans thought of human nature, left unfettered, than they do about African culture. Surveying the literature on Africans in the fifteenth and sixteenth centuries, Katherine

George found only one favourable report, written by a Dutch visitor to South Africa.

> I am astonished that... those half-truths that are spread about our [sic] Africans should have reached even your ears. I found this people ... living in harmony with nature's law, hospitable to every race of men, open, dependable, lovers of truth and justice, not utterly unacquainted with the worship of some God, endowed ... with arare nimbleness of mother wit, and having minds receptive of instruction. ... It is through the faults of our own countrymen . . . that the natives have been changed for the worse. . . . From us they have learned . .. misdeeds unknown to them'before, and, among other crimes of deepest die, the accursed lust for gold, (quoted by George, in Dundes, 1968, p. 32).

The history of race relations in this country suggests how far this observer was ahead of his times.

As conscious as Americans are of the shame of slavery, most have forgotten (or never knew about) the history of Oriental-Americans. In the mid-nineteenth century, Samuel Gompers, president of the American Federation of Labour and American Manhood Against Asiatic Coolieism, became famous for his attacks on Orientals. Why did he oppose "coolie" labour? Not because the Orientals, brought here to work on the railroads, threatened to take jobs away from Americans, but because - as everyone "knew" - Orientals are congenitally immoral. "The Yellow Man found it natural to lie, cheat and murder and 99 out of every 100 Chinese are gamblers," wrote Gompers. He went on to describe in intimate detail how the Chinese enticed little white boys and girls into their opium dens, where they remained, "condemned to spend their days in the back of laundry rooms, yielding up their virgin bodies to their maniacal yellow captors." Visions of the Mongolian hordes rising up to conquer the world lurked throughout the American West. In fact, Gompers was so successful that in 1902 Congress extended the Chinese Exclusion Act to quiet widespread fear of the "yellow peril." Although political motivation was substituted for racial epithets in the 1960s, the war in Southeast Asia was closely linked to ethnocentrism.

Cultural Integration

A people's customs, beliefs, values and technology are *interdependent*. Changes in one area invariably affect other areas, sometimes throwing the entire system off balance. For example, missionaries succeeded in converting large numbers of Madagascans to Christianity. The result? Theft, which was practically unknown in the pre-Christian days, became commonplace; people stopped caring for their homes and villages. The reason? "The fear of hell and the police are a poor substitute for the fear of ancestral ghosts who know everything and punished the evil doer with sickness on earth and exclusion from the ancestral village in the hereafter" (Linton, 1947, p. 357).

Similarly, the introduction of steel virtually destroyed the highly integrated Stone Age culture of aboriginal societies in Australia. To the Europeans who brought them, steel axes were clearly an improvement over stone implements. But to the aborigines the ax was more than a tool: relations between families and tribes were based on the ceremonial exchange of cherished stonework (Arensberg and Niehoff, 1964, p. 50).

Cultural integration refers to the degree of internal consistency in a culture. In a well integrated culture, there are few contradictions between the way people think and the way they act; established traditions enable them to make efficient use of the environment and to carry on the daily business of living with minimal inner conflicts. The Yapese, for example, once ruled the thousands of Caroline Islands that stretch across the western Pacific. Huge stone fish traps in the lagoons and a system of fresh water irrigation for taro patches (the Yap staple) enabled the island of Yap itself to support some 40,000 people in the nineteenth century. Women tended the gardens while the men fished. Men had special houses for their ceremonies and parties; women isolated themselves during menses and childbirth. The Yapese were divided into two classes, land-owning chiefs and landless servants. Every family and every individual was ranked according to the property he owned.

Only a few old people on Yap remember this past. Yap was claimed by Spain in 1886, sold to Germany in 1899, captured by Japan during World War I, and lost to the United States in World War II. Today it is part of the American Trust Tefritory of the Pacific Islands, under mandate from the United Nations. The Yapese resisted Western ways for centuries and a visitor today may still see women in grass skirts and men in elaborate loin clothes. Nevertheless, Yap culture has given way to "a new set of material wants, needs and satisfactions and a new set of social relations" (Labby, 1973, p. 35).

Motorboats have replaced outriggers, and the lagoons are polluted; villages in the interior have been abandoned along-with yam and taro patches. The people depend on expensive imported food (paid for largely with income from scrap metal salvaged from the wrecked military equipment of World War II). The land-based hierarchy of social status has given way to a job-based hierarchy that centers on American employers. Old people, who disapprove of American ways, nevertheless encourage the young to seek jobs and education in the city of Colonie; but they feel cut off. Those young people who adhere to traditions do so only to please their grandparents. High rates of juvenile delinquency and drunkenness testify to the difficulty new generations are having in coping with the loss of old values, in finding new patterns of authority, and in maintaining a sense of identity in the midst of cultural confusion and change.

What do the Yapese tell us about culture? Does their example indicate that a well-integrated culture is good and that a poorly integrated one is bad? Not necessarily. In *The Study of Man* (1947), Linton notes that a highly integrated culture, where religious, economic and family life are all of one piece, is extremely vulnerable. The Comanche were able to adjust to the ways of the white conquerors more easily than other Indian tribes precisely because their traditions were comparatively weak (pp. 364-65). Linton writes, "Cultures, like personalities, are perfectly capable of including conflicting elements and logical inconsistencies" (p. 358). We needn't go very far to illustrate this point, for American culture is truly a study in paradox.

AMERICAN CULTURE

Attempting to write the definitive profile of American culture is attempting the impossible. This country is unquestionably one of the most heterogeneous nations on earth. For every pattern one identifies, there will be myriad exceptions and contradictions. In addition, one of the dominant themes in our culture is change; it is Americans who have spread the gospel of progress around the world. Almost anything we say today will seem outdated next year. Nevertheless, certain basic orientations emerge, and certain forces of the past can be identified that are still active today. The portrait that follows describes these basic patterns. While it cannot possibly describe all the details, it does highlight the variations and contradictions in American culture.

Basic American Values

We begin with the sacred triad American children learn in first grade: freedom, equality and democracy. Polls indicate the Americans are far more likely than people of other nationalities to mention freedom and "our system of government" when asked what they are proud of in their country, and that the majority believe this *is* the land of opportunity (Williams, 1970, pp. 491, 478).

By freedom, Americans generally mean freedom *from* external controls, and freedom *to do* something in a mannel they see fit (to pursue happiness, success, and so on). But the emphasis is on noninterference. There is a tendency "to think in terms of rights rather than duties, a suspicion of established (especially personal) authority, a distrust of central government, a deep aversion to acceptance of obvious coercive restraint. . ." (Williams, 1970, p. 480). This aversion can be seen in President Eisenhower's warnings about the military-industrial complex, in George Wallace's successful campaigns, in the vilification of the Establishment in the 1960s, in the generation gap and the concomitant rebellion against the constraints of traditional marriage. Indeed, the American system of checks and balances is based on a strong fear of tyranny. Whether the founding fathers feared the tyranny of one of their peers acting like a king, or the tyranny of the landless mobs beneath them is debatable. On the personal level, freedom means autonomy and voluntary isolation: each person or couple takes care of themself.

The cluster of values that center around the ideal of equality in American culture is very complex. On one level, equality connotes a belief in the inalienable rights of all, in the inherent dignity of all people. The celebration of the average person runs deep in America: people say, "I'm just an average, run-of-the-mill guy," with a hint of pride. A strong tradition of humanitarianism (for example, helping people recuperate from natural disasters), a tendency toward generosity, gregariousness, and informality are linked to the belief in equality. People think of this country as a haven for the downtrodden, and enjoy seeing the underdog triumph. On the other hand, Americans have never interpreted the word equality to mean equality of condition: the idea of levelling, of equal distribution of wealth, arouses a fear of governmental control. Rather, Americans take equality to mean that every individual has (or should have) an equally good position at the starting gate. The fact that some horses tart the race lame has, until recently been ignored.

Racism, which surely is as American as apple pie, is problematic for just this reason. Americans in general are highly ethnocentric - both in the sense of seeing the United States as "bigger and better," and in clinging to their "own kind" within the country. At the same time, however, Americans go to considerable lengths to deny prejudice and discrimination. (We hasten to add "without regard for race, creed, colour, national origin," and most recently, "sex," to every statement. In the want ads, companies now print "equal opportunity employer" in bold type.) This conflict between equality and discrimination is but one of the contradictions built into American culture (see Myrdal, 1944).

The word *democracy* is conspicuously missing from the Constitution; nevertheless, this document symbolises democracy to most Americans and to people throughout the world. The protection of individual rights (principally from government infringements) and of private property, rule by law (as distinguished from personal rule), and faith in the electorate are all part of the democratic creed. Every school child is taught to respect Patrick Henry's plea for liberty or death, and each July Fourth evokes new speeches celebrating the freedoms guaranteed by the Constitution. Yet, the results of a national survey indicate that many Americans favour curbs on some of the basic tenets of the Bill of Rights (see the Box 4.2).

Box 4.2

How much do we Value Freedom?

The majority of Americans seem willing to restrict some of the basic freedoms constitutionally guaranteed by the Bill of Rights. Specifically, about three-fourths (76 per cent) of the 1,136 people interviewed in the nationwide CBS News telephone survey (March 10 - 12, 1970) believe extremist groups should not be permitted to organise *demonstrations* against the government, even if there appeared to be no clear danger of violence. Moreover.... over one-half of the people (54 per cent) would not give everyone the right to *criticise* the government, if the criticism were thought to be damaging to our national interest; and, a comparable number (55 per cent) feel newspapers, radio and television should not be permitted to *report* some stories considered by the government to be harmful to our national interests (wartime censorship was excluded in the question).

Two additional freedoms that people would restrict involve "double jeopardy" and "preventive detention." In the case of the former, nearly three out of every five adults (58 per cent) feel that if a person is found innocent of a serious crime, but new evidence is uncovered after the trial, he should be *tried again*. In the case of the latter, three out of every five adults (58 per cent) also feel that if a person is suspected of a serious crime, the police should be allowed to *hold* him in jail until they can get enough evidence to charge him with the crime. (Note the date of this poll, 1970, following the turbulence of the sixties and Richard Nixon's presidential campaign of 1968, which was conducted on a platform of "law and order.")

Box 4.2–*(Contd)*

On the other hand, other constitutional guarantees involving the judicial process appear to be so deeply embedded in our way of life that Americans emphatically uphold them. In particular, four out of five people (82 per cent) feel that guilt or innocence in a criminal case should be decided by a *jury,* not by the judge alone; three out of four (75 per cent) believe that the government should never be allowed to hold a *secret trial;* and two out of three (66 per cent) feel that the police should not be allowed to enter someone's home without a *search zoarrant* even if they suspect that drugs, guns, or other criminal evidence is hidden there.

Less strongly, but nonetheless acceptable to most people, are the rights of defendants in criminal cases to avoid self-incrimination and to confront witnesses against them. In both cases, more than one-half of the people (54 per cent) feel that the individual should have the right to *refuse to answer* questions if he feels his answers may be used against him, and that the prosecution should never be allowed to keep the *identity of witnesses* secret during a trial.

Source: Robert Chandler, *Public Opinion: Changing Attitudes on Contemporary Political and Social Issues,* New York, Rowker, 1972, pp. 5-6.

Another survey found that six out of ten young Americans believe that this society is democratic in name only, with most of the power residing in special interest groups (Yankelovich, 1973). Nevertheless, the word democracy still carries sacred overtones in this country.

Put together, this triad - freedom, equality and democracy - leads to two very different brands of patriotism. On the one hand, there are those who, believing this country has been good to them, define all criticism and protest as un-American (by which they mean treasonous). This American-first-ism, with its emphasis on rituals and symbols (the sacred flag), its inquisitions (the McCarthy hearings, for example), and its unquestioning loyalty, approaches the level of a religion. On the other side, there are those who see unquestioning loyalty as antithetical to freedom and democracy, and count criticism and protest among the citizen's moral obligations. For example, the most militant critics of the war in Southeast Asia - those who refused the draft, left the country, renounced their citizenship - defended their actions by pointing to violations, which they maintain were committed by the American government, of the principles of freedom, democracy, self-government and humanitarianism. The American government had lost legitimacy in their eyes, but their allegiance to American ideals motivated their behaviour.

"The business of America is business," said Calvin Coolidge, and indeed, Americans value success the way other people value holiness, family, or military prowess. Success is our primary measure of self-worth.

> The comparatively striking feature of American culture is its tendency to identify standards of personal excellence with competitive occupational achievement. .. . The value attached to achievement does not comprehend the person as a whole but only his accomplishments, emphasising the objective results of his activity. Because of the preoccupation with business, the most conspicuous achievements have been centered in business enterprise. (Williams, 1970, pp. 454-55).

Such expressions as "business is business," and the persistence of organised crime and the relative toleration of white-collar crime indicate the extent to which Americans suspend other values in their admiration of people scrambling for success. In addition to its practical significance, wealth has symbolic significance in this country, for it is one of the only measures of personal merit.

The rugged individualism of American culture finds its fullest expression in occupational competition. We still enjoy rags-to-riches stories; the idea that anyone who works hard and takes advantage of his opportunities can make it to the top dies hard. The problem is, of course, that in reality there is not much room at the top. This is the darker side of the American dream. The myth that any boy who tries can grow up to be president implies that there is something *wrong* with those who do not. Success and failure are personalised to an enormous degree in American culture; the individual who does not rise above his origins has only himself to blame. To be sure, many Americans are content with their work and their standard of living, but many others are haunted by a sense of personal inadequacy. Success in the land of unlimited opportunity is as elusive as the carrot on the stick dangling one foot beyond the proverbial donkey's nose. "The competitive life is a lonely one, and its satisfactions are very short-lived, for each race leads only to a new one" (Slater, 1970, p. 6).

Closely related to the achievement syndrome is the belief that work is a good thing in and of itself. Contemporary Americans have inherited their respect for purposeful activity from the Puritans, who endowed hard work and frugality with religious overtones and believed worldly success was a sign of grace.

According to a poll conducted in 1964, 80 per cent of labourers said they would continue working even if they were able to maintain their current standard of living without a job (Williams, 1970, p. 461). During the 1960s student protests, hippie attire, sexual freedom, and the call for new life-styles led many people to conclude that American youth were abandoning traditional values and social norms, including the work ethic. But the results of a nationwide survey of attitudes and values among American youth, conducted by Daniel Yankelovich in 1973, present a less clear-cut picture. The Box 4.3 reveals the way college youth feel about the work ethic.

Box 4.3

College Youth and the Work Ethic

79 per cent believe that commitment to a meaningful career is "very important" *but* 30 per cent would welcome less emphasis on working hard.

85 per cent agree that business is entitled to make a profit, *but* 94 per cent feel the business community puts profits too far ahead of social responsibility, and 54 per cent believe business should be overhauled or eliminated.

67 per cent maintain that "private property is sacred" and 62 per cent say that "competition encourages excellence," *but* less than half (44 per cent) agree mat "hard work will always pay off."

Source: Yankelovich Youth Study ©1973 by the JDR, 3rd Fund.

A practical people, Americans value innovation and efficiency - which has often meant "single-minded attainment of a goal or accomplishment of a task, with minimal attention to attendant costs, injuries, or disruptions outside the narrow zone of immediate attention" (Williams, 1970, p. 466). The pollution of our air and water in the name of progress testifies to this. However, it would be foolish to ignore the positive effects of pragmatism in medicine, for example, Americans have made dramatic advances in extending the science of curing.

The cult of progress is closely intertwined with the idea that science can and eventually will overcome all natural and man-made difficulties - an extraordinarily optimistic position, if you stop to think about it. The idea that some natural, social and psychological phenomena are beyond rational comprehension, that some things happen for no reason at all, disturbs most Americans. Witness, for example, the numerous task-force reports commissioned by the federal government, or the heavy reliance of the Kennedy and Johnson administrations on experts during the war in Southeast Asia. Even when Pentagon calculations were proving highly inaccurate, no one apparently raised the possibility that political behaviour cannot always be measured and qualified.

We said earlier that values are the criteria people use in assessing their daily lives and in choosing between alternative courses of action. It is likely, then, that the conflicts between social conscience and competitiveness, equality and racism, the myth of opportunity and the realities of stratification - to name just a few - all contribute to a restless undercurrent in American culture.

Subcultures

Another reason for the inconsistencies and exceptions in American culture is that this country includes a wide range of subcultures. When a group's perspective and life-style are significantly different from other people's in their culture, and when they define themselves as different, we say they belong to a *subculture*. Members of a subculture share a set of norms, attitudes and values that give them a distinct identity within the dominant culture. Subcultures may develop in occupational groups, ethnic or religious groups, socioeconomic groups, or age groups. Adolescents, for example, build a private world out of their peculiar position as not-quite-adults and no-longer-children; medical students share common experiences, goals, and problems, and hence a common viewpoint. Subcultures grow among people who are isolated together from the conventional world - isolated physically (adolescents in school, inmates in prison, soldiers on a base, or poor people in a ghetto), or isolated by what they do and think, by their world of meanings.

Jazz musicians are a perfect example of the subculture. Although often called *the* American art form, jazz has never gained the respect or popularity in this country that it has enjoyed in Europe. Blues, Dixieland, ragtime, and other schools of jazz were once considered just "whorehouse music," something nice people looked down on (Mezzrow and Wolfe, 1972, p. 51). Pianist Eubie Blake, for example, tells how his mother threw him out of the house when he was about six because she heard him playing *that* music. Even today, beyond a relatively small cult of admirers, jazz is usually linked to rock and other pop music, as opposed to so-called serious music - a custom that spurred trumpet player Dizzy Gillespie's comment, "What do they think we're doing up there, kidding?"

Howard S. Becker, a sociologist who doubled as a dance-hall pianist when he was in college, studied the jazz world in the late 1940s and published his observations in *The Outsiders* (1963, chaps. 5 and 6). With few exceptions, the people Becker met had become musicians against the wishes of their families - jazz not being an altogether respectable profession in the estimation of most people. Although many of the musicians had married, their hours (usually 9 p.m. to 3 or 4 a.m.), frequent travelling, generally low pay, and chronic job instability (except for the very few at the top) made family life problematic. As a subculture, jazz musicians contribute to the variety in American culture. Typically this group places little emphasis on the American dream of wealth and suburban success, but they are very tolerant of individual differences. Jazz players think of their music as art - an attitude the public generally does not share. But it is this public who, by their patronage, control the musician's livelihood. Jazzmen inevitably find themselves forced to choose between "playing what they feel" and thereby earning the respect of their peers (but little "bread") and "playing what the people want to hear" and perhaps losing their own self-respect.

In reaction to this uncomfortable dilemma, musicians practice what Becker calls "self-segregation". They tend to be suspicious of and often hostile toward the music-consuming public and toward the conventional world in general. At the same time, they are inclined to be extremely tolerant of their own. It is a rule among jazz musicians, for example, never to criticise a fellow player's music or life-style, whatever you think of it. Eccentricity, flouting convention, a devil-may-care approach are highly valued among players, whom Becker found to be self-styled outsiders.

People who engage in activities that are unusually demanding; isolating, unconventional, rebellious, or highly specialised often invent a language of their own - a jargon or argot. Jazz musicians are no exception:

I'm standing under the Tree of Hope, pushing my gauge. The vipers come up, one by one.

First Cat: Hey there Poppa Mezz, is you anywhere?

Me: Man, I'm down with it, sticktn' like a honky.

First Cat: Lay a trey on me, ole man.

Me: Got to do it, slot. *(Pointing to a man . . .)* Gun the snatcher on your left raise - the head mixer laid a bundle his ways, he's posin' back like crime sure pays.

First Cat: Father grabs him. I ain't payin' him no rabbit. Jim, this jive you got is a gasser. I'm goin' up to my dommy and dig that new mess Pops laid down for Okeh. I hear he rifled back on Zakly. Pick you up at The Track when the kitchen mechanics romp.

Translation:

I'm standing under the Tree of Hope, selling my marijuana. The customers come up one by one.

> First Cat: Hello Mezz, have you got any marijuana?
> Me: Plenty, old man, my pockets are full as a factory hand's on payday.
> First Cat: Let me have three cigarettes (fifty cents' worth).
> Me: I sure **will,** slotmouth [a private interracial joke]. Look at the detective on your left - the head bartender slipped him some hush money, and he's swaggering around as if crime *does* pay.
> First Cat: I hope he croaks [dies], I'm not paying him even a tiny bit of mind. [Literally, "father grabs him" suggests that the Lord ought to snatch the man and haul him away; and when you "don't pay a man no rabbit," you're not paying him any more attention than you would a rabbit's butt as it disappears hurriedly over the fence.] Friend, this marijuana of yours is terrific. I'm going home and listen to the new record Louis Armstrong made for the Okeh company. I hear he did some wonderful playing and singing on the number *Exactly Like You.* See you at the Savoy ballroom in Harlem on Thursday. [That is, the maid's night off when all the domestic workers will be dancing there.] (Mezzrow and Wolfe, 1972, pp. 187, 316.)

In-words and usages, as the passage above suggests, serve multiple purposes: they pin down ideas that are only vague in everyday language; describe events and experiences for which no word exists; promote in-group solidarity; and keep outsiders out. As Becker points out, hip talk expresses new meanings, conceals meanings, and makes the speakers feel separate from other groups. For example, there is no dictionary synonym for "square," a word Becker found jazz musicians used to describe most, if not all, non-musicians. The word connotes ignorance, intolerance, conventionality, and a general lack of enlightenment. Other words in the jazz man's lingo - "gig," "bread," "gauge" - do have everyday equivalents - a job, money, marijuana - but they do not have that special quality of in-words that enhances a musician's feelings of being special and different. And, as Harold Finestone writes, the earthy colourful terms of hip talk convey "an attitude of subtle ridicule towards the dignity and conventionality in the common usage" (1957, p. 4). The jazz world, with its own view of reality and its private jargon, is but one of the subcultures that flourishes on American soil, giving our culture its complex and heterogeneous flavour.

Culture Against People

After all that we have said in this chapter, the phrase "culture against people" would seem to be a contradiction in terms. How can culture be against the people who create it, who live in and by it? In Jules Henry's view, people have been so preoccupied with finding ways to feed and protect themselves, "inner needs have scarcely been considered. . . . [This orientation] toward survival, to the exclusion of other considerations, has made society a grim place to live in, and for the most part human society has been a place where, though [people have] survived physically [they have] died emotionally" (1965, pp. 11-12).

Sigmund Freud, too, believed that discontent was built into the human condition, that the conflict between the individual and society would never be completely resolved. He questioned the possibility of people ever finding satisfaction. Freud argued that by nature, people are egocentric, irrational, antisocial: without coercion, we would never consent to the "instinctual sacrifices" that are necessary in any social order (1961, pp. 6-7). However, he believed that overcivilisation - the complete subjection of the self to social demands - was destructive. People can become neurotic when they give up too many of their desires and impulses.

Box 4.4

In the News
Fight Pollution and Feed the World: Use Manure

Pollution and food shortages, two of the severest problems facing people throughout the world, may be eased considerably by a new use for an old product - manure. Cattle waste, recycled to produce animal feed, has been hailed as "an agricultural milestone that could substantially reduce a growing world protein shortage, transform the beef raising industry, virtually eliminate animal feed lot pollution and lower meat prices."

Cattle in feed lots produce some 600 million tons of manure a year, but hardly anyone has wranted manure since synthetic fertilisers became popular.

Box 4.4 - *(Contd)*

Researchers for the United States Department of Agriculture estimate that the protein extracted only from this feed-lot manure would equal the protein contained in this country's total yearly soybean crop.

The soybean is the leading source of plant protein and the United States grows 75 per cent of the world's supply. It is the chief protein source in animal feed in this country and in human food in poor countries.

Even partly replacing soybean meal with manure-derived feed in farm animal diets would greatly increase the amount of soybean protein left over for people. And as soybean prices rise, it may become uneconomical to use them for animal feed

For the food industry, which Ralph Nader has called one of the most polluting in the country (because of animal wastes), this new use for manure solves rwo problems at once. The recycling process, developed by an economist and a nutritionist "converts the manure to protein feed simply, cheaply and without pollution." Not only can cattle raisers rid their feed lots of polluting manure, they can also purchase its protein-rich by-product at a considerable savings over the cost of traditional feed. The one snag in the process is "image". Will cattle-raisers and consumers accept recycled manure as a protein-source for their steaks and chops? A traditional value - waste not, want not - may be called upon to increase public acceptance of the new product, but with a new twist - waste yes, want not.

Source: James P. Sterba, "Cattle Fed From Own Waste to Cut Protein Shortage," *The New York Times* (September 9,1973), pp. 1 and 40.

The question today seems to be whether the conflict between individuals and society isn't "escalating," whether in our expansiveness we haven't created a cultural monster that will ultimately destroy love, quietness and fun. Mental illness and crime flourish in big cities, and it is difficult to forget how thirty-eight people sat silently by as a woman was stabbed to death in New York in 1964. Social and physical mobility have cut people off from the families and communities that once gave them a sense of who they were. The pace of technological change continues to accelerate. Increasingly we live by the rhythms of machines, whose pace and timing bear little relation to human rhythms. In W.H, Auden's words:

... this stupid world where
Gadgets are gods and we go on talking,
Many about much, but remain alone
Alive but alone, belonging—Where?
Unattached as tumbleweed.

Yet, if people have the ability to create cultural problems, they also have the ability to solve them. Our values, of course, will affect how and if we choose to seek solutions.

5

SOCIALISATION

BIOLOGY, CULTURE AND SOCIALISATION

Ideas about the origins of human nature are a story in themselves. Once the nineteenth century overcame its initial shock at the idea that people and apes shared some distant ancestors, it accepted Darwin with all the devotion of true believers. Humans, after all, are animals. Then, like other animals, people reasoned, they must be born with instincts, or innate predispositions toward certain kinds of behaviour. The herding instinct was used to explain the fact that people everywhere lived in societies; the maternal instinct explained mothering; the acquisitive instinct, the pursuit of private property; the aggressive instinct, war; and so on. A similar kind of reasoning was used to explain individual differences. Why did one person become a thief, one a saint? Because the first, it was held, inherited criminal tendencies (just as he or she inherited brown eyes and a crooked nose), while the second inherited holiness. The notion that human behaviour is biologically determined dominated nineteenth-century thought.

Then, near the end of the century, a Russian physiologist named Ivan Pavlov upset the entire scheme by calling attention to the fact that much behaviour, even among lower animals, *is learned. A* hungry dog salivates instinctively when it sees food, but Pavlov showed that a dog could learn to associate the ringing of a bell with food and to salivate whenever it heard the bell, whether or not it saw food. With this experiment, Pavlov cast a shadow of doubt over the instinct theory of human behaviour. In time the idea that the infant is a *tabula rasa* (a blank slate) and that people are *products* of their environment gained a considerable following. Nowhere is this position better stated than in psychologist John B. Watson's manifesto:

> Give me a dozen healthy infants, well-formed, and my own specific world to bring them up in and I'll guarantee to take any one at random and train him to become any type of specialist I might select - a doctor, lawyer, artist, merchant chief, yes even 3 beggerman and thief, regardless of his talents, penchants, tendencies, abilities, vocations, and the race of his ancestors. (1924, p. 104).

Today, the vast majority of social scientists reject both biological *and* environmental determinism (Clausen, 1967). Neither heredity nor environment (learning) *alone* can explain the behaviour patterns that distinguish one person from another, and the members of one society from those of another. The key to individuality is socialisation, where biology and culture meet.

Biological and Cultural Interaction

Socialisation begins with the people who care for an infant, attending to the child's many needs. Dependency is one of our biological givens. Newborn children are totally incapable of providing for themselves: they must be fed and sheltered from the environment. But food and shelter are not enough: infants also need to be handled and loved.

Psychologist Hairy F. Harlow demonstrated the need for body contact in his famous experiments with rhesus monkeys. Harlow took infant monkeys away from their mothers and raised them in isolation. Each was given two wire "mothers," one equipped with a bottle, one covered with soft terry cloth. Surprisingly, the young monkeys became attached to the cloth "mothers" rather than to the "mothers" with bottles. Clinging to something soft meant more to them than food. Most significant, however, was the fact that *none* of the animals raised in isolation developed normally. When given the chance to associate with others of their species, all were frightened and hostile (Harlow and Zimmerman, 1959).

For obvious reasons, no similar experiments have been performed with human infants. However, we do know of at least one child who was raised in near-total isolation. Anna was the illegitimate child of a farmer's daughter. After trying to place the child in a foster home or institution, Anna's mother brought her home as a last resort. No one in the family was very proud of the new member; in fact, her grandfather refused even to acknowledge her existence. To avoid his violent disapproval, the mother put Anna in an attic room, where she remained for nearly six years. Except for feeding the child just enough to keep her alive, the mother ignored her. When social workers discovered Anna, she could not sit up or walk, much less talk. In fact, she was so apathetic, so uncommunicative, they assumed she was deaf, mentally retarded, or possibly both. However, the progress Anna made once she was placed in a special school indicated that she was capable of coordinating her body, communicating, and learning. With help, she began to talk and eventually learned to care for herself, to walk and run, and to play with other children. What Anna proved in the four-and-a-half years between the time she was discovered and her premature death was that practically none of the behaviour we associate with human beings arises spontaneously (Davis, 1948, pp. 204-205). Without attention; infants do not develop normally, either physically, mentally, or emotionally.

Although we know, from the case of Anna and from studies of children in foster homes, that socialisation should begin with mutual trust between parent and child, every society has ideas about the right and wrong ways to satisfy an infant's basic needs. There are as many ways of holding, feeding, clothing and training children as there are cultures. Moreover, each parent interprets child-rearing norms in his or her own way - in part because of the kind of person he or she is, in part because of the kind of infant the child is.

This brings us to another point about biological givens - each human being comes into the world with a unique genetic make-up. In large part, morphology (size and shape), facial features, and rate of physical and sexual development are genetically, determined. Differences in temperament are also apparent at birth; some infants like to be handled and cuddled, some kick and scream whenever they are picked up. These characteristics influence socialisation in several ways.

Size and strength will limit the activities a person chooses and the roles for which he or she is recruited. A frail person cannot realistically expect to participate successfully in activities that demand strength - for example, rowing against stiff currents or playing professional football. In addition, most, but not all, people still distinguish between male and female activities. More subtly, disposition, appearance, and rate of development affect the way parents and others respond to a child. If the community into which a boy is born values aggressive men, a male infant who energetically explores his surroundings and struggles vigorously, resisting any sort of constraint, will please his parents: "He's a 'go-getter,' they will proudly conclude. A placid baby boy, on the other hand, will cause his parents to wonder: Will he be able to keep up with the others? Similarly, if a community expects young people to assume adult responsibilities at the age of twelve or thirteen, the child who matures slowly will be considered a misfit. A girl whose family and peers consider her exceptionally pretty has different experiences than a girl who is considered homely.

The point is that all communities project *meaning* onto any number of physical characteristics. People respond differently to bright and slow, homely and attractive, frail and robust children, and their, expectations subtly shape a child's self-image. In the next section we focus on these influences to show how the child develops a sense of self and a feeling for his or her place in a community.

THE SELF AND SOCIALISATION

In the course of growing older, people develop a kind of amnesia about their early years. Perhaps a few incidents stand out, like being taken to a strange place full of strange children and suddenly realising your mother intends to leave you there. But how many people actually remember being put on a toilet and having no idea what it was for, or banging a spoon on a highchair table, or lying in a crib watching a toy circle overhead and feeling pleasant gurgles inside?

One reason why these early memories fade is that infants are fundamentally different from the people they become as they grow. As adults it is almost impossible for us to recall being speechless, uncoordinated and unselfconscious. For the first month or two of life, babies do not distinguish between their own bodies and actions and the people and objects around them. Nor do they feel happy and sad, proud and ashamed. Infants cry spontaneously when they are wet or hungry or cold. Only gradually do they realise that they are making these sounds, that they can turn crying on and off, that turning it on brings someone running, and much later, that crying is "baby stuff". The emotions and thoughts and sense of identity that adults take as givens emerge, step by step, during the process of socialisation. The analyses of socialisation that we examine in this section all focus on interaction - on the dialogue between children and the people around them, and on how this dialogue shapes the sense of self.

Charles Horton Cooley: The Looking-glass Self

Charles Horton Cooley (1864 - 1929) won a permanent place in the annals of sociology with his insights into the ways in which people establish and maintain a sense of personal identity. Adults take the words "I" and "me" for granted; we experience ourselves as distinct persons, separate from all others. But can there be an "I" without a corresponding "they"? Cooley thought not. The "self", he believed, is a social product that emerges as the child interacts with other people. He used the image of a looking-glass to explain how others influence the way we see ourselves:

Each to each a looking-glass
Reflects the other that doth pass.

By this, Cooley meant that we gain a feeling about ourselves by imagining what others think about the way we look and behave. For Cooley, the self has three main elements, our imagination of the way we appear to others; our perception of the way others see that appearance; and the way we feel about those judgments.

In Cooley's view, a person's self-image and self-esteem depend heavily on the feedback he or she receives as a child, a student, a worker, a parent, and so on. Without the social mirror, there can be no sense of self.

George Herbert Mead: Taking the Role of the Other

Taking his cue from Cooley, George Herbert Mead (1863 - 1931) traced the development of self-awareness back to the interaction between mother and child. At a very early age children begin to realise that they depend on other people (usually their mothers) to keep them comfortable, and that their behaviour influences the way these important people act toward them. Infants learn that crying brings food, smiles bring cuddling, and so on. Gradually, as they explore different ways of arousing desired feelings and responses in others, their vocabulary of significant gestures and sounds expands. As children learn to understand other people's attitudes, they gain some control over what happens to themselves.

By the time children begin to walk and talk, they have already acquired strong impressions about the world around them - impressions they work out in play Children at ages two, three and four spend much of their time in the world of make believe. For hours on end they play at being mothers and fathers, mailmen and doctors - often embarrassing adults with the accuracy of their imitations. Mead called this form of play "taking the role of the other." In effect, the child becomes one of the people who figure importantly in his or her social world, whom Mead called *significant others*. Exploring various roles firsthand, children learn how different activities look from the perspectives of parents, brothers and sisters, and others. One minute the child is a father demanding his dinner; the next, a mother saying she is too busy to cook. By so doing, children learn to look at themselves through the eyes of other people. Children at this age seem especially fond of playing mothers fussing at babies who have wet themselves, and at lecturing other children on their behaviour.

In time the characters children pretend to be become part of their internal landscape. They learn to imagine how people will respond to them without actually having to act out the situation. Thus, a five- or six-year-old will stop with his hand halfway to the cookie jar and say to himself, "No, you will spoil your appetite." Thinking, as Mead conceives it, is an internal conversation between the self and others who have become part of the self. The individual becomes aware of himself or herself, Mead wrote, "not directly or immediately . . . [but] only by taking the attitudes of other individuals toward himself within a social environment or context of experience and behaviour in which he and they are involved" (p. 138).

Gradually, as children move out from their family into the world of other children and adults, they begin to develop a generalised impression of what people expect from them and of where they fit in the overall scheme of things - what Mead called the *generalised other*. At the age of eight or nine, children leave the land of make-believe for the world of games. They learn to play for real. Mead explained this transition by calling attention to the complexity of organised games. To play baseball a child must understand the rules of the game -anticipate what will happen if the batter slugs a ball into right field - and adjust his or her own behaviour accordingly. Similarly, to "play the game of life," that is, to participate in the social world of the community, children must be able to understand their position in terms of the community as a whole. The values and attitudes of the community become an integral part of the child's personality.

Mead was among the first to conceive of psychology in social terms. He believed the self was composed of two parts: the active, spontaneous, idiosyncratic self, which he called the "I", and the social self (the internalised social expectations and demands), which he called the "me". Without these two parts, Mead reasoned, we would not be able to reflect on our own behaviour and develop a sense of inner continuity, or identity. "The self is something which has a development; it is not initially there, at birth, but arises in the process of social experience and activity, that is, develops in the given individual as a result of his relations to [the social] process and to other individuals within that process" (p. 135).

Sigmund Freud: The Psychoanalytic View

No discussion of socialisation would be complete without some mention of Cooley and Mead's famous contemporary, Sigmund Freud (1856 - 1939). Although the number of orthodox Freudians in psychology today is relatively small, Freud's work did represent a turning point in our conceptualisation of human behaviour and personality. Americans, especially, seem fond of invoking the doctor's name as well as ideas rightly and wrongly associated with him. (We often speak of Freudian slips, Freudian symbols, and so on.) Freud did not enjoy this popularity in his lifetime.

Freud shocked - perhaps outraged is more accurate - the Victorian world with his first papers on infant sexuality. These papers were based on Freud's impression that many of the female patients he was treating had been seduced by their fathers in early childhood. In this writings, Freud attacked the common belief that infants and children are asexual. Instead, he described the family circle as a hotbed of passions and the scene of guilt-ridden father/daughter, mother/son romances. No sooner were these ideas published, however, than Freud realised that he was wrong; his patients had *imagined* - not experienced - seduction, but the effect on their inner lives was much the same. This realisation led to Freud's unprecedented exploration of the unconscious mind, surely one of the most significant discoveries of the last century.

Throughout his life Freud's primary concern was to establish a science of the mind that compared with the physical sciences. He assumed that every aspect of human behaviour could be explained rationally, in terms of cause and effect. This wcrakl even apply to seemingly accidental slips of the tongue and to the most bizarre dreams and hallucinations. His clinical work led him to conclude that childhood experiences have a determining effect on personality.

Freud's description of socialisation begins with amoral, egocentric, aggressive, pleasure-seeking infants. In the first years of life all of the energies of children are directed toward oral gratification (sucking and eating), the pleasurable release of tension in defecation, and the joys of masturbation. Freud used the word *id* to describe not only sexual and aggressive urges, which he believed were inborn biological givens, but all bodily pleasure. Society - by way of parents - interferes with children's pleasure-seeking: their demands for food are met only at certain times; they are forced to control their bowels; and they are punished for masturbating. As children struggle to accommodate to these and other social demands, there begins to develop what Freud called the *ego*. The ego is the rational part of the self that interprets information obtained through the senses and finds realistic ways of satisfying biological cravings. However, the pleasure-seeking infant is not yet "tamed".

At the age of four and five, children's desires are still powerful, but so are their fears. Realising that their parents have enormous power over them, they imagine violent reprisals for their sexual and aggressive impulses. Striving to be what their parents want them to be is one way of protecting themselves. The *superego,* or conscience, develops in this period. Children begin to internalise their parents' ideas of right and wrong, including their moral ideals. They learn to repress socially unacceptable desires and, ideally, to redirect their energies into approved channels. For a time, during what is called the latency stage, children seem to be asexual. This is not to say, however, that their impulses disappear; the id has simply been forced underground. The desires and fears of childhood, which are stimulated by the reemergence of sexuality in adolescence, remain active in the unconscious, influencing the way the person behaves throughout life.

Freud's view of the process of human development is thus radically different from Cooley's and Mead's. Where they saw socialisation as the gradual, complementary merger of individual and society, Freud argued that socialisation was forced on small children, very much against their will. Moreover, Freud believed that socialisation is never complete. The id continues to press for gratification. The ego's function is to control these lustful, antisocial drives, while at the same time modifying the unrealistic demands of the perfection-seeking superego. Driven one way by biology, the other by society, we are- in Freud's view - eternally discontent (see *Civilisation and Its Discontents,* 1930).

Erik H. Erikson: The Eight Ages of Man

In the late 1940s and early 1950s, Erik H. Erikson, one of Freud's greatest students, began to expand both the scope and content of his teacher's theory of human development. One of Erikson's most significant contributions to the study of socialisation is his vivid description of the problems of adolescence and young adulthood. It is he who gave us the familiar term *identity crisis*. But this concept is only a small part of Erikson's comprehensive theory of human development, which brings Cooley, Mead and Freud together, integrating the physiological, psychological, and social elements of the process. Erikson does this by focusing on the ego in its role as mediator between the individual and society.

Erikson's central concern is with the feelings people develop toward themselves and the world around them. He describes socialisation as a lifelong process, beginning at birth and continuing into old age. In *Childhood and Society* (1950) Erikson describes eight stages of human development. Each stage constitutes a crisis, brought on by physiological changes and new social environments, to which the growing person must adapt. Erikson describes positive and negative responses to those crises, but emphasises that elements of both exist in most people. When things go well, the maturing ego works out solutions to these crises that build up to a stable identity.

Trust* vs. *Mistrust (Infancy) - During their first year children are totally dependent on adults, primarily their mothers. Even their own sensations of comfort and discomfort are unfamiliar, unpredictable. Children whose mothers respond warmly and consistently to their needs begin to develop feelings of *basic trust*. Comfort becomes what Erikson calls an inner certainly, and Children come to believe that the world is reliable. If mothers are patient when infants bite while nursing or grasp so hard that it hurts, allowing children to develop control at their own pace, they also begin to trust themselves. Infants whose mothers are undependable and rejecting find the world a fearful place; there is no one they can count on to ease their discomforts. If mothers are erratic, about caring for them, children may be afraid to let mother out of their sight, fearing that she might never return. The quality of maternal care in this first year shapes infants basic orientation toward themselves and other people.

Autonomy* vs. *Shame and Doubt (Early Childhood) - For the first two years of life children spend endless hours trying to make their bodies do what they want them to do. By the age of three their muscles and nerves have developed to the point where they are capable of grasping, reaching, crawling, controlling their bowels and so on - delightful accomplishments from their point of view. However, while these accomplishments bring new autonomy, they raise doubts as well. A child crawls around the corner to another room, then realises he is alone and cries out. Besides the doubts of going it alone, there is the shame of losing self-control, as when a toilet-trained toddler wets the neighbour's rug.

Much depends on children's parents. If adults allow the young ones to explore and develop at their own pace, they gain confidence in their ability to govern themselves - what Erikson calls *autonomy*. On the other hand, if children interpret constant supervision as a sign that they cannot take care of themselves, they may begin to overdiscipline themselves to avoid punishment or ridicule and shame (the feeling of being exposed). Neglected children, whose parents allow them to get into situations where they are hurt, may experience similar feelings of self-doubt. Erikson suggests that to develop self-confidence, children should be encouraged to "stand on their own feet," but they must also be protected from experiences of shame and doubt.

Initiative* vs. *Guilt (The Play Stage) - At four or five, children begin to extend their mastery over their own bodies to the world around them (if, that is, they have developed some sense of autonomy). They enjoy attacking and conquering the material world: in their play and fantasies they begin to act out adult roles, transforming (and hence mastering) the world in their imaginations. Most important, in Erikson's view, children begin to *initiate* purposeful activities on their own. Earlier, their play consisted mostly of exploring and imitating others.

Children's feelings of self-worth grow if their parents and others who are important to them respect their efforts. Ridicule and disinterest make children wonder about the values of their actions and goals; they may punish themselves for their failures. There is a danger, then, of children developing more or less permanent *guilt* feelings about any self-initiated activities at this age. Ideally, children begin to turn from their attachments to their parents to the world beyond - without losing the exuberance of early childhood.

Industry* vs. *Inferiority (School Age) - The social setting now shifts from home to school and the larger community. At six, if not earlier, children enter the impersonal world of unrelated children and adults, of rules and organised games. As they begin to acquire the skills and technology of their society, they "learn to win recognition by producing things"

(p. 259). Ideally, they come to enjoy the exercise of mental and physical skills, and take pride in *industry*. However, if they are not emotionally prepared for school, if they fail to do well in school, if they find that their race or family background or looks or even the way they dress automatically disqualifies them in other people's eyes, the experience will be negative. Some children develop a deep sense of *inferiority* in this stage, a fear of being required to perform and failing. Some overcommit themselves to the sphere of work, trying to compensate for feelings of inadequacy.

Identity* vs. *Role Confusion (Adolescence) - With childhood drawing to a close and adulthood looming ahead, adolescents become preoccupied with the question of *identity*. It is not that they don't know who they are before this time, but rather that they have been changing and shaping themselves in many different ways. The time has come to draw together all that has made up their lives, to give a more permanent shape to who they are and where they are going as adults. What Erikson means by *identity* is being able to derive a sense of continuity about one's past, present and future, coordinating feelings about the self with the image reflected in the social looking-glass. There is also the danger, however, that a person will not be able to integrate his or her various roles into a clear identity. The self, then remains diffuse.

Intimacy* vs. *Isolation (Young Adulthood) - Erikson sees young adulthood, like each of the stages before it, as a turning point. Think how many young people fall madly in love at twenty, only to find that after a few months they feel stifled by so much closeness. The other person seems to be taking over their life, swallowing them up. They can't find that comfortable sense of self anymore, someone sees through their acts - and they pull back. This is true in close friendships as well as in love affairs. As Erikson suggests, *intimacy* requires vulnerability; caring deeply for another person always involves some risk - the risk of being hurt, of losing that person. Without a clear sense of identity, without an ability to trust, it may be difficult to take these risks. Young people who are unsure of themselves, who fear commitment, find intimate relationships anxious and stormy - however much they desire love and companionship isolation - keeping to oneself or moving from one intense but short-lived relationship to another may feel safer, but it limits personal and social growth.

***Generativity* vs. *Stagnation (Young Adulthood and Middle Age)* -** In young adulthood, there is still time for exploring and dreaming; the future is still an open book. In middle-age, however, realistic alternatives seem limited; a way of life has been chosen. Erikson identifies the "need to be needed" as the central theme of adulthood. Perhaps nothing satisfies this need so much as an infant, whose helplessness seems to cry out for intimacy and giving. This is one of the points where the needs and desires of one stage mesh with those of another. An infant satisfies and adult's desire to give, while an adult satisfies the infant's needs for warmth and security. This is why Erikson speaks of a *life cycle.*

Generativity is the feeling that one is making a significant contribution, that one is guiding new generations - either directly, as a parent, or indirectly, by working to better society. The better people feel about themselves, the closer they are to other people, the more likely they are to feel productive or industrious, to work creatively, to take on social commitments. For some people, however, middle-age is painful. Childish seif-absorption and "early invalidism, physical or psychological" (p. 267) are signs that a person has not found generativity. It is almost as if they were reliving unresolved crises of earlier stages. Yet as with all stages, Erikson points out that elements of both resolutions -generativity and stagnation - are found in even the healthiest person.

***Integrity* vs. *Despair (Old Age)* -** The last stage in Erikson's "Eight Ages of Man" is one of reflection and evaluation In a very real way, coming to terms with death means coming to terms with life - with where one has been, with what one has done with one's time on earth. By *integrity* Erikson means that a person sees meaning in both the good and bad, the joys and pain of his or her life; that he or she has arrived at a higher level of self-acceptance. The despair that comes from looking back and seeing one's life a's a series of missed opportunities and realising that it is too late to start over is difficult for a younger person to imagine.

In describing the "Eight Ages of Man" Erikson focuses on the potential for negative as well as positive developments in each stage, and how the growing person's adjustment in one stage affects his orientation in the next. Thus, gaining a sense of initiative aids a person in being industrious, though the sequence is not rigid. Erikson believes that the concerns of every stage are present throughout a person's life, though each pair has its time of prominence. This means that a person can overcome an early sense of shame or mistrust by working at it later, or that a person can lose an early strength like initiative through great strain later on. No crisis is completely resolved once and for all; the most the growing person can do is to achieve a positive balance of healthy and pathological tendencies. Moreover, no one can maintain feelings of trust, autonomy, or initiative in isolation. Positive feelings toward the self and the world must be verified and reinforced in each stage.

Table 5.1
Erikson's Eight Stages of Life

Age	*Psychological Crisis*	*Predominant Social Setting*
Infancy	Basic trust vs mistrust	Family
Early childhood	Autonomy vs. shame and doubt	Family
Four to five	Initiative vs. guilt	Family
Six to twelve	Industry vs. inferiority	School
Adolescence	Identity vs. role confusion	Peer group
Young adulthood	Intimacy vs. isolation	Couple
Young adulthood and middle age	Generativity vs stagnation	New family; work
Old age	Integrity vs. despair	Retirement

Source: Adapted from Erik, Erikson, *Identity Youth and Crisis* (New York: Norton, 1968).

Erikson pictures the social order as growing out of (and therefore in harmony with) developmental stages. In his view, as a people work out the solutions to developmental problems, the solutions become institutionalised in the culture and are thereby available to future generations.

> The underlying assumptions ... are (1) that the human personality in principle develops according to steps predetermined in the growing person's readiness to be driven toward, to be aware of, and to interact with, a widening social radius; and (2) that society, in principle, tends to be constituted as to meet and invite this succession of potentialities for interaction and attempts to safeguard and to encourage the proper rate and proper sequence of their unfolding. (p. 270)

This interrelationship between personal crises in growth and social structure is the most striking part of Erikson's theory, which he has applied to studies of Hitler, Luther, Gandhi and others.

Jean Piaget: Cognitive Development

Anyone who has spent time with children knows the drama of a (Child's first words, the frustrations of trying to reason with a three-year-old, the delight on the face of a ten-year-old who has just grasped a new concept. Learning to talk, to think, and to reason are among the basic processes of socialisation. For this reason, we turn to the great child psychologist Jean Piaget, whose insights into cognitive development are unsurpassed. Fiaget was one of the first to recognise that cognitive development is a social as well as a psychological phenomenon. The stages he outlines complement and reinforce the theories of personality development we have been discussing, adding a new dimension to our picture of socialisation.

Sensorimotor Stage (Infancy - Two Years) - In the sensorimotor stage, roughly corresponding to Erikson's first stage, children gradually acquire what Piaget calls *motor intelligence* - that is, a physical understanding of themselves and their world. At first, infants do not realise that shaking a rattle produces the sound they hear; they experience the shaking and the noise that results as separate phenomena. In time, however, they learn to associate the two, and shake a rattle deliberately. The main cognitive development in this stage is the discovery of object *permanence:* infants learn that mother, their toys, and other objects do not dissolve when they leave their range of vision. They also begin to distinguish their own body from the environment. This cognitive development (object permanence) parallels the emotional development of trust. Each involves the growing familiarity of children with the people and objects in their world.

The Intuitive Stage (Early Childhood) - The acquisition of language is the single most important development in this period (Erikson's second and third stages). Language enables children to communicate with other people, to think, to represent the external world, the past, and the future. With language, children can carry out mental experiments and evaluate themselves (by assuming the attitudes of others through words). In short, words make it possible for children to conjure up mental images o(objects and experiences not present in their immediate environment, thus dramatically widening their horizons.

This is not to say that the two- to seven-year-old thinks and reasons like an adult. Typically, they cannot consider more than one point of view, more than one dimension, at a time. For example, J.L. Phillips (1969) asked a four-year-old boy if he had a brother. The child answered, yes, he had a brother named Jim. "Does Jim have a brother?" Phillips asked. Pausing a moment, the child answered, "No." In addition to not being able to consider various points of view simultaneously, young children tend to jump to conclusions: they do not try to test and prove their ideas.

With language, children can assert themselves more aggressively than they can with their bodies, which are considerably smaller than those of the authorities in their lives. Language is also the primary medium for self-evaluation. Taking the role of a parent, children begin to chastise themselves - hence the possibility of developing feelings of doubt and guilt in this stage.

Stage of Concrete Operations (School Age) - In Piaget's third stage (Erikson's age of industry vs. inferiority), children's thinking matures markedly. As they learn to manipulate the tools of their culture (what Erikson calls *industry),* they begin to understand the rule of cause and effect; to comprehend the law of conservation (that mass remains consistent, despite changes in form); to classify objects along more than one dimension, and to perform other logical operations. All of this development is a direct result of their experiences with the material world. Children also learn to consider other people's viewpoints., and most important, to coordinate them with their own (Mead's game stage).

In this stage, children are extremely concrete: that is, they think in terms of real objects and situations that they can handle physically. They know the difference between internal events, such as dreams, and real things. This concreteness in part explains children's susceptibility to feelings of inferiority, which Erikson described. Children evaluate themselves in terms of physical size and prowess, and in terms of other objective achievements, such as the things they can do and make. Less observable qualities or attributes count little in the value systems of young children. Feelings of pride or inferiority develop as children compare their bodies and skills with their peers' and observe their reactions.

Stage of Formal Operations (Adolescence) - The most obvious cognitive change in this stage is that at eleven or twelve, children begin to think in terms of abstract concepts, theories and general principles. Whereas younger children test their ideas by trying them out, adolescents can formulate hypothetical problems in their heads.

The development of abstract thinking has emotional consequences. Younger children tend to experience their emotions as direct responses to people and events: you love people because they are good to you, hate people because they are mean. The discovery of ambivalence - feeling hate and love for the same person - is a direct outgrowth of the ability to think in abstract terms. The development of abstract or formal thinking also explains adolescents' ability to reflect on their self-image and future hopes. Trying to combine personal desires and social demands, adolescents strive for an identity, as Erikson suggested.

In summary Piaget shows that there are very real differences in the *way* children think at different ages. Is cognitive development "wired into" the growing person? Or do these stages reflect the influence of culture on children and the way they are socialised? Neither of these would be accurate in Piaget's view. "Stages are . . . the products of *interactional* experience between the child and the world experience which leads to a restructuring of the child's own [cognitive] organisation" (Kohlberg and Gilligan, 1971, p. 1059). Is the development of abstract reasoning (and, by extension, an identity crisis) inevitable? Lawrence Kohlberg, who has devoted much of his career to investigating Piaget's theories empirically by testing large numbers of people at different ages and in different cultures, found that "the adolescent revolution is extremely variable in time, [and] that for many people it never occurs at all" (Kohlberg and Gilligan, 1971, p. 1065). He estimates that perhaps 50 per cent of Americans never develop formal reasoning at all. Kohlberg is mainly interested, however, in questions of judgment and the development of moral thinking. Building on Piaget's pioneering work in this field, Kohlberg describes six stages of moral development. Aiongwith psychological and cognitive growth, moral development adds a third dimension to the process of socialisation.

Lawrence Kohlberg: Moral Development

Kohlberg's investigative methods are quite simple: he presents children with a moral dilemma. For example, he describes an episode like the following. A man's wife is dying and there is only one drug that can cure her, but the small dose that is needed costs $2,000. Unable to raise the money, the man asks the druggist to let him pay part now, the rest later. The druggist refuses, and in desperation, the man breaks into the drugstore and steals the medicine. Is he right or wrong? After presenting this and similar questions to

American, Chinese, Malaysian, Turkish and Mexican children. Kohlberg concluded that the way people think about moral issues is not simply a reflection of their culture, but, like emotional growth and cognitive skills, something that develops in stages as the child gains experience in the world.

The Preconventional Level **-** Kohlberg uses the term *preconventional* to describe children who may behave well, but who have not yet developed any sense of right and wrong. The preconventional level includes two stages. In *stage 1,* children do as they are told solely because they fear punishment; they are simply deferring to superior power. In *stage 2,* they begin to realise that certain actions bring rewards. But "human relations are viewed in terms like those of a market place. . . . Reciprocity is a matter of 'you scratch my back and I'll scratch yours, not of loyalty, gratitude, or justice" (Kohlberg and Gilligan, 1971, p. 1067). Malaysian boys at this second stage, for example, thought that the man in Kohlberg's story "should steal the food because he needs his wife to cook for him."

The Conventional Level **-** As children grow they become increasingly concerned about what other people think of them. As a result their behaviour becomes largely other-directed. In *stage 3,* children begin to seek their parents' approval by being "nice." Gradually, ideas about right and wrong - whatever they may be in the child's society - take on a meaning of their own. Children have entered *stage 4* when they begin thinking in terms of rules. A child in this fourth stage might, for example, say that the man in the story above should not have broken into the drugstore because it is always wrong to steal. Rigidly conventional thinking characterises this stage.

The Postconventional Level **-** As growing children move out from their homes and begin to associate with people whose ideas may be different from their own, their perspectives widen. In *stage 5,* children recognise moral conflicts and evaluate different points of view in terms of general rules and legal principles. For example, they understand why the man decided to break into the drugstore, but wonder: Suppose everyone decided to steal, what then? Following this line of reasoning they begin to question the morality of charging so much money for drugs. As the conflicts between individual needs and the need for social order, between the norms adults profess and those they practice, become clearer to them, children begin late in the fifth stage to sense strong feelings of good and evil within themselves. At this point the young person is becoming self-directed: he or she behaves one way instead of another to avoid self-condemnation. Gradually, they develop "universal principles of justice, of the reciprocity and equality of human rights, and of respect for the dignity of human beings as individual persons" (Kohlberg and Gilligan, 1971, p. 1068). (This is Kohlberg's *stage 6)*.

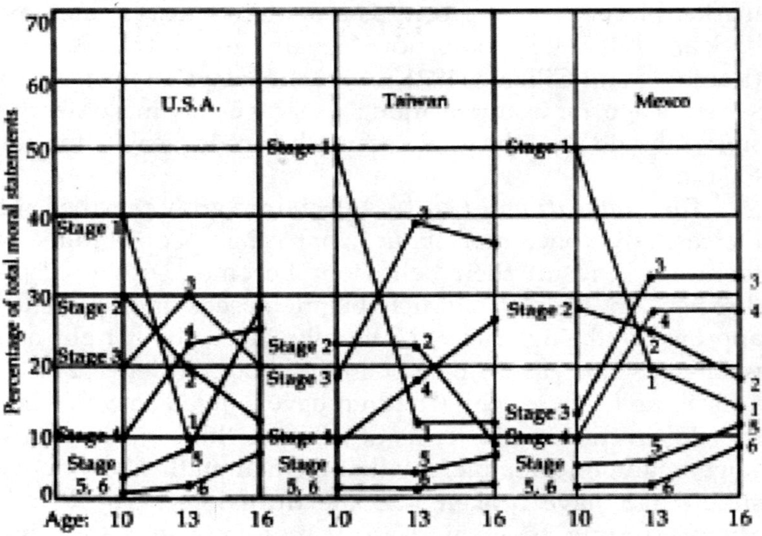

Figure 5.1: Cross-cultural patterns of moral development for middle-class burban boys in the United States, Taiwan, and Mexico.

At age ten, in each country, stages are used in order of difficulty, with most responses in stage 1. At age thirteen, stage 3 is used most. At age sixteen, American boys have reversed the order of age ten stages (with the exception of *stage 6)*. *Stage 5* thinking is used more by the American boys at sixteen than by the Taiwan or Mexican boys. But it is present in these countries, so it is not only an American way of thinking.

It is no coincidence that as children's ability to think about moral issues matures, as their identity and cognitive skills develop, they are meeting many children and adults outside their home. In the next section we will consider the family, schools and peers as agents of socialisation.

AGENTS OF SOCIALISATION

The concept of childhood did not exist in the Middle Ages, a time when infants were considered "nonpersons". High infant mortality meant that they simply didn't count for society. Those children who did survive were pushed into the adult world as apprentices of one kind or another as soon as possible. People expected a seven- or eight-year-old to work for a living (usually in his father's occupation), just like everybody else (Aries, 1962, p. 128).

Growing up in the modern world takes sixteen, twenty, and sometimes even more years-primarily because there is so much to learn, both technologically and socially. The separation of work and family, specialisation, social mobility, the lack of fixed traditions; proliferating subcultures, and the generation gap all contribute to the complexity of modern life. A person must learn to play many roles, and socialisation has become a lifelong process, as Erikson described so well in his "Eight Ages of Man". The family, schools, peers, lovers and spouses, even children (if people have children), all play a part.

The Family

People have children for any number of reasons: to watch a young person grow; to perpetuate their family name; in the hope that a child will fill some vacancy in their own lives, perhaps by realising their own frustrated dreams; because they assume all *normal* people marry and raise families; to prove their virility or femininity; or perhaps because their method of birth control failed (Stone and Church, 1973, p. 145). Parents' motives - subtly communicated in the way mothers hold their newborn infants, satisfy their needs, respond to their first explorations - make a difference to their children.

Self-image and Self-control - The self-image that children eventually develop begins to take shape during their struggle to master their own bodies and the world around them. At the same time, children try to reconcile their own desires with the demands placed upon them - as we saw in the discussions of Mead, Cooley and Erikson. The family is the whole world to children in their first years of life. The people who raise them - both parents, a single parent, a grandmother or older sister or a governess - are the only looking-glass that matters. Am I lovable? Am I a good person? Am I competent (can I control myself)? Should I trust other people? Is the world a good, safe place, or is it full of troubles, pain and deceit? Who am I and who am I not? Directly and indirectly; the 'people' who care for small children answer these questions. Well before children are able to talk and question and examine the facts, they form a picture of themselves and their world, which is based on their family' attitudes and feelings.

Values and Roles - Parents teach children what matters in life, and who counts, often without realising the full impact of their value messages. The desire to achieve and to excel; the need for popularity at all costs; the belief that a girl must be pretty, accommodating, and coy instead of bold and direct, and that catching a husband is the only goal worth seeking for a female, are passed from parent to child. Gordon Allport's accounts of kindergarten children trying dutifully to express the "correct" prejudices, although they had no understanding of the concept of race whatever, poignantly illustrate the way attitudes are learned (1954). One little boy told his mother, "No, Mother, I never play with niggers. I only play with white and black children." A little girl, confused but anxious to please, came running home one day in a flurry. "Mother, what is the name of the children I'm supposed to hate?" Allport concluded, "It takes a child well into adolescence to learn the peculiar double-talk appropriate to prejudice in a democracy."

The behaviour adults encourage and discourage and the ways in which they discipline children also affect their basic orientation toward the world. But values and child-rearing styles are not uniform from family to family. A study by Melvin Kohn (1963) suggests that they are influenced by social class. The working-class parents he studied value obedience, neatness, cleanliness and respect. They want their children to conform to traditional standards of behaviour; they demand that children do as they are told. Focusing on the immediate consequences of a child's actions, they tend to enforce discipline with physical punishment. Middle-class parents, in contrast, are more concerned about the child's motives and intentions than with actions per se. Usually they attempt to reason with the child, trying to make him understand why he should or should not do this or that. Why? Because they value curiosity, happiness, and, above all, self-control. They want the child to be self-directed. However, middle-class parents often practice a psychological punishment - the withdrawal of love and emotional support.

Kohn suggests these different approaches are directly related to the parents' occupations. Whereas most white-collar jobs require some measure of initiative and independence, as well as an ability to get alongwith people and to manipulate ideas, blue-collar jobs usually consist of carrying out a supervisor's directions. Success in the blue-collar world depends on following rules and orders, and working-class parents train their children to follow orders. Similarly, middle-class parents try to prepare children for the social reality they know.

Authoritarian and Permissive Parenting - Discussions of the relative merits of authoritarian parenting (forcing a child to obey) and permissive parenting (giving a child more or less free reign) tend to take on moral overtones. Allport (1954) argues that authoritarian parents give children the impression that "power and authority dominate human relationships - not trust and tolerance." Moreover, children who are taught not to have tantrums, and not to masturbate, learn to mistrust their own impulses - and, by extension, to "fear evil impulses in others". In contrast, "the child who feels secure and loved *whatever he does* . . . develops basic ideas of equality and trust" (italics added). Obviously, Allport is advocating permissiveness; No doubt he would agree with English educator A.S. Neill, founder of Summerhill, who stated categorically, "1 believe that to impose anything by authority is wrong" (1960, p. 114).

Diana Baumrind (1966) disagrees. The permissive school of child-rearing is based on the idea that by not interfering with the child, parents communicate their approval and respect for him. But isn't it possible that the child experiences noninterference as indifference? Baumrind suggests that permissiveness handicaps the child in two ways: first, by depriving the child of the chance to learn the costs of nonconforming behaviour; second, by not giving the child opportunities to argue and rebel, thereby formulating his own positions. In Baumrind's view, parents should be authoritative, not authoritarian - enforcing their own rights as well as the child's "in a rational, issue-oriented manner," so that the child learns how to balance responsibility and freedom.

Of course, the bet intentions and theories may fall by the wayside in the day-to-day interaction of parent and child. Parents learn to be parents, "the hard way, by practicing on their first-born" (Stone and Church, 1973, p. 146). Research by Hilton and others indicates that new mothers are more anxious, and therefore more attentive and interfering than experienced mothers. Their behaviour is more extreme. By the time a second or third child arrives, the mother is more relaxed: she knows what to expect and how to handle most problems that arise. Experienced mothers tend to rely on the child to express his needs and make his way; they do not fuss so much. Thus, no two children, not even members of the same family, are socialised in exactly the same way.

The Schools

In modern societies the school is the primary agent for weaning children from home and introducing them into the larger society. Life in school is a drastic change from life at home. In the family, relations are built around emotional ties ("I'm spanking you because I love you"). At school, children are expected to obey - not because they love their teachers or depend on them - but because rules are rules and they exist to be obeyed.

> The students walk into the room the teacher has been assigned. The school year has begun. Usually the class sits down before the teacher makes his first remark. Sometimes the class stands up, waiting. Whatever happens, the first move of the year is the teacher's.
>
> He introduces himself, calls the roll of pupils' names (usually in alpru betkal order), and then assigns seats....
>
> The first day of class is used to familiarise the students with the routines and rules the teacher intends to impose upon the class throughout the year.. .. The "do's" and "dont's" are paraded out. Don't leave your seat without permission; don't talk out; do raise your hand if you want something; do remain cjuiet at the beginning of class; don't chew gum . . . .(Kohl, 1969, pp. 22 - 25)

School thus socialises young people to a uniform set of values and to the organisational life they will experience as adults. Everyone is expected to obey the same rules. Students are rated more for what they do than for who they are, and their ratings become a matter of record. In the words of one high-school student:

> "The main thing is not to take it personal, to understand that it's just a system and it treats you the same way it treats everybody else, like an engine or a machine. ... Our names get fed into it - *we* get fed into it - when we're five years old, and if we catch on and watch our step, it spits us out when we're 17 or 18." (Noyes and McAndrew, in Silberman, 1371 p. 155).

In most schools, every moment of the students' day is planned and scheduled for them. Students do not participate in decisions about rules or curricula or other issues that affect their lives; they don't even have the right to speak up, move around, or go to the bathroom without permission. An extensive study of today's schools concluded:

> There is no more firmly rooted tradition than the one that holds that children must sit still at their desks without conversing at all, both during periods of waiting, when they have nothing to do, and

> during activities that almost demand conversation. Yet even on an assembly line, there is conversation and interaction among workers, and there are coffee breaks and work pauses as well. (Silberman, 1971, p. 128)

The contrast between the traditional classroom and the home is dramatic.

The avowed purpose of school, of course, is to teach young people technical and intellectual skills and cultural values and attitudes, to prepare them for their roles as adults in a subordinate position vis-a-vis a knowledgeable teacher. Whether this system works is debatable.

Peer Groups

One of the most important side effects of entering school is that children begin to spend more and more time among peers. Power in the family and the schoolroom is one-sided; parents and teachers can force children to obey rules they neither understand nor like. But peers are relatively equal. By virtue of their age, sex and rank (as child and as student), peers stand in the same relation to persons in authority" and therefore "see the world through the same eyes" (Davis, 1948, p. 217). Among equals, children learn the true meaning of exchange and cooperation. Peers share forbidden knowledge including sex lore and ways to evade and manipulate parents and teachers.

The importance of peer groups increases over the years, reaching a climax in adolescence, when popularity becomes all-important for most young people. James Coleman (1961) believes this happens because parents and other adults abdicate, leaving young people largely to their own devices. Adolescents develop a society of their own - with their own jargon, symbols, heroes, values, and "only a few threads of connections to the outside adult society." Most of the young person's time is spent in the clannish and sometimes cruel peer group. Coleman argues that in some ways the adolescent society is subversive - that is, it subverts the goals adults get for young people. For example, hard-working, conscientious students are rarely the most popular; teenagers are not very kind to overachievers. On the other hand, Coleman found that the cliques or in-crowds that form among young people usually reflect the adult world's emphasis on economic background and family status. Having a car (for boys) and nice clothes (for girls) count as much in adolescent society as standing up to authority and other acts of bravery. Coleman suggests that the youth subcultures of the late 1950s were almost a parody of adult society, where, after all, intellectual prowess is not always valued.

In peer groups young people can defend themselves against the ambiguities of adolescence. In most nontechnological societies, children win adult status early by undergoing the traditional rites of passage. When they emerge from such ceremonies, boys are men and girls are women, with all the accompanying rights and responsibilities. In our society, adolescence is a no man's land.

> Just when [they are at their] peak sexually, adolescents must remain celibate; just when they have the most strength and energy, they are given no productive, satisfying work to do; just when they are at their intellectual height, and when their need for power is greatest, they are denied the right to participate in society's decision-making. (Boroson, in Newkirk, 1971, p. 86).

By aligning themselves *with* peers and *against* adults, young people who are still financially dependent on their parents (and who may remain so for years if their parents finance college and graduate education), who are still practicing instead of participating in the work of society, can achieve some sense of autonomy.

In the last decade peer groups have become important agents of socialisation during post-adolescence, as growing numbers of people consider "singlehood" as a way of life, not just a temporary condition. [*Newsweek* magazine (July 16,1973, p. 52) reported that 12.7 million Americans between the ages of twenty and thirty-five are single, an increase of 50 per cent over the last ten years.] Many single men and women live in a subculture of their own, built around clubs and apartment complexes, transitory relationships, and the continuing search for identity (as opposed to the traditional search for a mate). To some degree, the peer group - the people who frequent a club or bar, the group that works or plays together -becomes an extended family.

ADULT SOCIALISATION

Socialisation does not end at age nineteen or twenty. Entering the work force, moving into one's own apartment, marrying, becoming a parent, changing jobs or neighbourhoods or spouses, and growing old all require learning new roles. For example, when a couple move in together, they are still the same people they were the week before when they lived separately. Yet there are changes. One may find it difficult to reassure the other that wanting some time alone is not rejection - a problem that may never have come up before. Arguments take on a new significance - they can't go home to cool off for a week anymore. Similarly, when a couple decide to separate, each has to relearn the role of being single. After six or eight years of marriage, dating may feel as awkward as it did in early adolescence.

Adult socialisation builds on the norms, values and habits learned in childhood and adolescence. For an adult, learning new roles is largely learning new ways of expressing existing behaviours or values. For example, if a woman who has spent many years as a wife and mother and working for the PTA and various charities, becomes active in Women's Liberation groups, she is still seeking the pleasures of belonging to an organisation, still working for a cause in the hope of making things better. Of course, she may seem quite different to her family and friends and even to herself, but adult socialisation is largely a reshaping of existing orientations.

Marriage and Parenthood

Not too long ago, marriage was a step into the unknown- very few couples lived together before their wedding. In many cases one or both were virgins. Today, most couples know a great deal more about one another than their parents

Table 5.2
Proportions of Creative Output Produced in Each Decade of Life

Field	*Number of men*	*Number of works*	Age *20s*	*30s*	*40s*	*50s*	*60s*	*70s*
Scholarship								
Historians	46	615	3	19	19	22	*24*	20
Philosophers	42	225	3	17	*20*	18	22	20
Scholars	43	326	6	17	*21*	*21*	16	19
Means			4	18	20	20	*21*	20
Sciences								
Biologists	32	3,456	5	22	*24*	19	17	13
Botanists	49	1,889	4	15	*22*	*22*	*22*	15
Chemists	24	2,120	11	21	*24*	19	12	13
Geologists	40	2,672	3	13	22	*28*	19	24
Inventors	44	646	2	10	17	18	*32*	21
Mathematicians	36	3,104	8	*20*	*20*	18	19	15
Means			6	17	*22*	21	20	15
Arts								
Architects	44	1,148	7	24	*29*	25	10	4
Chamber musicians	35	109	15	*21*	17	20	18	9
Dramatists	25	803	10	27	*29*	21	9	3
Librettists	38	164	8	21	*30*	22	15	4
Novelists	32	494	5	19	18	*28*	23	7
Opera composers	176	476	8	30	*31*	16	10	5
Poets	46	402	11	21	*25*	16	16	10
Means			9	23	*26*	21	14	6

Note: Maximum values are shown in italics. Total output in each field = 100.

Source: Wayne Dennis, "Creative Productivity between the Ages of 20 and 80 Years," *journal of Gerontology,* vol. 21 (January 1966): 2 Data gathered by analysing published biographies of contributors to the fields listed above.

Declining productivity and old age do not necessarily go together. Much of the total contribution to scholarship, science and art made by men who live to old age comes in their later years. For the men represented in the above table (all of whom lived to age seventy-nine and over) 20 per cent of their output in scholarship, 15 per cent in the sciences and 6 per cent in the arts was made during their seventies.

did when they got married. This is not to say that learning to be married is easier now than it was then. On the contrary. In the past people got married because they wanted a respectable sexual relationship and a family. Today marriage is not a prerequisite for sex or respectability, and the population explosion makes having children a dubious virtue, so there is now less reason to get married in the first place.

Premarital sex surely makes wedding nights less awkward and embarrassing. On the other hand, contemporary couples may be more self-conscious about their sex lives than their parents were. They expect more. A great many couples think something must be wrong if they do not make love as often as they did when first together, or if they do not experiment as they read others do. In some circles, the husband or wife who resents his or her spouse's extramarital activities finds little support. In addition, the traditional roles of wife-nomemaker mother and husband-bread winner-father are no longer givens. Although more and more people today accept women's rights to pursue their careers, we have not, as a society, resolved the question of who is going to take care of the children. Finally, with divorce becoming more common and more acceptable, marriage itself is not the final commitment it once was. So to a large extent today, the absence of clear models forces couples to define their roles as husband and wife on their own. For some people this freedom is welcome; for others, however, it is a trying experience.

The process of defining roles begins anew when a child is born and the family of two becomes three. Having worked out a routine for living with one another, the couple now must learn how to deal with the frustrations and interruptions of a young child. In a very real sense, their live is not their own any more (they can no longer just "pick up and go")-Relationships in the family continue to change as children grow up; the couple faces middle-age; the children leave home and Mom and Dad learn to be a couple again; one spouse dies. Each change brings new roles to be learned.

Box 5.1

In the News
Growing Old Alone Together

Age-segragated adult communities may not be what either Margaret Mead or Erik Erikson had in mind when they considered older people's needs for institutional support, but such communities are growing throughout the country. At present, 1.5 million retirees live in "adult mobile-home parts," and another 500,000 live in retirement villages. Instead of continuing to participate in the social life of the communities in which they spent most of their adult lives, 10 per cent of Americans over sixty-five are now living in communities open only to others of their own age group. Children are allowed by invitation only. Anthropologist Sheila R, Johnson writes:

> As recently as fifteen years ago there were no such communities, and in the early 1960, when they first began to be built, sociologists made dire predictions about them. They argued that it was mentally unhealthy for older people to live apart from young people and children, and that it would deprive society of much valuable experience.

One of the reasons for the growing popularity of such communities may be that our society has not paid enough attention to meeting the needs of older people. Old people do not have the institutionalised social roles that Margaret Mead suggests they should have. Perhaps in reaction to being ignored by a youth-oriented culture, old people are doing some ignoring of their own.

Sheila K. Johnson suggests that "residents of retirement communities ... [may be] helping to create a new subculture of aging," which would have a positive effect on the way old people feel about themselves.

> It has been said that our youth-oriented society has long treated the elderly much as we treat minority groups, with the strikingly similar result that the elderly have accepted society's derogatory definition of their status. But now, with large numbers of active, not-so-old, retired individuals living together in separate communities, it may become possible for them to forge a new and more positive self-image.

Source: Sheila K. Johnson, "Growing Old Alone Together," *The New York Times Magazine* (November 11,1973): 40-59.

Growing Old

For many people in our society, socialisation to old age is socialisation to withdrawal (see Riley *et ai,* 1968). Whereas in many traditional societies old people are revered, in ours they are usually shunted aside. The elderly are expected to exchange their authority as parents for the pleasantries of grandparenting. Giving advice to their children may be seen as interfering. They are expected to leave their jobs, making room for younger men and women with families to support. Retirement, a "roleless role," is particularly disorienting in a society where a person *is* what he or she *does*. Expectations are reduced; the older person may actually be reprimanded for performing chores that were once performed as a matter of course (for example, mowing the lawn). In addition, old people must learn to cope with their diminished physical capacity.

Anthropologist Margaret Mead suggests that much of the loneliness old people experience stems from their own desire to remain independent, at all cost. Living all their lives in a country that values independence and frowns on dependency, old people become victims of their own socialisation:

> We have reached the point where we think the only thing we can do for our children is to stay out of their hair, and the only thing we can do for our daughters-in-law is to see as little of them as possible. Old people's homes, even the best, are filled with older people who believe the only thing they can do for their children is to look cheerful when they come to visit. So in the end older people have to devote their energies to "not being a burden." (1971, p. 242).

In peasant communities, where change was slow, old people had valuable knowledge to pass on to younger people. But today, "such memories are no longer useful. We can be dead certain," says Mead, "that when our grandchildren reach [old] age, they will not be living as we live today." But, old people *can* contribute their memories of a changing society to give younger people a broader perspective on current social changes. Older people have lived through wars, riots, economic depressions, and other upheavals. Many of them have witnessed the first automobiles, airplanes, and other modern inventions and can assure young people that change does not mean an end to the world, but merely an end to parts of the world as they knew it.

Mead suggests that old people can reduce their loneliness and despair by utilising their independence and experience. Society should encourage older men and women to work in day care centers and other community service organisations. In the Soviet Union people who have had experience caring for others are paid to be "grandmothers" in housing projects, where they assist young mothers. This country, too, can find ways to institutionalise meaningful social roles for old people.

6

SEX ROLES

On February 8, 1964, the eight-one-year-old chairman of the House Rules Committee, Howard W. Smith, introduced what he liked to call "my little amendment" to Title VII of the Civil Rights Bill, which prohibited discrimination in employment because of "race, colour, religion of national origin". Smith proposed including the word "sex" in this list - and hastened to add, "Now I am serious about this amendment. . . "The Virginian settled back to listen to the clerk read through the bill, adding the word sex at appropriate points.

Emanuel Cellar of New York, who headed the pro-Civil Rights coalition in the House, took the floor. Would the amendment mean that women would be subject to the draft, he asked. What about alimony and child custody? "You know the biological differences between the sexes. In many States we have laws favourable to women. Age you going to strike these laws down?" But Cellar could not resist injecting humor into the occasion. "I can say as a result of forty-nine years of experience - and I celebrate my fiftieth wedding anniversary next year - that women indeed are not the minority in my house. ... I usually have the last two words, and those words are, 'Yes, dear.'" Frances P. Bolton of Ohio proposed transferring the sex issue to Title X. *Miscellaneous,* but Smith objected. "I think women are entitled to more dignity that that." The traditional assumption that men and women are born with different abilities and temperaments which make them naturally suited for different social roles is a myth. Although genes determine sex, the fetus is sexually undifferentiated until about three months, when hormones begin to act. But sex (that is, male or female biology) does not determine either *gender* (the psychological characteristics associated with femininity or masculinity) or *sexuality* (erotic responses and activities). The biological differences between the sexes are not as clear-cut as most people imagine. The-discovery that children who have been assigned the wrong sex grow up believing in the assignment substantiates this conclusion.

If testosterone is recognisable made is born testosterone is not produced, a female is born. Interestingly, both males and females produce hormones of the opposite sex. There is abundant evidence that testosterone stimulates libido or sex drive in *both* sexes. The difference seems to lie in the concentration of sex hormones at critical periods. If a female fetus is given testosterone, she will develop male-like genitalia. If a male is castrated before puberty (a brutal form or sterilisation, at one time applied to some male singers and haremkeepers), he will not develop secondary sex characteristics (such as a beard) or genital sexuality. But sterilisation of an adult male eliminates the produc ion of sperm but has no effect on sexual appetite or behaViour (Gergen, in Vincent, 1968, p. 190). In other wcrds, sex differentiation is multidimensional: genetic sex, fetal and pubertal hormones, internal and external anatomy do not necessarily coincide. There is much variation within the sexes, as well as between them (Money and Ehrhardt, 1972).

Do sex hormones influence behaviour? Every so often something goes *awry* during prenatal development and an infant is incorrectly classified as female or male at birth, creating a "natural experiment". The parents accept the doctor's sex identification and raise the child as a boy or girl - whichever they've been told. The child grows up to be, in his or her own mind, this sex - sometimes despite contrary evidence. John Money and Anke Ehrhardt studied matched pairs of her- aphrodites (children born with the internal organs of boexes) who were biologically identical, but had been assign to different sexes. The contrasts between those raised as females and those raised as males were so complete, "the ordinary person meeting them socially or vocationally has no clues as to the remarkable contents of their medical history." Money and Ehrhardt conclude, "nature has ordained a major part of gender-identity differentiation to be accomplished in the post-natal period" (1972, p. 18). Robert Stoller cites the even more remarkable example of a boy who was born without normal male sexual organs, but nevertheless developed a strong and enduring sense of maleness (1968, p. 42). Although exceedingly rare, such cases are instructive because they show that anatomy does not guarantee that a person will grow up thinking he or she is the sex his or her biology indicates. If gender identity were genetically or hormonally determined, misidentification would not be possible. But with these children, upbringing had more impact than biology.

Gender Identity and Socialisation

Socialisation to gender begins virtually at birth and continues into adolescence, with its biological changes and fumbling discoveries and adulthood. The groundwork for gender differentiation is laid in infancy.

Infant Care - In large part, infant care is non-discriminatory. All infants must be fed, bathed, diapered, cuddled and rested. There is no sex-typing in these basic activities, but there is some evidence that parents respond differently to male and female infants. Sears, Maccoby and Levin (1957) found that parents tend to handle infant girls more warmly and affectionately than infant boys, and to be more tolerant of assertiveness and physical aggression in infant boys than in infant girls.

Parental preferences for one sex or the other may also influence infant care. Richard Green found that parents who had hoped for a daughter but gotten a son tended to feminise their child. One boy who had what most people would consider female interests told Green:

> Well, my problem to begin with is of very long standing. In fact, all my conscious life, 1 have been aware that I was of the wrong sex, and I can remember quite clearly back as far as my third birthday. I have scattered little memories of this and that, beginning with my parents. They were sort of expecting a girl when I arrived. (1974)

Thus, patterns we suggested above may be reversed: parents who wanted a son may play roughly witn an in infant girl, encouraging her to display assertive behaviour, which most parents suppress in girls. Or, a boy or girl may resist his or her parents lessons.

Gender Training - When the child reaches the age of two or three, these casual, half-conscious distinctions become explicit lessons. Parents begin to address the child as "Daddy's little girl" or "Mommy's big boy" and to actively discourage (or at least ignore) behaviour they consider inappropriate. In some ways the change is greater for boys than for girls. Boys are expected to outgrow dependency and clinging, whereas this kind of behaviour is accepted from girls (Bardwick and Douvan, 1971). A mother may begin to ignore a boy's whimpering. If he persists, she may ask him, "Did you ever see your father cry? Do you think Joe Namath or Muhammad All cries? Of course, not." Gradually boys learn that only girls are supposed to cry. A little girl finds that her parents are genuinely angry when she uses a "nasty" word, but chuckle if her brother does. The message is clear. Sometimes the difference in the ways boys and girls are raised is dramatic. In traditional Puerto Rican families, for example, parents expect boys to fend for themselves and rarely interfere with their wanderings. But a girl's life is closely supervised; daughters are not allowed out of an adult's or brother's sight (Simpson and Yinger, 1972, p. 479). In other families, the differences are subtler, but all children develop concrete notions of girl and non-girl, boy and non-boy even before they understand the facts of life. Girls are supposed to be pretty, clean, neat, sweet and popular; boys should be clever, strong and fearless. For most children, striving to live up to these ideals is the path of least resistance.

Of course, parents are not children's only source of information on how they are supposed to act; brothers and sisters, other children, teachers, television and books provide additional models. Even before children can read, books have a special fascination and magic: they open doors to a world beyond their own experience, and show them what other children do and think, as well as the consequences of such behaviour. Lenore J. Weitzman and Deborah Eifler (1972) found that nearly all prize-winning children's books present highly stereotyped and unrealistic images of girls and boys, men and women. Females are decidedly underrepresented in the winners and runners-up for the prestigious Caldecott Medal. Although 51 per cent of the population is female, the ratio of male to female pictures was eleven to one; and one-third of the books involved *males only*. It would be perfectly reasonable for children to conclude that females are not very important, for if they were, more books would be written about them.

When girls did appear in the children's books, they were nearly always indoors, helping, watching, or loving the book's hero. The one exception was a book about a little girl named *Sam* who convinced a boy to act out her mischievous fantasies. But most of the girls were like pretty dolls, concerned only with pleasing others. In contrast, boys were shown rescuing helpless animals and girls, riding turtles into underwater kingdoms, outwitting the gods, and the like. Similarly, men were farmers, housebuilders, kings, fishermen, gods, spiders. They *never* cried. Women were mothers (with the exception of one fairy godmother, who was the only adult woman engaging in any activities that vaguely resembled a career). One set of books, called *Mommies* and *Daddies*, was not very complimentary to mothers: "Daddies," the author wrote, "know you're big enough and brave enough to do lots of things that mommies think are much too hard." Not one of the books mentioned working mothers or showed fathers helping around the house; not one dealt with death or divorce or any of the problems that might trouble children.

Parents, relatives, friends and books are not the only means by which children learn to be boys or girls. Sex roles are also taught in school. On a typical day at the Educational Alliance Child Care Center in New York City, a visitor can find little girls busy in sawing, and little boys rocking doll cradles and setting tables. This daycare center is exceptional. (The very thought of boys playing with dolls would strike terror into the hearts of many parents.) The teachers, who are participating in a demonstration project to combat sex stereotypes, had to make their own books with pictures of women working and fathers cooking, cleaning and caring for children. Their biggest problem, however, was learning to identify their own, unconscious biases. Even the children, though only four or five years old, resisted innovation. The girls shied away from building blocks - until, that is, they visited a construction site where a woman was working as an engineer *(The New York Times,* April 19,1974, p. 40).

In most schools, boys and girls are segregated in sports (hardball for boys, softball for girls) and such classes as shop and home economics. In *Sisterhood is Powerful* (Morgan, 1970) one young woman describes her experience as the lone female in shop.

> The first day I started Shop I was very apprehensive about how boys were going to react to me being in the class. I had two very good friends in that class .. . and they congratulated me on my success. One of the boys is very condescending toward me, always speaking in a patronising, gentle voice that really makes me angry. "Connie, let me help you," they say. Well I just want to tell you - (expletives deleted). "Quit it!" I say furiously, but silently But Shop is fun if the teacher isn't paying attention because you can goof off all you want to. One thing I realised when I walked into the room the first day was that I could *never* cut, because my absence would be too noticeable, (p. 365)

The irony in keeping girls out of shop is that the girls who do become housewives need to know how to use tools as much as or more than their husbands, who may not be home when things break.

In the early 1970s, parents around the country began organising to combat discrimination in curricula and teaching materials. A group in Kalamazoo, Michigan, for example, is working with the Houghton Mifflin publishing company to create children's readers showing women working and men in the home *(The Wall Street Journal,* October 9,1973, pp. Iff). But it is difficult to say whether teaching children of both sexes the same skills in the same classes will alter the personality/attitude dimension of gender training. Harriet Holter (1970) believes that by the time children reach school, such personality dispositions as emotional expressiveness, self-reliance, or competitiveness may be relatively fixed. Studies of the kibbutzim in Israel tend to confirm this view. Despite the conscious attempt to eliminate sex-typing in work and recreation, men and women on a kibbutz are as different from each other as men and women in Ohio or Manhattan. One reason is that although kibbutz pioneers tried to create "occupational unisex," they did not try to alter sex stereotypes - the idea that men are strong, responsible and rational and that women are soft, nurturant and decorative. The contradictions between women's occupational and personal roles (woman as strong worker but pliant individual) in part explain the reemergence of the "woman question" on the kibbutz today (Keller, 1973).

We can conclude then, that a child's gender identity - the feeling, "I am a girl" or "I am a boy" - seems to be established before she or he enters school. Gender identity does not develop naturally and inevitably as a by-product of physical maturation, it is acquired gradually through experience (Stoller, 1968; Money and Ehrhardt, 1972). It involves an awareness of physical distinctions (anatomy and appearance); a consciousness of sex-specific activities, skills and modes of self-preservation; and covert feelings of liking or disliking for the interests reserved for one's sex (Kagan, 1964). *Sex* (male or female biology), *sexuality* (erotic response and activities) and *gender* (the psychological characteristics associated with masculinity and femininity) do not necessarily coincide with gender assignment. A person may be anatomically male but feel feminine and be erotically drawn to women, or conversely, be classified as female but feel masculine and be erotically drawn to both sexes.

Gender identity does not depend on an awareness of the facts of life, but sex-role identity does. Gradually the child learns that certain reproductive, erotic and social activities are appropriate for his or her gender by watching same-sex models and observing how others react to the way he or she dresses, talks and plays. The role the child is expected to learn depends on the culture and community into which he or she is born.

THE SOCIOLOGY OF GENDER: SEX ROLES AND SOCIETY

> Why, generally, do European actresses present multi-dimensioned personalities while our American stars flatten out like uncorrugated cardboard? ... We caricature screen heroines ... we categorise .. . overplay ... overdress. Our women slide into easy character niches.
>
> But European moviemakers don't give us such easy signals ... in the course of the films their women often reveal themselves as rich, complex human beings. . . . Nothing stagnates, and no one is readable at a glance. (Rosen, 1973, p. 352)

Why do Swedish or French women behave differently from American women, on and off the screen? As the preceding discussion suggested, we will not find the reason by examining their genes, hormones, or anatomies; they are all biologically female. The reason lies, rather, in culturally patterned expectations about what is appropriate for women or men. This is what we mean by *sex roles:* they are guidelines for gender appropriate appearance, dress, interests, skills and self-perceptions; models of what men and women should be like.

Clues to sex-role standards in a society range from laws governing marital relations (and perhaps restricting women's rights) to contests and awards (such as the Miss America pageant) to humor. Why do people laugh at the image of men wearing aprons and doing dishes? Why do so many

American organisations issue awards to the Mother of the Year (but not the Father - or even the Parent - of the Year)? How can we explain the emotion-charged responses of a few years ago to young men letting their hair grow long -responses ranging from ridicule to suspension from school? Reactions to deviations from group norms are an index of the strength of those norms, a measure of how far people will go to safeguard gender ideals. Such clues give us a generalised image of how men and women are *supposed* to lock and act in this or another society. But perhaps the best way to illuminate sex roles is to contrast our standards with those in other cultures.

Cross-cultural Variation

When anthropologist Margaret Mead left for New Guinea in 1931, she "shared the general belief in our society that there was a natural sex-temperament which at most could be distorted or diverted from normal expression" (1950, p. xvi). After living with and studying the Arapesh, the Mundugumor, and the Tchambuli, her attitude changed, and she explained why in *Sex and Temperament in Three Primitive Societies* (originally published 1935).

The mountain Arapesh are a very mildmannered people. They regard competitiveness and aggression as aberrations. An Arapesh may fight to defend a relative, but he would be ashamed to show anger on his or her own behalf. What interested Mead most about this tribe was that they have no idea of any temperamental difference between men and women. They expect all people to be gentle and home-loving; they believe men and women are equally inclined to younger or weaker, and to derive personal satisfaction from giving of themselves. No Arapesh can bear to hear an infant cry; the nearest man or woman rushes to cuddle and feed an unhappy child. Often, relatives borrow a youngster for the sheer pleasure of participating in his or her upbringing. In short, they are what we would call a maternal tribe. "To the Arapesh, the world is a garden that must be tilled, not far one's self, not in pride and boasting, not for hoarding and usury, but that the yams and the dogs and the pigs and most of all the children may grow" (p. 109).

The neighbouring Mundugumor are as fierce as the Arapesh are gentle. The Mundugumor assume a natural hostility between members of the same sex; relations between sexes are only slightly less mistrustful. "The Mundugumor man-child is born into a hostile world, a world in which most of the members of his own sex will be enemies, in which his major equipment for success must be a capacity for violence, for seeing and avenging insults, for holding his own safety very lightly and the lives of others even more lightly" (pp. 146-47). The birth of a child is an ambiguous event among the Mundugumor. If the child is a boy, the father considers him a rival. Members of this tribe obtain brides by exchanging sisters and daughters, and a father and son have an equal claim on the females that are their daughters and sisters, respectively. If the child is a girl, the mother begins worrying that the father will exchange her for a new, rival bride. Often a couple offers a child for adoption. The children they keep receive only minimal attention and are expected to fend for themselves as soon as they can walk, while their parents plot and scheme ways to satisfy their lust for power, position and revenge. The aggressive, combative Mundugumor ideal applies to *both* sexes. All Mundugumor exhibit what we might call exaggerated *machismo*.

Members of the third tribe Mead studied did believe the sexes are temperamentally different, but the roles they prescribe for men and women are the exact opposite of ours. Tchambuli women are "solid, preoccupied (with practical matters), powerful, with their shaven unadorned heads." Every dawn they set out for the lagoons to fish and trap, returning at mid-morning to work on the crafts they exchange with other tribes. Tchambuli men drift about the fringes of the women's circle, hoping for an approving word, an invitation, a gift. It is the women who pull the economic strings in Tchambuli society and the men who devote their lives to self-adornment and the arts of "languishing looks and soft words"; the men who bicker and pout, exhibiting the emotional ups and downs and employing the wiles we call feminine. These roles naturally carry over into mating, where women take the initiative.

> A young widow is a tremendous liability to the community. No one expects her to remain quiet until her remarriage has been arranged. ... This is the comment that is continually made in Tchambuli: Are women passive sexless creatures who can be expected to wait upon the dilly-dallying of formal considerations of bride-price? Men, not so urgently sexed, may be expected to submit themselves to the discipline of a due order and precedence, (p. 193)

Tchambuli sex roles are thus a mirror image of our own. Mead describes Tchambuli women's attitude toward men as "one of kindly toleration and appreciation"; they do not take men terribly seriously.

Commenting on these surprising discoveries, Mead concludes that strange as it may seem "to a civilisation that in its sociology, its medicine, its slang, its poetry and its obscenity accepts the socially defined differences between the sexes as having an innate basis," the characteristics we tend to regard as belonging to one sex or the other are "mere variations of human temperament to which members of either or both sexes may, with more or less success in the case of individuals, be educated to approximate" (p. xvi).

Although published in 1935, *Sex and Temperament* (and other illustrations of different conceptions of proper male and female behaviour) received relatively little public attention. In part this was because researchers tended to stress universals and consistencies rather than differences across cultures; in part because ethnocentrism (and androcentrism, or male-centeredness) created unconscious blinders. The data accumulated over the past century, however, leave little doubt that the existence of universal gender prototypes is a figment of our imagination.

Some of the most puzzling cross-cultural variations in attitudes toward sex and sex roles are found in the Trans-Fly region of New Guinea. The Etero prohibit sexual intercourse for 295 days of the year. Their neighbours, the Marind-amin, prefer homosexual to heterosexual relations. Obviously their birth rate is very low; most Marind-amin children have been captured, not born into the tribe. Societies also vary in the degree to which they enforce the roles they prescribe. Many American Indian tribes, for example, institutionalised the *berdache* - a man who dressed and lived like a woman. If a man was not suited to be a fearless male warrior, he had an alternative (Mead, 1935, p. 103).

If men and women *are* born with distinct interests and talents, how do we account for the fact that *76* per cent of the physicians in the Soviet Union but only 6 per cent of their American counterparts are female (Sullerot, 1971, p. 151)? (See Table 6:1.) The recruitment of Soviet women for employment outside the home is unique in the modern world. Marx Engels, and other communist thinkers equated the subjugation of women with the oppression of the workers: under capitalism, women were chattel. In the early days of the Soviet experiment, women were seen as natural allies, and their role in the Revolution was idealised. In fact, ideology coincided with need in Russia. War had created a shortage of manpower; if the country was to modernise, women had to work. Indeed, women were doubly valuable - as workers and as mothers, who in bearing children would contribute needed population.

Table 6.1
A Cross-cultural Comparison of Women in the Medical Profession

Country	*Per cent of Female Physicians*
USSR	76
Great Britain	15
France	22
West Germany	20
Austria	18
Sweden	13
USA	6

Source: Evelyn Sullerot, *Women, Society and Change* (New York: McGraw-Hill, 1971, p. 151.

Box 6.1

Woman's Place in Old Japan

1. A girl should be gentle, obedient, chaste, faithful, kind of heart and quiet.
2. A girl should observe the distinction between man and woman from childhood, and should not be shown or fold of flirtation. She should not associate with anybody without the instruction of her parents.
3. Woman has to regard the home of her husband as her own. No matter how poor or humble her husband's home may be, she must not complain but consider it heaven-sent because of her misfortune.
4. Woman should regard her husband as a master. Her way lies in obedience. She should never be irritable, luxurious or rudely behaved. She should never contradict his orders; she should regard him as heaven. If he leads a dissolute life, she should advise him to the contrary, but never with anger.
5. Woman should get up early in the morning and go to bed late at night. Even though she may have servants, it is in accordance with the manner of woman to do manual work.
6. Woman should not be overclean or conspicuous to attract the attention of others, nor shall she use conspicuous colour or dyestuff for her ornamental apparel. She should communicate with no young men other than her husband on business.
7. Being stupid in nature, woman shall stay at home as much as possible. Seven out of ten women have the following mental defects: disobedience, resentment, slander, jealousy, and a shallow brain. These weaknesses place her beneath man and she must correct them by self-reflection. She should go nowhere without her husband's permission.
8. Woman must ever remember three obediences: to her parents as a child, to her husband as a wife, and to her son in old age. She should never get offended when she is despised or looked down upon, but should show prudence by forbearing criticisms. Then she will live long in congenial happiness with her husband and her home will be peaceful

In old Japan both males and females were dedicated to their social roles in a way Westerners find hard to conceive. "In the past, a Japanese would feel uncomfortable in thinking of his 'self as something separable from his role" (De Vos and Wagatsuma, 1970, p. 336). A Japanese woman married to become a member of a family more than to fulfil her own individual psychological needs. Being a correct and proper housewife was indeed a full-time job in traditional Japan, given

Box 6.1 - *(Contd)*

the complex rituals associated with all relationships and activities. And there were alternatives to the housewife role, notably the profession of geisha. As an entertainer a woman could be dominant, self-assertive. But in the home women deferred, remaining as inconspicuous as possible. Why? "One might almost equate the Japanese housewife in the traditional family to an efficient secretary in an American business company, where any undue emphasis on the sexual aspects of the secretary as an attractive young woman could become disruptive to the smooth functioning of role relationships within the office". (De Vos and Wagatsuma, 1970, p. 360). A disruptive wife could be sent back to her family in disgrace.

Source: "Woman's Code of Conduct (originally published 1729), trans, by Kalbara Ekiken; George De Vos and Hiroshi Wagatsuma, "Status and Role Behaviour in Changing Japan." In Georgene H. Seward and Robert C. Williamson, eds., *Sex Roles in Changing Society*, New York: Random House, 1970.

Today a"Russian woman who chooses not to work is stigmatised as a kept woman, a parasite. But conditions for woman are far from ideal in the Soviet Union. Russian men consider housework degrading; as a result, Soviet women are housewives as well as workers. And although women have entered many professions (the Soviet Union had the first female astronaut), they are underrepresented in executive and managerial positions in industry and in the Communist party (Field and Flynn, 1970). Nevertheless, the number of female physicians, engineers, and the like in the Soviet Union shows clearly that society, not biology, determines what women can do.

Before Europeans invaded West Africa, most tribes believed men should hunt and women should till the fields. However, when the British and French decided to introduce modern agricultural techniques to Africa, they "naturally" instructed the men. Deprived of their independent economic function, many women became traders and prospered. Today women constitute 80 per cent of Ghana's traders, and 50 per cent of eastern and western Nigeria's traders. A Yoruba girl does not consider marriage until she is able to earn her own

Box 6.2

The Swedish Experiment

As early as the 1930s, the Swedish government prohibited employers from discriminating against women for being married or because they might become pregnant. Numerous reforms followed. Unlike their counterparts in the Soviet Union, China and the Israeli kibbutzim, Swedish reformers did not believe that child-rearing should be taken out of the home. Rather, they argued that fathers should play an active role in child care. "Both men and women have one main role, that of a human being. For both sexes, this role would include child care" (Dahlström, 1967, p. 179). The work week was shortened and vacations lengthened to give men more time at home. Women were awarded paid leaves of absence at childbirth, and the government provided part-time child care and part-time jobs for working mothers. The state also assumed some of the financial burden of parenting, out of the belief that home- and child-care should be paid like any other work. But although the legal barriers to equality have been removed, other obstacles remain. In general, men have not given up the desire for full-time wives; girls tend to drop out of school earlier than boys and to enter traditionally female occupations such as nursing; and for young people "the fear of going too far in behaviour not typical of one's own sex is very great." Surveying the current situation, Dahlström concludes that so long as women retain "a special status from the standpoint of maintenance," they will not shed their image as dependent, supported housekeepers. He adds, "Equality cannot or realised as long as the majority of women are content to bear by themselves the main responsibility for the care of home and children" (1967, p. 178).

Source: Edmund Dahlström, "Analysis of the Debate on Sex Roles," in Edmund Dahlstrom, ed., *The Changing Roles of Men and Women,* Boston: Beacon Press, 1967.

living. Although the Philippine government provides equal opportunity for education to both sexes, many girls drop out at nineteen for fear of not being able to find a husband of equal or better educational status. Thailand, in contrast, has instituted a quota on women medical students to prevent that profession from becoming all female. In Moslem societies where the sexes are strictly segregated, females are forbidden to study with male teachers or to visit male physicians; these professions are therefore open to women. Over 20 per cent of women working in nonagricultural fields in Moslem countries are professionals. This is a higher percentage than in the United States, where only 14 per cent are professionals (Leavitt, 1972).

The comparative study of sex roles challenges the implicit equation between women's biological make-up and their worldly achievements. In single-society research, the sociological determinants of sex-based achievements often remain hidden, tempting researchers to attribute sex differences to genetic or hormonal endowment. Cross-cultural data show that this assumption is false. The different rates of women's participation in professional and public life can hardly be attributed to biology, which, as far as we know, does not vary nationally.

Subcultural Variation

Even within a single society, norms about masculinity and femininity vary from one subculture to another. For example, in American society the idea that men should be breadwinners and women homemakers is realised primarily in middle-class settings. Neither image fits the lower class, where both spouses are likely to be working, or the upper class, where neither spouse may have to work. Homebound and child-oriented (at least in principle), middle-class wives do many chores that upper-class women consider unladylike and leave to servants. Not surprisingly, these different milieus present differing definitions of femininity to little girls growing up in them. In one case it means scrubbing floors, washing, ironing and cooking three meals a day; in the other, it means supervising the people who do such work.

Mirra Komarovsky's *Blue-Collar Marriage* (1967) highlights the differences between working-class and middle-class (college-educated) gender ideals. She found that many working-class husbands and wives got married because they were unhappy living with their parents or because they thought it was time to settle down (marriage being a symbol of adulthood). Middle-class couples, many of whom leave home before they marry, cite a desire for companionship and intimacy as motivations. Although some working-class wives are troubled by the low levels of communication in their marriages, most feel that if a husband is a good provider and a wife a good homemaker neither has any grounds for complaint. They do not expect friendship and understanding from their spouses. After all, they told Komarovsky, men and women are different:

> "When I was first married, half of the time I didn't know what she was driving at, what it was all about," confessed a 23 year-old grade school graduate. "Sometimes I'd think I'd got her all figured out and then I don't make her out at all. The women in her bunch understood her pretty well though," he added. They seemed to understand her better than I did sometimes. They'd tell their husbands about her and the fellows would tell me." His 22 year-old wife remarked, "Men are different. They don't feel the same as us."
>
> "You're supposed to tell your husband everything," said one young wife, "but you don't. Nobody can tell you what you ought to tell him. Sometimes you can tell him just the little old nothings and it is as wrong as it can be. And sometimes you tell him something you think will bring the roof down and he won't even bat an eyelash." (p. 33)

Working-class wives tend to confide in their female relatives and friends, husbands in their men friends; on social occasions, the men and women separate into two groups. Middle-class couples do not make so sharp a distinction between men's and women's worlds. Interestingly, however, working-class mothers were less likely than their middle-class counterparts to feel guilty about taking a job. Working-class mothers who took jobs explained that they needed the money or, simply, that they wanted to get out of the house.

Regional variations in attitudes toward appropriate male and female roles are also apparent. Why, for example, did Wyoming grant women the right to vote fifty years before the country as a whole saw fit to do so? The diversity of state laws on marriage, divorce, alimony, employment and health standards all attest to the existence of special subcultural and subgroup definitions of masculinity and femininity.

History and mythology reveal changing images of men and women. Women have been variously portrayed as powerful and independent, or as submissive and weak (Neumann, 1963; Lederer, 1968). Some mythologies emphasise traits we consider feminine, such as love, compassion and fecundity (for example, the earth-mother goddesses); others portray women as awesome, blood-thirsty, cruel and vengeful (for example, the Indian goddess Kali). Men, too, have taken on a number of antithetical characteristics, appearing here as powerful fathers or suppliant sons, there as bold warriors or effete courtiers. In feudal societies men of privilege, who had serfs or slaves at their command, considered work as a mark of social inferiority. Men earned their reputations through glorious deeds in war and statecraft. But feudal knights also exhibited many traits we now consider feminine. Exempt from gainful employment (like contemporary housewives), they dedicated themselves to service, compassion and erotic love; they were given to temper tantrums and fits of weeping (Ossowska 1970, p. 18). What seems clear is that societies that do differentiate between male and female roles tend to regard their way as the only "natural" or right way, and devote substantial collective energies to enforcing sex-typed behaviour. But if differences in feelings and capacities were inborn, their social elaboration, reinforcement and supervision would not be necessary.

SEX ROLES IN AMERICA

There is no doubt that sex roles are changing, in this country. In the past few years television, magazines, and other media have begun presenting alternatives to the man who gets a job, marries, fathers two children, and settles into the comfortable respectability of being a hard worker and a good provider, and the woman who, having realised the wedding of her dreams, devotes her life to her husband, her children and her home. Indeed, as we suggested earlier, these stereotypes never applied to many lower- and upper-class people. But even though we can discern some important changes in sex roles it is still possible to identify certain basic beliefs about men and women that have widespread approval and official (legal) support and that affect all Americans to some degree. The core values we will describe are not absolutes. Subtle and flexible, sex roles operate on several different levels and are open to varying interpretations.

The American Woman

What do Americans believe about the capacities and destinies of women? Popular wisdom holds that all "normal" women want to marry and have children, and that whatever other interests women pursue are secondary. This belief may be expressed in pseudoscientific theories about maternal and nesting instincts, or in humor about women trying to trap husbands, whose instincts are thought to be quite different. Women who don't want to marry or mothers who don't enjoy their children are thought to be irregular - or worse. Until quite recently having children was in itself an honourable occupation, and one of the chief ways for a woman to validate her femininity and fulfil herself as a person. What happened to a woman after her children were grown was not important. (See Bernard, 1971, pp. 80-81).

A woman's status depends on the men in her life (first her father, then her boyfriends, husband and sons); she has no independent social standing. Taking her father's name at birth and her husband's name after marriage symbolises this dependency. We consider it perfectly legitimate for a woman to depend entirely on her husband for support. Indeed, some husbands feel that their wife's taking a job would impugn their masculinity. Other related customs include a man paying for everything on a date.

Homebound and financially dependent, a woman is urged to live vicariously, sharing the triumphs and sorrows of her husband and children, rather than seeking her own goals. Although "the pursuit of self-interest is almost a virtue in the world men inhabit," a woman is expected to sacrifice her own needs for those of her family - and she is supposed to enjoy doing so (Bernard, 1971, p. 26). Open expression of self-assertiveness or aggression are considered unfeminine -

unless a woman is defending her home and family, in which case she is allowed to be ferocious. There is a similar ban on a woman taking direct initiative in sexual rejections.

A capacity for sympathy, caring, love and compassion (exemplified in such occupations as nurse and teacher) is central to the female role in America. Women are associated with nurturance and life-preserving activities, such as bearing children and taking care of the helpless and the ailing. *Stroking* - building up another person's ego by downplaying one's own talents - is one of woman's chief functions (Bernard, 1971, pp. 88 - 94). Whereas men are expected to be achievement oriented, women are raised to be people-oriented, to place personal loyalty above other considerations. For example, a woman is not condemned for protecting her child, even if he or she is a criminal. Finally, women are encouraged to actively cultivate beauty and sex appeal and to be concerned with personal adornment (traits that not incidentally perform the latent function of stimulating consumption, as well as stimulating men).

Put together, these supposedly feminine characteristics lead Americans to treat women differently than men. "The first step has been taken when feminine gender is ascribed to the female infant. A lifelong train of consequences then ensues. She is thereafter dealt with on the basis of what she is - a woman - rather than on what she does, on her [feminine] qualities rather than on her performance" (Bernard, 1971, p. 26).

To be sure, there have always been exceptions to this role. Intentionally or not, career women, working wives and working mothers have defied the "rule" that women should be economically dependent on men. Many as married women, lesbians, and call girls have rejected being sexually dependent on men (Call girls, of course, depend on men, but not on one man.) The Women's Movement has questioned the entire system of female/male relations. But until now, conforming to the conventional ideals of femininity was the path of least resistance for most women.

Costs and Benefits of the Female Role - With all the talk about sexism and discrimination against women these days, it is easy to forget that the woman's role includes privileges as well as liabilities (and *vice versa* for the male role). What are some of these privileges or benefits?

Most obviously, women are not obliged to work forty hours a week all of their lives to provide for others. Furthermore, they have the legal right to claim support from their husbands. In many states, a man is liable for his wife's debts, but she is not responsible for his. Men cannot sue for nonsupport, alimony, or child support (in the rare case where a divorced man is awarded custody of his children), but women can. Of course, women do work; but although employment may be an economic necessity for women, it is not yet a *moral* duty.

Nor do women suffer from the same pressures to achieve that haunt men in our society. Although a woman may strive to reach the top of her profession, there is little shame in failure or in achieving only moderate success. Women do not suffer from the career syndrome. Philip Slater elaborates:

> When we say "career" it connotes a demanding, rigorous, preordained life pattern, to whose goals everything else is ruthlessly subordinated - everything pleasurable, human, emotional, bodily, frivolous.... Thus, when a man asks a woman if she wants a career ... he is saying, are you willing to suppress half of your being as I am neglect your family as I do, exploit personal relationships as I do, renounce all sponteneity as I do? Naturally she shudders a bit. (1970, p. 72)

Women also have more emotional freedom than men, in the sense that they are permitted to express a wider range of emotions and have more outlets for tension and anxiety. The sphere of intimacy and close human contact is more accessible to women; the exercise of nurturance, warmth, and sympathy, which is to some extent denied men in our society, can be its own reward. The fact that women do not very often participate in the "rat race" and are not required to inhibit their emotions may partially explain why women live longer than men and have fewer heart attacks, ulcers and other health problems associated with tension and stress. Women are treated and institutionalised for mental illness more often than men, however, perhaps because housewives have only one source of gratification whereas men have work and family; because housework is frustrating and demeaning for educated women; because the role of housewife is unstructured and invisible, leaving much time for brooding; and because women's role expectations are unclear and diffuse (Grove and Tudor, 1973; see also Chesler, 1972).

The cult of beauty and erotic love is largely woman's domain. Arousing admiration is an intrinsically satisfying and creative experience for some women. For others, however, being a sex object - or not being one - is dehumanising. Moreover, the glamour-girl ideology implies that beyond the age of twenty-five everything is downhill for women. Which brings us to the costs of the woman's role.

Women are denied autonomy in most spheres of American life. To channel small girls' talents into domestic/maternal interests, parents subject them to more restrictions and constraints than their brothers. Girls are not supposed to be independent or adventuresome, and the economic dependency they experience as grown women may lead to passivity, timidity and weakness. (For example, a woman who has no profession or trade and has not worked in ten or fifteen years will think twice before she decides to leave an unhappy marriage.) The taboo on self-development and self-assertion is especially trying for independent, self-propelled women who are not content with the traditional female role.

In her article entitled "Fail: Bright Women" (1969), Matina Horner argued that many women consider success and femininity to be mutually exclusive, and that bright women especially are afraid of success. This conclusion was based on a study of male and female undergraduates. The women were asked to write a four-minute story about Anne, who, at the end of her first term of medical school, was at the top of her class. Over 65 per cent wrote stories about Anne losing her friends or feeling guilty and unhappy, and some denied that such a person existed (they suggested that Anne was a code name for a group of students). Only 9 per cent of the male subjects wrote negative stories about John (the counterpart of Anne) being at the top of his class. Horner then gave women who showed high "fear of success" two anagram tests, one in which they worked alone, one involving "mixed-sex competition". Thirteen of seventeen women did better working alone.

Not surprisingly this study attracted a great deal of popular and professional attention; the idea that women fear success seemed to click. But Horner's study is far from conclusive. First, it is unscientific to generalise from a sample of less than two hundred undergraduates to the entire female population, as many people have. (*Ms.* magazine, for example, reported: "Psychologists found women's data indicated a hopeless will to fail.") Horner did not study the women whose stories indicated they did not fear success; nor did she study the *men* who feared success. [Other studies have found that as many or more men than women fear success and that a substantial percentage of male students associate high grades with "endless drudgery and premature coronaries" (Prescott, 1971; Robbins and Robbins, 1973).]

David Tresemor, who reviewed the many studies on this topic (1974), found that the percentage of women who wrote stories that suggested a fear of success varied from 11 to 88 per cent; the percentage of men, from 14 to 86 per cent. His own study of high-school students indicated that students wrote different themes for different stories, mixing positive and negative responses to success stories with little consistency. Tresemor also questions Horner's definition of success. Citing another definition: "He has achieved success who has lived well, laughed often, and loved much," he asks whether the ability to solve anagrams or being first in medical school is truly a measure of success. One question about a woman's being number one in her class at medical school is simply too limited a test. Isn't it possible that Horner's female subjects would have responded differently if they had been told half of Anne's fellow students were female, or that she was in the top ten of her class? Isn't it possible they were expressing fear of failure (that is fear that she would not remain number one throughout school) rather than fear of success?

In a recent survey of 21,000 college students conducted by the Educational Testing Service (The Graduates, March 1973), researchers found startling differences between the aspirations of college men and women (see Table 6.2). As many men with C+ averages planned to attend graduate school as women with B+ and A averages. Although the proportions of female and male students planning graduate study in the arts and sciences were about equal, twice as many men as women planned to enter professional schools

Table 6.2
Future Plans by Sex and Undergraduate Grade Average, 1971 (by per cent)

	Women-Grades[1]			*Men-Grades*[1]		
	C+ OR Lower	*B*	*B+ OR A*	*C+ OR Lower*	*B*	*B+ OR A*
Highest Degree Expected						
Bachelor's	30	21	14	29	12	6
Master's	62	65	61	49	46	33
Academic doctorate[2]	4	8	17	8	19	31
Professional doctorate[3]	1	4	6	11	22	28
Other and No answer	3	2	3	3	2	2
Immediate Postcollege Plans[4]						
Full-time work (including military)	85	76	64	80	59	41
Graduate study	11	18	27	11	21	29
Law or medicine	1	3	5	6	14	24
Other professional study	7	8	9	11	16	14

[1]Question: Approximately what overall average grade have you received so far in college?
[2]Includes Ph.D., Ed.D. and D.Arts.
[3]Includes M.D., LL.B., J.D., D.D.S., D.V.M. and D.D.
[4]Some respondents indicate more than one activity.
Source: Leonard L. Baird, Mary Jo Clark, and Rodney T. Harnett, *The Graduates*, copyright © 1973 by Educational Testing Service. All rights reserved. Adapted and reproduced by permission.

(for example, in business, law, medicine and engineering). The authors found that the approval of relatives and friends was the greatest influence on students' career decisions. This suggests that although women may not be *actively discouraged* from entering the profossions, they receive less encouragement to do so.

The percentage of women working has risen steadily over the years. In 1972, 49 per cent of women between the ages of thirty-five and forty-four were employed (less than 20 per cent were in 1940), but women are overrepresented in low-paying jobs and do not earn equal pay for equal work. *The Economic Report of the President,* submitted to Congress in February 1974, indicated that women's salaries are about 66 per cent of those of men with the same age and education. Perhaps half of this differential can be explained in terms of unequal experience. Often women drop out of the labour force to raise children, returning to an unfamiliar job market in their late thirties or early forties. But this still leaves the remaining difference unexplained. The government report refutes the common notion that women who take jobs are only working for "extras". In reality, three-fourths of working women are either single or are married to a man who earns less than $7,000 a year. Strangely, the tax laws penalise working wives (a working couple pays higher taxes than a one-worker family with the same income). Similarly, most banks will not count a wife's income toward a loan or mortgage. Their reasoning seems to be that a woman may stop working at any point (after all, they think she is only working for "extras") or become pregnant. Indeed, the biological capacity to bear children is an economic liability for American women. In many states a pregnant woman cannot draw unemployment insurance even if she is laid off for reasons other than pregnancy. And of course, housewives and mothers are not paid for their work. According to one estimate, if they were, the gross national product would be increased by 38 per cent (Bernard, 1971, p. 75). Economic restrictions, such as no pay or low pay without the ability to get a loan, tend to make women permanent minors not only in their own eyes, but in the eyes of sQciety as well.

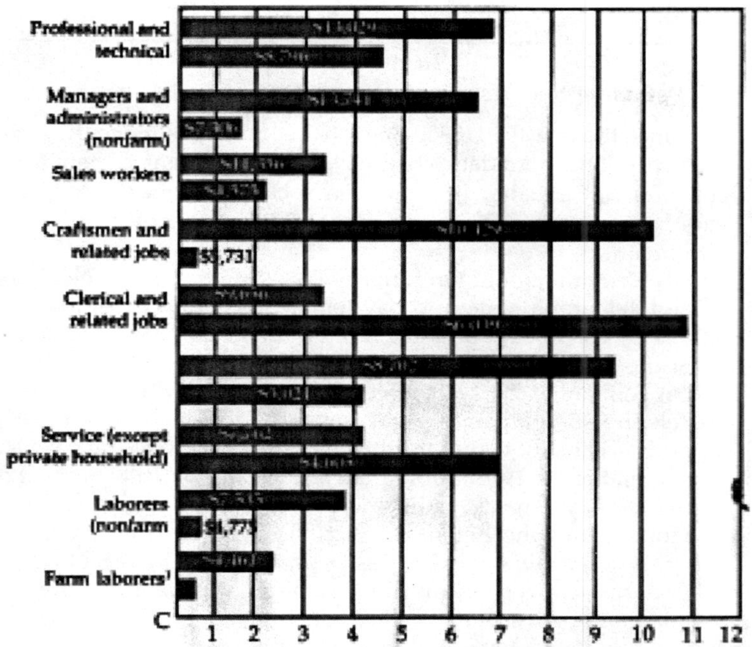

[1]Too small to calculate for women

Figure 6.1: Millions of year-round full-time civilian workers and their median income for 1972.

This is not to say, however, that American women are powerless. Many observers take the formal dependency and subordination of women rather too literally, overlooking the possibilities that women have for exercising power behind the facade of male supremacy. The literature on Jewish, Italian, and black mothers, and the jokes about henpecked husbands attest to the fact that women do dominate in some spheres. Housewives exercise power by running households, dominating kinship networks, arranging a couple's social life, making demands on husbands, supervising their children's lives, and disposing of the family budget. Indeed, housewives may resent intrusions on their territory.

Box 6.3

In the News

Ending Sex Discrimination: A Few Steps Forward

Since the late 1960s women have begun to challenge the legal and institutional boundaries that have always prevented them from achieving full equality in American society. Within the last few years some progress has been made although many restrictions still remain.

Job Discrimination: On January 18,1973, American Telephone and Telegraph agreed to pay female and minority employees $15 million in back pay stemming from the company's violation of the Equal Pay Act (*The Wall Street Journal,* April 18, 1974). On September 29, 1973, a federal court ordered the New York Telephone Company to pay seventy women between $ 450 and $1,000 in compensatory wages (*The New York Times,* September 29, 1973). More than a year later only 48 per cent of the money American businesses owed women because of violations of the Equal Pay Act had actually been paid. Not one woman was working as a professional in the Office of Federal Contract Compliance, which is responsible for preventing government contractors from discriminating against women and members of minority groups.

Maternity Leave: In 1974, by a vote of seven to two, the United States Supreme Court ruled that school boards could not set a mandatory date for pregnant teachers to leave their jobs, but the court did not say that women could decide this matter for themselves.

Religion: In 1973 the Committee on Jewish Law and Standards of the Conservative branch of Juoaism ruled that women could be counted in the quorum of ten required for a communal service (*The New York Times,* September 11,1973). A month later the House of Deputies of the Episcopal Church rejected, for the second time, a proposal that women be admitted to the priesthood (***The** New York Times,* September 26,1973).

The Family Name: More and more women are keeping their own name after marriage, adopting a hyphenated name (theirs and their husband's), and in a few cases using their mother's first name as in Sarachild (single or maiden names being, after all, their father's name). Hawaii is the only state that prohibits this. However, many women are running into difficulties: banks refuse to give them and their husbands joint accounts; airlines refuse them family rates (*Time,* May 13,1974).

> The traditional woman's self-esteem would be seriously threatened if her husband were to play a role equal to her own in the lives and affections of her children or in the creative or managerial aspect of home management.... The lesson is surely not lost on her daughter, who learns that at home father does not know best though outside the home men are bosses over women. (Rossi, 1964, p. 15)

The difference is that women's influence is often personal indirect (covert and perhaps manipulative), and emotional (women today cry much as their grandmothers fainted). But the female role does not, as is often claimed, preclude the exercise of power.

Finally, a number of conflicts are built into the female role. Women are supposed to depend on men but to be resourceful in times of crisis, to be domestic and also glamorous, to be faithful to one man but to make themselves irresistible to many. Not surprisingly, a growing number of women are fighting for a relaxation of standards and the eventual elimination of distinct sex roles. But some respond to these conflicts by clinging to the customs and beliefs that make the sexes separate and unequal. So do some men.

The American Man

The male role is as deeply tied to the family as the female's, although the connections are not always so obvious. First and foremost man is expected to be a good provider for his wife and children. Financial independence is a prerequisite for manhood in our society respect goes to men who are reliable, hard-working and achieving. Americans do not think it odd for a man to sacrifice leisure, his time at home, even his health to a career. His accomplishments and property are a measure of his worth. Initiative, ambition and strength are all part of the "masculine mystique". We say a man is mature if he accepts obligations for dependents, takes necessary risks, makes decisions, and provides security and protection for those in his care.

It is no wonder, then, that so many American fathers encourage their sons to excel in sports (sometimes ignoring that they are not interested in or built for athletics). Sports are not an end in themselves: very few boys will go on to become professional athletes, and few fathers expect them to. But sports teach a boy to be assertive, aggressive and competitive - all of which are thought to be essential masculine qualities, as Normal Mailer's description of boxer Muhammad Ali suggests: "Ali had shown what we all had hoped was secretly true. He was a man. He could bear moral and physical tortue and he could stand" (Mailer, 1971).

Most elementary-school teachers are female and most fathers spend relatively little time at home, so contact with and acceptance by male peers may be especially important to a young boy. To a large degree boys depend on one another for information about the male role. The "locker-room culture" of adults (nights off with the boys, drinking, playing cards, going to a ball game) is reminiscent of youthful team sports. As Joseph Pleck suggests: "It seems hard to get a group of men together for very long without someone suggesting a competitive game" (1972, p. 10). For many American men, realising that it is too late to become a professional pitcher or linebacker is a sobering reminder that they are growing old.

Sports are one of many object lessons in self-reliance and stoicism. Weakness, doubt and compromise are signs of failure for men who are raised to conceal or deny such feelings. The taboo on expressing emotions and self-doubt explains the strong silent type in American lore. The 100 per cent American he-man is happiest when he is with his buddies or riding the range alone on his horse. Courteous to women, he is also detached and prefers dealing with them on a "man-to-man" basis. (Humphrey Bogart's expression of love to Ingrid Bergman in *Casablanca,* "Here's lookin' at you, kid," would hardly be considered romantic in other countries.) Impervious to pain as well as feelings, he is rugged, resourceful and enjoys combating overwhelming odds. John Wayne, of course, is the prototype for this "ideal man".

> The on-screen John Wayne doesn't feel comfortable around women. He does like them sometimes - God knows he's not *queer.* But at the right time and in the right place - which he chooses. And always his

> car/horse parked directly outside, in/on which he will ride away to his more important business back in Marlboro country. (Manville, 1969, p. 111).

In recent years the cowboy has been resurrected as the playboy: suave, urbane, shrewd - in a word, cool - who treats women like consumer products, never becoming involved (Balswick and Peek, 1971). Paradoxically, the cowboy and playboy ideals may strengthen the family. "By acting as the cowboy or playboy . .. the married male may effectively rob extramarital relationships of their expressiveness and thus preserve his marital relationship" (Balswick and Peek, 1971, p. 366). Compelled to act unfeeling, a man may "save up" his emotional needs for the woman in his life (Pleck, 1972). Or he may be as cool in his marriage as he is on the outside.

The ban on male emotions does not extend to sexual matters, however. Heterosexual prowess is essential to American manhood. Men are expected to have nearly unlimited appetites for sexual adventure and to enjoy sex for its own sake (unlike women, who are thought to require at least some romantic feelings). Far more stigma is attached to the effeminate boy than to the masculine girl, who can play the role of tomboy. A woman who displays little interest in heterosexual relationships may be labelled prissy or frigid; a man is assumed to be homosexual. And there is no worse insult to an American man - except perhaps the imputation that someone is "trespassing on" his woman.

Costs and Benefits of the Male Role - Like the female role, the male role has mixed effects. American men have access to the pinnacles of institutional power; men (white men, that is) not women run the nation's government, churches, corporations, professions, universities, even theaters and art galleries. Men are free to exercise legal and social powers that are denied women and children. With the notable exceptions of the now defunct draft law and alimony statutes, neither law nor custom restricts or discriminates against men solely on the basis of their sex. Men have more opportunities than women to develop their talents and acquire special skills and knowledge to cope with the world. (If a family has only enough income to send one child to college, in all likelihood it will choose their son. Men are overrepresented in all professions.) In general, men earn more than women performing the same work, and are more likely to be promoted to powerful and lucrative executive positions (where they enjoy the ministrations of secretaries, who are nearly always female). The fact that men are encouraged to display initiative and independence from the time they are small must also be counted among the benefits of the male role. Finally, the pervasive myth of male supremacy cannot but buoy the male ego.

It is important to remember, however, that although these potentialities are built into the male role, they are not available to all men. Opportunities for training, economic self-support, and power are clearly more accessible to men at the top of the social pyramid than to those at the bottom. To generalise from the privileged few to the struggling many distorts the actual situation for the vast majority of men, who are not in control of their lives nor anywhere near the seats of economic and political power.

The responsibilities that attach to the male role in America can be a source of great stress and anxiety as well as a source of satisfaction and pride. Being in a position to make decisions is fine if a person knows what he is doing, but it may seem less of a privilege to a man who is uncertain of himself. Complicating this is the fact that men are supposed to maintain the impression of strength and courage at all times. Fear of inadequacy and failure is the dark side of the pressures on men to prove themselves.

Equally costly is the competitive syndrome that asks men to consider all other men as either inferiors or rivals and requires substantial mobilisation of psychic aggression. Famed as male solidarity is, male friendships are not necessarily easy relationships.

> When stripped of male sex role "props," such as baseball scores, automobiles, and masculine sex boasting and fantasy, many men find great difficulty in relating to other men. A man in a group said, "You know, I have a pretty good idea of what I can get in a relationship

> with a woman; but I just don't know what I could get from a man. I just don't know." (Pleck, 1972, pp. 8-9)

In very concrete terms, men do not live as long as women and suffer more heart attacks. It is also very revealing that they have more psychosomatic diseases, such as ulcers, spastic colons, asthma and migraine headaches. The male suicide rate is triple the female rate, and men are fourteen times as likely to become alcoholics. Moreover, men commit 95 per cent of all violent crimes and eight times as many murders as women do. Men also have to fight the wars other men make.

Finally, as with the female role, a number of conflicts are built into the male role. Men are supposed to be single-minded in the pursuit of success but not neglectful of their families; they should be simultaneously interested and disinterested in women; and they must be strong and self-reliant, yet require the care of a nurturant wife.

As a result, masculinity is in many ways a rather vulnerable and precarious status. The male role is demanding and difficult and the rate of "failure" is high in the best of times. In American society, as in other industrial societies few men can in fact achieve the wealth, power, and positions of leadership that are held out as ideals for all. *Machismo,* or compulsive masculinity, may be a last resort for men who accept the traditional masculine role but cannot fill it. Machismo has two faces, an overt and a covert one. Overtly it consists of a show of strength and sexual prowess as well as the denigration, exploitation, and often brutalisation of women. Covertly, this display masks fears and doubts about self-worth. As an effort to convince other men, women, and above all himself that he is truly all-male, machismo is a front for insecurity, self-doubt and worldly failure (Aramoni, 1972, pp. 69 - 72).

Serious doubts and anxieties about masculine identity and purpose are bound to occur as many women forego the need for male protection and successfully compete with men in spheres previously considered off-limits to them. For example, 30 per cent of male undergraduates in one study experienced some conflict between the desire for female intellectual companionship and the notion that as men, they should be intellectually superior (Komarovsky, 1973).

Some men have begun to see these changes in the female role as a welcome liberation. Is traditional masculinity worth the price? These men seek a new male ideal, less geared toward competition and dominance. Men will be better off, they argue, if they can learn to acknowledge their human vulnerability and limitations and escape the posturing and pretense of the male role. However, others see change as a dethronement from a previously privileged status. The more they feel they have to lose, the more likely men - and women - are to resist change. The days ahead will not be easy for those who are wedded to traditional gender ideals. There is bound to be anger, conflict, misunderstandings - a tug of war as traditional roles change for both men and women.

CONDITIONS FOR CHANGE

Social necessity has always been a prime agent for change. During both World Wars, for example, American women suddenly became capable of performing work they were thought unsuited for, a year earlier; they "manned" the nation's defense plants. In the past, most religions emphasised men's and women's procreative roles. After all, life was precarious, and many children did not survive infancy. Except for priests and other celibates, family and sex roles were interdependent. The moral/religious formula read: female=potential wife and mother; male=potential husband and father. However, the threatening possibility of standing room only on this planet and the easy availability of reliable birth-control devices have diminished the importance and desirability of reproduction. Procreation is no longer an imperative. And while sexual relations are still desirable for conception (artificial insemination can now be used), the reverse is less and less true: conception is no longer the typical outcome of sexual relations.

Other changes are also apparent. The nuclear family has lost many of the functions it once performed, such as education, production and to a large extent recreation. While important, the functions it retains - the partial socialisation of children and the provision of a sense of belonging - have become romanticised and ritualistic. As a result the family-centered female role is less significant and gratifying than nonfamilial roles. Similarly, the emphasis on egalitarian family relations has undercut the dominance of the father-husband; and the pressure for nondiscrimination in employment is eroding the male monopoly in high-paying and prestigious careers. Women are breaking into occupations that used to be labelled "men only," and men are entering female-dominated spheres (such as nursing, and teaching in elementary schools).

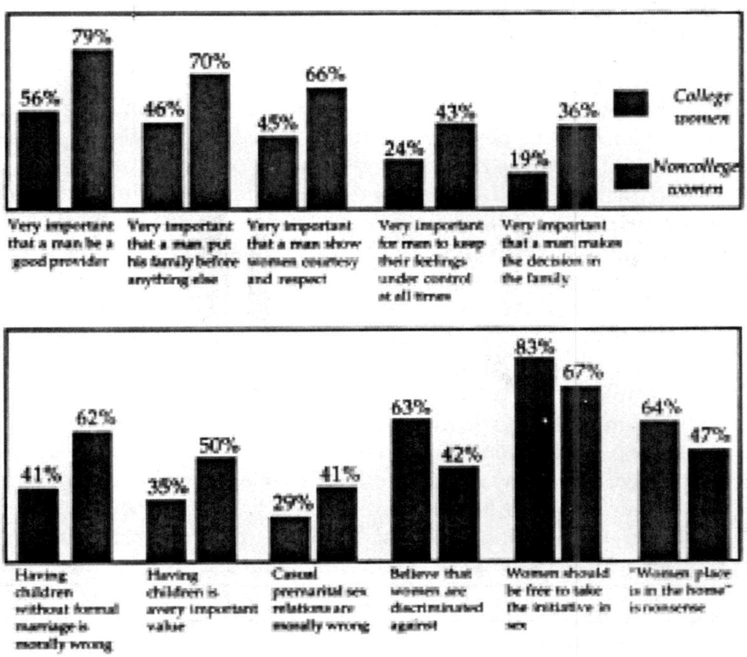

Figure 6.2: College and noncollege women's beliefs about sex roles (1973).

Box 6.4

The "New Values":
The Liberated Generation?

How has the Women's Liberation movement affected today's youth? A nationwide survey of college and noncoUege youth found a majority believe that men and women are bom with essentially the same human nature and that any differences between them can be attributed to upbringing. A majority also feel that the idea that women are less logical and more emotional than men is "ridiculous". Women should receive equal pay for equal work, and they should be as free as men to take the initiative in sexual relations. A majority also agree that women's relationships with other women are as important as their relationships with men. Young people are not totally liberated, however. A majority reject the ideas that women can do almost any job as well as men and that women can be happy without men.

Attitudes toward masculinity have also changed. A majority of the young people questioned do not believe that physical strength, keeping emotions under control, or making decisions in the family are essential masculine qualities. Survey results show that 55 per cent believe men should be concerned with women's sexual satisfaction, and 59 per cent say that a man should satisfy a woman sexually. At the same time, over 70 per cent believe a man should be a good provider and hold strong moral views; nearly 65 per cent believe men should show women "respect and courtesy" and 60 per cent do not feel it is very important for a man to be willing to help with household chores.

Breaking the data down into four categories (college men, college women, noncollege men and noncollege women), Yankelovich found college women are the most liberated, noncollege women the least. For example, 64 per cent of college women characterise the statement "A woman's place is in the home" as "nonsense," compared to a minority of 47 per cent of noncollege women. Yankelovich suggests this is because, for women who lack a college degree, a job is little more than a way to help make ends meet. The idea that wifehood and motherhood alone are not fulfilling roles a central theme of Women's Liberation, is especially threatening to their self-esteem.

Source: Yankelovich, Youth Study © 1973 by the JDR 3rd Fund.

Opportunities and expectations are changing. New attitudes toward sex and innovative family styles are also chipping away at the traditional roles. Of late we have seen men winning paternity leaves and alimony suits, and numerous changes in adoption, divorce and the legal rights of spouses. Finally, the "togetherness" ideal in American society desegregates the sexes in play and work, accentuating shared rather than separate experiences.

Thus, sex roles are changing because society is changing. Altered occupational, personal and familial styles reflect the emergence of new priorities and goals, which no longer depend on a hard-and-fast sex-typing of appearance, behaviour and identity. Eventually, when no more than a fraction of the population participates in producing the next generation, the traditional equation between gender and parenthood will seem less obvious. Patterns of marriage and family life may become more flexible, and childless couples, single parents, and new modes of child-rearing will be more common. Already there are fewer and fewer absolute indicators of gender. Should a man help a woman into a car, light her cigarette, open doors for her? Should a woman expect her husband to support her? While the physical distinctions between the aexes remain intact, their social significance has blurred. A nationwide survey suggests that attitudes toward gender are indeed changing. Whatever one's view, the momentum of change is bound to create inconsistency and instability. The outcome of efforts to change the gender map will depend on our knowledge and understanding of how sex differences develop and what part they have played in human societies.

7

SOCIAL GROUPS

WHAT ARE SOCIAL GROUPS?

Like many of the terms sociologists borrow from everyday conversation, the word *group* has no single, commonly understood meaning. There are several ways to distinguish among the various meanings of this term. One way is to focus on the patterns of interaction among the members of the group. Thus, we may think of commuters who board the same bus every morning as a minimal group. These travellers see each other every day, know each other's time schedules, and are aware of each other's stops. But beyond this minimal contact, accompanied, perhaps, by a smile or a nod, these passengers have limited amounts of interaction. They comprise a loosely knit group, and their daily contact has little significance for any of them. The group is together by chance, not by choice. They have neither a task to accomplish nor any meaningful bond that unites them. We are all members of many such casual groups but unless something unusual (like an emergency) occurs to change our patterns of interaction in these groups, they have little effect on our daily lives.

When the patterns of interaction become somewhat more involving, however, we begin to assign different meanings to our notion of the group. Think, for instance, of a college classroom. Students usually sit in the same general area for each lecture. They exchange greetings and share information with each other, and they are treated as a group (at least for the semester) by both the lecturer and the college administration. The class has a distinct sense of its "groupness," even though interactions among the students may not carry over into activities outside the classroom. While this kind of group may have some effect on our personal lives (the classmates, for instance, may be lively or listless, attentive or disruptive, cooperative or competitive), our emotional involvements in the classroom are, nonetheless, usually minimal.

Sometimes we become members of groups without realising it. When we order a meal in a restaurant, we become part of a team that is organised to accomplish a task. The customer, waiter, headwaiter, busboy, chef and dishwasher are all cooperating to serve a meal. The restaurant staff, which is together all day as a task group, may not think of itself as a group. The employees may relate to each other only in terms of their assigned work roles and they may not see each other after work, yet, they are decidedly an on-going group with extensive (though not necessarily emotional) patterns of interaction.

Thus, the amount and kinds of interaction among group members can range up and down several scales: the scale of time spent together; the scale of task-oriented interdependence; the scale of multiple shared activities; and the scale of emotional involvement. The higher the score on each of these scales, the more meaningful will the group be for its individual members. It is no wonder, therefore, that groups like combat platoons, which score high in all these dimensions become so involving that their members will sacrifice their lives in order to preserve the group. Several studies, described in the Box 7.1, have found that military heroism really stems from the need for group preservation and not from individual striving for glory.

Group Membership

Given the welter of possible meanings for the deceptively simple word *group,* how can we possibly produce a single working definition? Many sociologists have tried their hands

Box 7.1

The Power of Social Groups

Why does a soldier risk his life in a foreign war? Common sense suggests many possible answers: men endure the horrors of combat because they love their country and believe in the cause of the war; men enjoy being soldiers and identify with the symbols and rituals of military life; men are afraid to desert or to show fear because they will be labelled "unmanly"; men assume they will be jailed or even shot if they refuse to obey commands. Studies of German and Allied infantrymen in World War II and of American soldiers in Korea and Vietnam indicate that few of these assumptions are true.

Two sociologists, Edward Shils and Morris Janowitz (1948) shattered the "love-of country, belief-in-the-cause" theory when they discovered that World War II German infantrymen, far from being Nazi fanatics, were largely apolitical. As one German POW put it: "Nazism begins ten miles behind the front line." The Americans who fought these Germans were hardly any different. Shils (1950) found that only a handful of American soldiers in World War II were motivated by ideological conviction, by hatred of the enemy, or by fear of punishment for desertion.

As for identifying with the rituals of military life. Roger Little concluded, after fifteen months with a rifle company in Korea, that soldiers' attitudes toward the military were ambivalent at best. Soldiers tended to be suspicious of bravery, courage, heroism, and other so-called manly virtues. As one soldier told Little: "You shouldn't stick your neck out unless you have to.... If a guy gets a medal for doing his job, it's O.K. But if he's taken a chance or exposed his men, he's no hero because he's made it more risky for everyone" (1970, p. 366).

What matters most to soldiers is staying alive. This primary concern with survival links every soldier to every other soldier with whom he eats, sleeps and fights. Cut off from civilian life, soldiers begin to think of their platoons as families: buddies speak of one another as brothers. "The men in my squad were my special friends. . . . We bunked together, slept together, fought together, told each other where our money was pinned in our shirts.... If one man gets a letter from home, the whole company reads it. Whatever belongs to me belongs to the whole outfit" (Shils, 1950, p. 18). Soldiers obey orders that ask them to risk their lives not for love of country, not for devotion to cause, not for allegiance to the army, but to support and protect the close-knit group that now supports and protects them.

In the Korean War, American POW's learned from their captors about the importance of close human ties. Prisoners were prevented from forming intimate groups. As a result of their social isolation, many

Box 7.1 - *(Contd)*

of the prisoners broke down physically and mentally and 38 per cent of them died in the camps. Once again, the fate of each prisoner depended not so much on the individual's personal characteristics as on his social group experiences.

During the Vietnam War, the crucial human need of group stability and intimacy was not met. One observer of the war (Moskos, 1970) attributed the low morale of American troops to the fact that soldiers served on a rotating basis and never formed intense relationships with comrades. In Vietnam, according to Moskos, it was very man for himself.

at definitions, and although there is not universal agreement on the meaning of the word, one noteworthy and frequently accepted definition has been provided by Robert K. Merton. He suggests that a *social group* is a number of people who define themselves as members of a group; who expect certain behaviour from members that they do not expect from outsiders; and whom others (members and nonmembers) define as belonging to a group) (Merton, 1968, pp. 339-40). This definition places a heavy emphasis on members awareness of their groupness. It *excludes* the following collectivities of people, who have the potential for becoming self-conscious groups but have not yet realised that potential:

1. Individuals with common characteristics - old people, smokers, bicycle riders, the poor.
2. Individuals who happen to be at the same place at the same time - theater audiences, pedestrians at a street crossing, shoppers in a supermarket.
3. Individuals who interact regularly but with limited involvement - tenants in an apartment building. Friday pay check depositers, patrons of a bar.

Any one of these nongroups can rapidly become a group -we need only think of senior citizens' clubs, welfare rights organisations, tenants' unions, and theater clubs to realise that the potential for groupness lurks everywhere.

In-groups and Out-groups - Merton's distinction between members and nonmembers as one criterion for groupness is not an accident of language. Ever since 1906, when William

Graham Sumner, an American sociologist, coined the terms in-group and out-group to describe the feelings of "we" and "they" generated by group membership, the notion of an *in-group* as a circle of people in which a person feels at home has been in common usage. In-groups breed a *consciousness of kind*. They are typified by families, friendship cliques, social clubs, and religious and ethnic groups. Consciousness of kind can also emerge among people who have never met. The feminist movement is beginning to create such a consciousness among women; election years generate such a consciousness among political allies; the war on poverty has brought this awareness to the poor.

In-groups usually develop their sense of "we ness" as a result of sharing common experiences. In one of the most, thoroughgoing sociological studies, conducted between 1927 and 1932 in a Western Electric plant, investigators observed in detail the social dynamics of a small group of factory workers whose job it was to prepare banks for telephone switchboards of wires (Homans, 1950). This group of men developed their own rules about how much work each man should produce and, despite the fact that all the men were paid according to the numbers of units the whole group completed overproduction ("rate busting") was as much discouraged as underproduction ("chiseling" the sense of togetherness among the workers was enhanced by an elaborate system of controls, which they designed to keep outsiders from securing information about the group's activities. These factory workers was a strong sense of "we-ness," and they defined nongroup members as outsiders.

An *out-group,* then, is a circle of people to which a person feels he or she does not belong. Out-groups surround us everywhere. If we are drug users, the out-group is the straight world; if we are black the out-group is the white world; if we are the out-group is the poor; if we are young, the out-group is the old. All these groups of individuals whom we sense differ from us in significant ways comprise our out-groups.

One of the reasons that we are even able to view other people as outsiders and other groups as out-groups) is that we tend, for convenience, to divide up our world in terms of stereotypes: "all long-hairs are hippies", "all politicians are corrupt". Carried to its extremes, stereotyping is a dehumanising process. The Nazis did not see Jews as people; they saw them as contaminating sub-humans. This dehumanising process also occurred in My Lai, Vietnam, the scene of the slaughter of unarmed villagers. The area around My Lai was declared a "free fire zone" in the mid-sixties, after attempts to "pacify" local villagers failed to rid the area of Viet Cong. What this meant was that any Vietnamese was fair game. Seymour Hersh (1970), who uncovered the My Lai incident, suggests that this dehumanising attitude rested on the GI's ignorance of Vietnamese customs; his inability to distinguish civilians from "the enemy"; and the fact that the body count was the only measure of victory in the war. One *Gl* summed up the essence of dehumanisation-by-stereotyping when he asserted: "Anything that's not dead and isn't white is VC" (Hersh, 1970).

To some extent everyone defines out-groups in terms of stereotypes. The existence of in-groups implies the existence of out-groups; the feeling of "we" implies awareness of "they". Groups are defined as much by a consciousness of the differences between insiders and outsiders as by a consciousness of the likenesses among members (Summer, 1906).

Reference Groups **-** Sociologically viewed, we may belong to groups we have never encountered. These groups are the ones to which we refer, either consciously or unconsciously, when we try to evaluate our own situations in life.

The groups to which we refer, but to which we do not always strictly belong, are called *reference groups*. Depending on what groups we select to compare ourselves with, we either feel deprived or privileged, satisfied or discontented, fortunate or unfortunate. When a student receives a B on an exam, he or she can either feel terrific in comparison to the C students or inadequate compared to the A students. When a basketball player reaches 6'4", he can either feel tall in comparison with average players or short in comparison with many professionals. When a woman becomes a general practitioner (M.D.), she can either feel accomplished in relation to most women or inferior in relation to neurosurgeons. Our feelings about ourselves are very much determined by what groups we choose as reference groups. Even our thoughts and beliefs can be molded by our real (or imagined) perceptions about the acceptable thoughts and beliefs of our reference groups.)

One long-term study of the dramatic effects of reference groups on individual behaviour and beliefs was conducted by Theodore Newcomb (1958) at Bennington College, a very liberal women's college in Vermont. Newcomb first studied the students at Bennington between 1935 and 1939. At that time most of the students came from extremely conservative political backgrounds. When the young women arrived at Bennington the liberal political atmosphere (particularly among the faculty) provided them with a new and conflicting set of values and ideas. Newcomb found that in most cases the longer the girls stayed at Bennington (from freshman to senior year) the more politically liberal they became. Those who remained more conservative continued to look to their famines for information and approval, even though they were physically separated from home.

The evidence of the Bennington studies is that our values, behaviour, and goals are influenced and altered by the people or groups whom we choose for our models. We need not necessarily be members of a group to choose that group as a model. Think, for example, of first-generation immigrants who relinquish the values and customs of their own countries in order to conform to the values of those Americans whom they select as their models - be they bankers or bank robbers. Although we like to think that we create our own standards of goodness and worth, if we look closely we find that our personal standards are strongly influenced by the standards of those to whom we look for approval, acceptance, leadership, or example.

Group Structure

When we talk about in-groups and out-groups or membership and reference groups, we are essentially talking about the *quality* of membership in these groups - about the ways these groups make particular members or nonmembers feel. But it is also possible to think about groups as social forms that are more than the sum of the individuals who compose them. When scientists look at cells, they may not be concerned with any particular molecule in that cell, but with how the cell is put together, what its properties and structures are. Similarly, it is possible to look at groups from the outside to see how they are put together, regardless of the particular characteristics of any specific member of that group. This is a structural way of looking at groups (what they *are)* rather than a functional way (what they *do).*

Group Boundaries and Conflict - One of the structural properties of groups is their boundaries. Without boundaries there would be no way of setting groups off, no way of distinguishing members from nonmembers, insiders from outsiders. A fraternity pin is a symbolic but tangible social boundary: those who own one are members, those who do not are nonmembers. When a "brother" (note the symbol of closeness) gives his pin to a woman, he symbolically extends the group boundary to include her. A college decal on a car window is a social boundary; it publicly differentiates insiders from outsiders. Skin colour can be a boundary and so can ethnic background. The one-time southern debate over how much African ancestry a person needed to be labelled a Negro was an attempt to define black-white boundaries when visible skin colour failed to serve as a boundary clue. Almost anything can be used as a social boundary to distinguish "in" from "out", "us" from "them". A dormitory can be used as a boundary marker and so can a sports car ("we" drive them; "they" don't). Hair, clothing, and music styles surely mark different groups off from each other. Sometimes a coloured strip of rag will do the trick. During the college uprisings of the 1960s, students with different political views (ranging from "Burn the place down" to "Restore law and order") were able to show their allegiances and create feelings of "we" and "they" just by wearing different-coloured arm bands to signify different political views.

If we recognise that all groups have boundaries, we can begin to ask questions about how these boundaries are created and maintained. One of the most effective ways of creating and maintaining group boundaries is through conflict with outsiders. A common enemy helps draw people together, and through confrontation with out-groups insiders begin to develop a sense of "we-ness". Georg Simmel, an inventive and provocative German sociologist, suggested that: "A state of conflict [with outsiders] pulls the members . . . tightly together. . . . This is the reason why war with the outside is sometimes the last chance for a state ridden with inner antagonisms to overcome these antagonisms" (Simmel, in Coser, 1956, p. 87).

Student activist leaders of the 1960s certainly learned this structural lesson in dramatic and unexpected ways. Because the actual number of activists on American campuses was very small, leaders were forever combating problems of inaction and apathy. However, when college administrators began calling in police and national guardsmen to halt demonstrations, entire student bodies went on strike. Through conflict, boundaries were drawn and students were forced to make choices about which side of the boundary they were on.

The paradox of cohesion through conflict is all around us, but often not recognised. We tend, like news reporters, to see only the drama of conflict and overlook the undercurrents of cohesion. The old union song, "Which side are you on, boys, which are you on," is an attempt to draw sharp boundaries through conflict. It is also an attempt to raise workers' consciousness about where they belong and where their allegiances should rest.

Conflict with out-groups, then, is one way in which social groups create and maintain their own boundaries. The sharper the conflict with outsiders, the tighter the internal cohesion is likely to be (at least until internal conflicts begin).

Because conflict is so useful for boundary definition groups may attract or invent threats where none exist in order to maintain cohesion. Lowis Coser, an American sociologist who elaborated on Georg Simmel's writings about conflict, suggests that white southerners at the turn of the century stiffened their ranks against the blacks through exaggerated stories of black crimes against whites. The actual numbers of crimes that blacks committed against whites were very small, but stories of rapes, murders and imminent race wars abounded. As Coser says, "Fear of the Negro, far from deriving from the Negro's actual behaviour, is a means of keeping the status system intact, of rallying all members of the white group around its standard" (1956, p. 109).

Of course, no amount of conflict with outside groups can sustain a group that is not a going concern. Unless a group has some basis for cohesion and consensus, it will fall apart and not be able to rally under external pressure. During the depression in America, for example, close families became closer and stronger as they united against their troubles, but weak families disintegrated (Komarovsky, 1971). This is not to say that on-going groups must be conflict-free. Sometimes internal conflict and its eventual resolution help to define and strengthen a group's boundaries. When a group successfully expels its "enemies from within," it publicly reaffirms its boundaries. During the Vietnam War for example, draft resisters presented American society with an acute problem of internal conflict: if individuals were allowed to follow their own consciences and not the edicts of the draft board, how would the nation remain unified in the face of conflict with outside groups? America's solution to this threat of internal dissension was to close its ranks against the dissenters. Draft resisters were either sent to jail or fled the country in self-imposed exile. Both "solutions" maintained the cohesion necessary to continue the war. Through expulsion of the dissenters, America established its boundaries as the type of social group that would not (or could not) tolerate in its midst men who refused to fight when they were called.

Box 7.2

In the News

Conflict and Cohesion

Greers Ferry, Ark.- "This has been a white fiefdom for a hundred years. They succeeded in keeping blacks out by just such tactics as they are employing now against us. And in the absence of any blacks, *we've become the niggers of Cleburne Country"* (italics added). - Dixon Bowles.

Dixon Bowles is the leader of a commune of men and women who call themselves The Group. For two years the commune lived in peace with the rest of the townspeople.

It entered commerce and became the owner or operator of seven thriving businesses. It started the town's first Chamber of Commerce and its first Optimist Club.

Its members became the entire volunteer fire department of the town, which has a population of 389. Other members became leaders of Boy and Girl Scout troops.

The men of the commune wore neatly trimmed short hair and dressed like the other men of the town. Unlike some communes elsewhere, The group, Inc., as it is called, rigidly prohibited drugs and free love. Several members joined the Baptist and Methodist Churches.

Then they made their mistake. The town held an election last fall, and for the first time since moving to Greers Ferry in 1971 the members of The Group voted. They turned out to be the balance of power between two fiercely contesting factions. The losing faction turned its anger on the commune and on the night of Aug. 23 The Group's home was attacked by a stone-thro wing mob.

Votes alone did not cause the people of Greers Ferry to turn so violently against The Group. Even though they were active in the town's economy and lived conservatively, the commune people were perceived to be different. The Group's children attended their own school, which caused some resentment. Townspeople felt that they held themselves aloof, especially intellectually.

But the main cause of the community's uneasiness seems to be its uncertainty over the commune's aims. Some think The Group intends to "take over the community" and turn it into one large commune. That idea is especially prevalent among the hundreds of Northerners, mostly retired people, who have moved here in recent years. The Northerners have stirred up the hill people, some of whom are violently inclined. Mr. Bowles .. .,described the method used by a certain retired Northerner to stir antagonism against The Group.

Box 7.2 -(*Contd*)

> "He goes up to these people who barely got out of the sixth grade and sign their name with an X," Mr. Bowles said, "and he says, 'That's a commune over there. You know what they do in communes? Let me read you this Reader's Digest article. Dah-de-dah, dah-de-dah-dah.' And this guy says, 'Well, son of a bitch,' and before you know it, it's out on the pick-up circuit that we have orgies over here, and dope and it's called commune, therefore it's corn-a-nist."

In short, The Group has become the out-group of Greers Ferry, the victim of stereotypes about communes. Fear of differences, it seems, has led the townspeople to create a threat where none really existed. By expelling their newly created out-group, the people of Greers Ferry reaffirmed and strengthened their social boundaries.

Interestingly, once before, The Group had shored up *its* boundaries in a similar way:

> Mr. Bowles and 14 other original members, all from Odessa, Tex., have always been "straight" by the standards of many communes. However, during the late nineteen-sixties The Group attracted a number of what Mr. Bowles calls "freaks," and their free-swinging style threatened to change The Group's direction. Mr. Bowles threw them out and The Group returned to its relatively conventional ways.

Source: Roy Reed, "Conformity Backfires for a Commune," *The New York Times,* September 22,1973, pp. 33, 36.

The expulsion from the Soviet Union of Nobel-Prize-winning writer Alexander Solzhenitsyn was another case of boundary drawing. For some years Solzhenitsyn had openly criticised the Soviet system. Finally, in March 1974, the Soviet leadership decided it was time to reestablish internal unity and to reaffirm the boundaries of acceptable behaviour for membership in the Soviet Union. By deporting Solzhenitsyn, Russia was saying it would not tolerate severe criticism from within.

Of course, internal conflict need not always be so threatening to group cohesion that the dissenter must be expelled in order for group unity to be restored. If a group is secure in its own basic cohesion, in its common value system, it can tolerate and adjust to relatively large amounts of dissension. In fact, it is this tolerance that often allows members to let off steam before so much pressure builds up that the whole system explodes. It is the rare family that expels its dissenting adolescents, and it is the rare professional organisation that excludes its critical or challenging members. On the other hand, though, the more intimate a group the more possibilities there are for conflict since more sides of each person's personality are involved in the group. But a group that is essentially stable can allow conflict within its boundaries because when "we are certain of the irrevocability and unreservedness of our feelings . . . peace at any price is unnecessary" (Simmel, in Coser, 1956, p. 81). Since each group eventually sets its own norms (which are either stated explicitly or implied) about the amount of dissension members may express, these norms help to define the group's boundaries and to reaffirm its sense of uniqueness.

***The Influence of Size* -** Although we rarely think of it, the size of a group very much affects our behaviour and feelings in that group. We generally tend to attribute our experiences in groups to the personalities of the group's members, but, in fact, the highly impersonal feature of group size often has a great deal to do with these experiences. A person's sense of security, for example, can be greatly altered by the size of a group to which he or she belongs. First children, for example, often resent the birth of a second child; similarly, the addition of a third friend may create uncertainty for the original two.

Comparing *dyads* (two-person groups) and *triads* (three-person groups) provides a dramatic example of the effect that group size can have on group experience. The very existence of a dyad depends upon the participation of both members. If either member withdraws, the group no longer exists. A three-member group, however, can survive the loss of a member. The effects of this purely structural feature - size -on the personal experiences of each group member are very strong. We need only think of the differences in our own responsibility when we are involved in a two-person or three-person conversation. In a dyadic conversation we can never lapse into reverie without jeopardising or destroying the interaction. But if a third person is present we can pass the responsibility of the conversation on to him or her and indulge in our mental wanderings. The very dependence of a dyad on the continuing participation of both members creates for its members unique intimacy, responsibility and pressure.

Contributing also to the uniqueness of the dyad is the inability of either member to "pass the buck" to other members. If, for example, two people are living together and one of them finishes off the last piece of cake, both members of the dyad know with complete certainty who did the eating. With three or more people in the house, however, only the cake-eater could know for sure who the culprit was. Groups larger than dyads, then, provide some anonymity and privacy for their members. The dyad participant "is much more frequently confronted with All or Nothing than is the member of the larger group" (Simmel, 1950, p. 135).

Another unique feature of dyads is that they cannot cast one member in the role of mediator. With three or more people, one person can reconcile the other two. Dyads also do not have to deal with problems of intruders or spectators. If two people are interacting directly, they cannot be performing for the benefit of a third party, nor do they have to be sensitive about giving a third party "air time". Also, in dyads there can never be a majority or minority and never a coalition of two against one. All these factors, entirely due to the properties of size, have enormous impact on private experiences.

We tend to attribute power in a group to the strength of individual personalities or talents, but here, too, a structural property - group size - plays a key role. Group size affects the formation of coalitions that may control the balance of power among group members, in his book aptly titled *Two Against One* (1969), sociologist Theodore Caplow describes all the possible outcomes of different coalitions among three people with differing amounts of power. If, for example, A is more powerful than B, and B has the same power as C, then the possibilities for winning coalitions exist between A and B vs. C; B and C vs. A; A and C vs. B. These possibilities for coalition prevent the nondyad group from becoming static. There is always the potential for new alliances. In a two-person group, however, the relationship is less volatile since no new coalitions are possible. Triads are marked by perpetual imbalance: "In most triads members tend to switch coalitions from one disagreement to another simply to maintain solidarity and avoid permanent exclusion of one member" (Hare, 1962, p. 242).

Adding a fourth member to a triad again changes things drastically. It opens up new possibilities for coalitions (for example, two vs. two; three vs. one). As the size of a group grows, the number of possible relationships increases geometrically. (In a group of three, there are six possible relationships; in a group of four there are twenty-five possible relationships; and in a group of five there are ninety! See Table 7.1.)

Table 7.1
Increase in Potential Relationships with an Increase in Group Size

Size of Group	*Number of* Relationships
2	1
3	6
4	25
5	90
6	301
7	966

Source: A Paul Hare, *Handbook of Small Group Research* (Glencoe, 111.: Free Press, 1962. p. 229.

By increasing group size many features other than pairings also change. In large groups, for instance, it is difficult for any one member to keep all the others in mind when he or she states an opinion or suggests an activity. Thus, statements made in large groups sound more like pronouncements than conversation: think of the formal way we discuss ideas in a classroom as compared to the informal way we share the same ideas with a friend. Because we cannot speak directly and uniquely to each member of a large group, our statements become more abstract and general so that they will be relevant to everyone. In large groups, too, individual opinions carry less weight, so to reach consensus, discussion must be limited and the group must resort to more formal means of reaching decisions (like taking a vote). Group size also influences the efforts of individuals to gain control and determines how much pressure there will be to reach a representative decision.

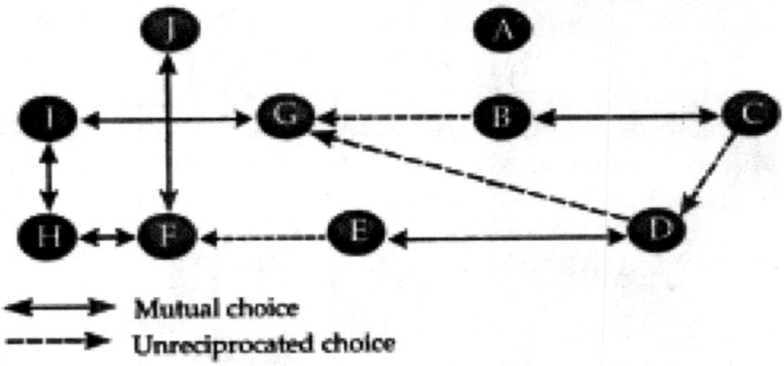

Figure 7.1 A sociogram

Some years ago, J.L. Moreno devised a technique for describing relationships within a group. The researcher questions each member of the group on his or her personal preferences. For example, he might ask each person: Whom would you like to work with on this project? Whom do you enjoy spending time with after hours? Whom do you consider to be your best friends? These preferences are then transcribed to a diagram. Each circle stands for one person. The solid lines with arrows at each end represent mutudal choices; the dotted lines stand for unrecriprocated preferences. The resulting *sociogram* enables the researcher to identify popular and influential individuals, cliques, dyads and triads, and isolates—at a glance. For example, in the group of ten pictured here, G is clearly the most popular four people chose this person. The number of mutual choices in the subgroup to the left (F, H, I, J. G) indicates the presence of a clique. B-C and E-D are dyads. A is an isolate who neither chose other people nor was chosen by them. Sociograms are extremely useful in clarifying communication networks and decision-making patterns in small groups.

From this very brief discussion we can see how important size is in determining our seemingly personal and unique experiences in different groups. Size, like boundaries, is a structural property of groups, and it influences the behaviour of members regardless of their individual psychological make-ups. Other such important features are (1) the purpose of the group - is it to accomplish something, to make decisions, or to provide pleasure and relaxation; (2) the hierarchial structure of the group - is it rigid and authoritarian or flexible and participatory; (3) the relations of the group with surrounding groups - is it secret or public, accepted or disapproved of, admired or scorned; (4) the history of the group - is it new or old, stable or changing. All these factors strongly influence our group experiences and help to define the nature and types of satisfactions we can derive from group life.

PRIMARY AND SECONDARY RELATIONSHIPS

If we think of the vast differences between life in a tribal village and life in a big city, we can begin to grasp the wide range of possibilities for organising our social group experiences. In a tribal village, all members may relate to each other daily. They share a common ancestry, as well as goals, values, aspirations and traditions. Everyone in the tribe is involved with the survival and welfare of the whole. In addition, each member of the tribe has a fixed position in the social order, usually assigned at birth. Geographic mobility is as limited as social mobility; a tribal member lives and dies within very restricted geographic boundaries. Such expressions of individuality as clothing, work aspirations, leisure activities, and friendship circles are all highly circumscribed by the rights and obligations of tribe members. The entire web of each person's relationships is interconnected and predetermined at birth. Since every aspect of an individual's life meshes with every other aspect (family, co-workers, neighbours and friends are all the same people), a tribal member's entire social identity is involved in each relationship. Personal, social and economic life are all rolled up together, and the notion of "self" is virtually indistinguishable from the notion of "my tribe".

We need hardly mention the dramatic differences between this type of group life and the kind we are so familiar with in our own urban, industrial society. For the mid-twentieth-century city dweller, social life is much more fragmented. Relatives may live far away, friends may live across town, fellow workers may live in a different town altogether, and neighbours may be anonymous. With no one group, except, perhaps, the immediate nuclear family, do we have regular, continuous, face-to-face interaction. Those who live around us may come from very different backgrounds and have very heterogeneous histories so that we do not necessarily share common goals, values, aspirations and traditions. The survival and well-being of one group is often antithetical to the survival and well-being of another (think of labour unions and management; cab drivers and bus drivers; industrialists and ecologists). And unlike tribal members who spend their entire lives in one village, we are so mobile that one out of ten Americans moves each year. We also move socially, leaving old friends behind.

Between these extremes lies the whole range of possibilities for human social organisation. We have learned to take these two ends of the spectrum for granted, but in earlier times, particularly in the nineteenth and early twentieth centuries, when the world was undergoing breathtaking changes as a result of modernisation (industrialisation, urbanisation and bureaucratisation), the switch from close, intimate villages (typified by rural agrarian communities) to fragmented heterogeneous cities was a source of great dismay, fear, curiosity and wonder.

From *Gemeinschaft* to *Gesellschaft*

In trying to make sense of the new and sometimes frightening changes in the old and familiar order of things, early sociologists often resorted to extremes of comparison between what was in the past and what would be in the future. The first of these notable commentators was Ferdinand Töennies, a German sociologist, who drew distinctions between what we now call *primary relationships* and *secondary relationships.* Töennies (1887; 1957) elaborated on the contrast between *Gemeinschaft,* or community, and *Gesellschaft,* or society. *Gemeinschaft* is characterised by close, intimate, overlapping, and stable relationships (as in tribal villages). *Gesellschaft* is characterised by the pursuit of self-interest, impersonal attachments, efficiency and progress.

Emile Durkheim was also concerned with the nature of social relationships within these two contrasting types of societies. He asked questions about the social bonds that hold people together under the two different kinds of social conditions. Although Durkheim intended to describe the distinctions as ideal types, that is, as generalised models, his perceptions about the distinctive nature of these two types parallel those of Toennies and remain powerful to this day.

Durkheim (1893) distinguished between what he called mechanical solidarity and organic solidarity. *Mechanical solidarity* describes the types of relationships that link together members of small, stable communities. These relationships are overlapping and interrelated, and members of the group are interdependent because of the common bonds and habits they all share, not because they exchange specialised skills both need. The relationships that characterise mechanical solidarity are based on personal, stable, intertwining emotional attachments. Our close friendship groups are based on mechanical solidarity. We turn to our friends for affection, support, help and advice *because* they are our friends and not because they are necessarily the most efficient supporters, helpers, or advisers in any particular instance.

In contrast, *organic solidarity* is characterised by relationships that are impersonal, transient, fragmented and rational. In a society marked by organic solidarity, different parts of the society are linked by efficient interdependence, *not* by the bond of homogeneity. Just as the parts of the body differ dramatically from each other in appearance, substance, and function and yet depend completely upon each other for survival, so the segments of an organically linked society differ drastically from each other, yet depend on each other for survival. In relationships marked by organic solidarity we do not relate to the whole individual, but to those qualities that pertain to the function of the relationship. For example, when we hail a cab on a city street we don't care who the driver is or what his personal characteristics are. All we ask is that he get us where we want to go. He, in turn, doesn't care who we are as long as we can pay the fare. The cab driver and passenger are briefly interacting in terms of a transaction, not in terms of an emotional attachment. The driver is interchangeable with any other driver, and the passenger interchangeable with any other passenger.

The consequences of such a drastic shift in human relations., brought about by the irreversible conditions of modernisation, have both fascinated and frightened a large number of social observers, and the total eclipse of human community has been forecast with gloom and doom for at least a century now. While no one would deny that the shifts from farm to factory, from village to city have brought great changes in human social organisation, the initial alarm over these changes has been tempered in recent decades by the discovery that modern relationships are not wholly isolating and alienating and that traditional relationships were not wholly intimate, supportive and integrating. Even when families are separated by great spaces and different value systems, they still stay in contact and help each other (think of how many college students go home for vacation; receive gifts on holidays, keep their parents informed of their whereabouts). Even in large urban centers people still make friends at work, in the neighbourhood through their children's schools. Even in the most bureaucratic organisations, work groups and friendship cliques form. While these relationships are clearly not as all-consuming as the relationships in a tribal village, they often have their own merits.

Erich Fromm has suggested that modern society promotes greater independence and self-reliance (1941, p.

124). What he means is that in a society where people have substantial freedom to select their friends, their jobs, and their leisure activities, they are more able to create their *own* identities, rather than being tied to the social roles into which they were born. On the other hand, this type of freedom often leaves us bewildered and confused by the choices at hand: "The structure of modern society affects man in two ways simultaneously; he becomes more independent, self-reliant, and critical, and he becomes more isolated, alone and afraid" (Fromm, 1941, p. 124).

It is likely that the debate over the virtues of *Gemeinschaft* and *Gesellschaft* relationships will continue for some time. People in traditional, small, intimate communities will rail against the narrowness and lack of privacy; and people in large, heterogeneous, anonymous cities will long for some sense of community and safety. As an elderly rural churchman said to a sociologist studying his once close-knit farming village in England: "Newcomers have broken down many of the old community ideas and people have become sentimental about the passing of ways and customs, although many of them were narrow, limiting, and bad. . . . (In the old days) they had sort of a code but all the natural human relations were covered by cruel and ugly taboos which obsessed some of them" (Blythe, 1969, pp. 69-70).

Primary and Secondary Groups

Although the terms *Gemeinschaft* and *Gesellschaft* were originally intended to describe the social organisation of entire communities, these concepts have also been adopted for the description of different types of smaller groups. The primary group is analogous to *Gemeinschaft* and the secondary group to *Gesellschaft*.

Primary Groups - Several interconnecting features characterise primary groups:

1. continuous face-to-face interaction
2. permanence
3. ties of affection

4. multifaceted relationships
5. non-task-oriented relationships.

The nuclear family, at least in theory, is the primary group *par excellence*. Members of the family are frequently in face-to-face interaction; the unit is enduring (even after members move away they are still members of the family); family members are bound together by love and affection; members of the family have many kinds of relationships with each other (ranging from exchange of services, "You set the table, I'll wash the dishes," to emotional support and physical protection); and the family is a unit *because* it is a family not because it is trying to accomplish something.

These are the structural features of the *ideal* family (or ideal primary group), at least as it is defined in contemporary American society. But between the ideal and the real there is, of course, often much disparity many families break up and therefore have neither continuous face-to-face interaction nor permanence. Many families spend more time in conflict than in love; many families have severely limited interactions (teenagers, for instance, are often reluctant to share their private lives with their parents); and many families are, in fact, united for the fulfilment of tasks (for example, bearing and raising children, working the farm, dividing up the chores of survival), rather than for the fulfilment of emotional needs.

Although not even the nuclear family therefore, always fulfils the requirements of the ideal primary group, the list of characteristics helps us to discern how much various groups actually differ from this ideal. These insights can then help us to understand the causes of satisfactions and disappointments in different groups.

Secondary Groups - In contrast to primary groups, secondary groups ideally have the following characteristics:

1. limited face-to-face interaction
2. nonpermanence
3. ties of exchange not of affection
4. limited relationships
5. task-oriented relationships.

But, just as for primary groups, this theoretical description is an ideal type. Secondary groups do, in fact, produce long, intimate friendships, and despite their initial task orientations, secondary groups can turn into primary groups. A perfect example of this is the highly task-oriented group of office workers that may become a close-knit primary group. Co-workers may develop strong friendships, spending much of their leisure time together.

If you join a secondary group, such as a political club, with the hope of developing enduring friendships, you may be disappointed. This disappointment will result not so much from the personalities of the club's members (or from your own social deficiencies) as from the structure of the group itself. To begin with, the club will meet infrequently and only for a few hours at a time, affording members little opportunity to get to know each other in a variety of situations. The members of the club are together for an explicit, task-oriented purpose and too many diversions from this task will be met with impatience and hostility. Membership in the club is voluntary and temporary, and turnover rates may therefore be high. Although members may hold similar attitudes and values, their basic ties to each other are intellectual and not emotional. For all these reasons friendships may be difficult to form, regardless of the personalities of group members.

Encounter Groups and the "Singles Industry"

The encounter movement, which gained momentum in the 1960s, is an attempt to heighten self-awareness and mutual human trust. Encounter methods vary weely, but a group typically consists of eight to eighteen persons led by a "facilitator". Members of the group are usually urged to express their emotions toward one another both verbally and physically. The by-words of encounter groups are mutual trust, openness, honesty and naturalness.

Although there are a growing number of techniques for conducting encounter groups, and although more than 6 million Americans have participated in some sort of encounter at some variety of "growth center", there is still a great deal of dissension about the consequences of such instant intimacy. While the effects of encounters on participants are, in the end, the crucial concern of those evaluating this startling new movement, the fact that such an untraditional form of community life has gained such a large following is, in itself, fascinating. We can only marvel at the types of self-exposure that millions of men and women make among total strangers in encounter groups. As one experienced observer has written:

> There is no denying the searing shock of what one sees and feels once the mask of everyday polite behaviour peels away: the smooth and powerful business executive finally cracking and confessing in wracking sobs that he has never had a friend, never really "talked" to his wife, is a stranger to his children; the "successful" housewife and club-woman gasping out the tragedy of what she feels is a "wasted life"; the smart junior executive, his tie askew, grimacing in anguish as he confesses aloud for the first time in his life the humiliation and anguish of being a closet homosexual; the beautiful young bride admitting through silent tears that she feels nothing - absolutely nothing - for anyone or anything. (Hoover, 1972)

Carl Rogers, one of the founders of the encounter movement, has tried to explain the popularity of this new approach to human relations.

> I believe it is a hunger for something the person does not find in his work environment, in his church, certainly not his school or college, and sadly enough, not even in the modern family. It is a hunger for relationships that are close and real; in which feelings and emotions can be spontaneously expressed without first being carefully censored or bottled up; where deep experiences - disappointments and joys - can be shared; where new ways of behaving can be risked and tried out; where, in a word, [people] approach the state where all is known and all accepted, and thus further growth becomes possible. This seems to be the overpowering hunger which [people] hope to satisfy through the experience of an encounter group. (1970, pp. 11-12)

Encounter groups, then, represent a mating of primary and secondary forms of group life. They are primary in their intimacy, emotional bases, and intensity, but they are secondary in their temporariness and short-term commitments.

Do encounter groups really change behaviour? Are they harmful or helpful? Within the last few years, researchers have begun to study the effects of encounter groups. Preliminary results of one study suggest that "encounter groups . . . consistently improve self-satisfaction, self-reliance and comfort with sexuality, and lessen loneliness, alienation and social inhibition" *(The New York Times,* January 13, 1974). The results of another study were more negative. Irvin Yalom and Morton Lieberman (1971) organised eighteen encounter groups at Stanford which were led by people with varied training in group leadership. Out of the 209 undergraduates who participated, 39 dropped out before the experiment ended. Of the 170 who completed the thirty hours of group encounters, 16 suffered "enduring, significant, negative outcomes, which were caused by their participation in the group." The study found that the most vulnerable students were those who had little self-esteem and who expected great changes from their group experiences.

The growth of the encounter movement, which is aimed at personal fulfilment through group experience, has been paralleled by the growth of the "singles industry". With the break-up of traditional communities, people who have reached adulthood without marrying (or whose marriages have been disrupted) are no longer incorporated into families or village communities. Urban life is not conducive to extended-family living, if only because space is so limited in high-density apartment houses, and the break-up of small communities has robbed people of the protection and sustenance of a community that assumes responsibility for its members. How then, do isolated individuals in a society geared to family units create or locate a community for themselves?

John Goodwin, in his book entitled *The Mating Trade* (1973), explores the many and diverse institutions that have sprung up to service the never-wed, separated, deserted, divorced, and widowed millions in America. Goodwin estimates that there are some 36 million single adults in America, and with the break-up of traditional communities, which often provided meeting places for the unwed, the singles industry has flourished as a means of bringing together unattached adults. There are singles bars, singles clubs, singles magazines, singles parties, singles weekends, singles cruises, and even singles encounter groups.

Once again, this is an example of secondary-group structures being used to foster primary-group relations. The computerised dating services, which Goodwin calls "electronic cupids," are "nothing less than the automation of the hallowed ritual of Boy meets Girl" (1973, p. 79). But that hallowed ritual, particularly for men and women cast adrift in urban settings, is working with decreasing effectiveness, and a modern world is turning to modernised means for filling the gaps that are created by the decline of long-lasting primary communities.

Communes: Old and New

Not all attempts at replacing lost community are based on modern means. The movement toward planned or intentional communities, given so much publicity in the last decade, did not originate with the hippies. The colonies at Jamestown and Plymouth were intentional communities, and the nineteenth century saw the birth of numerous religious communities, including the Shakers, the Hutterites and the Amana True Inspirationists. John Humphrey Noves founded Oneida, an experiment in ga ap marriage; industrialist Robert Owen put his ideas about social reform to work in New Harmony; and Fanny Wright set about buying farms for freed-slave communes (Lawson, 1972; Hinds, 1973). Only eleven of the ninety-odd intentional communities founded in the nineteenth century lasted twenty-five years or more. Why?

Curious about this high mortality rate among earlier communes, sociologist Rosabeth Kanter conducted a study of American communes. She discovered that the longevity of earlier planned communities was highly connected to personal sacrifices, including abstinence from alcohol or meat, plain dress, and celibacy, and to irreversible investments, such as turning property and income over to the group. "Sacrifice," writes Kanter, "means that membership becomes more costly and fa therefore not lightly regarded or likely to be given up easily" (1972. p. 353). Most successful communes demanded that members renounce all ties with outsiders and in some cases ties with insiders as well. (Both celibacy and free love helped to prevent the formation of exclusive ties that might undermine group cohesion). In long-lasting communes, privacy was discouraged or forbidden: common dwelling places, eating and recreational facilities, and group rituals were emphasised. Most strikingly, in those that endured, the community required total submission to authority, and most of these practiced confession, self-criticism, and strict conformity to programmed activities. In all cases, the more the participants invested (emotionally and otherwise) in the community, the greater were the chances of the community surviving.

Modern communes frequently lack these longevity-producing features. Despite the fact that the new wave of communes flourished in the mid-1960s, many of them did not endure. The emphasis in today's communes is on self-expression and autonomy, not submission; on freedom from routine and control, not discipline and communal labour. Exceptions are highly disciplined religious communes and Walden Two, a commune modeled on the older, enduring types (Kinkade, 1973). But for the most part, attempts at recreation of the traditional community have been short-lived and occasionally chaotic.

To say, however, that modern communes are not long-lasting is not to invalidate their existence. With the loss of permanence in other forms of community life, there is no reason to insist on permanence in communal living. Whatever group satisfactions and rewards can be gained from communal experiences should be appreciated on their own merits without reference to nostalgic standards of longevity and permanence.

8

SOCIAL STRATIFICATION

THE DIMENSIONS OF STRATIFICATION

The Siriono of Bolivia come as close to being a classless society as any people we know of. Like most hunters and gatherers, the Siriono have very few possessions - at most, a bow and arrow, a crude knife, a bone or stick for digging roots, a bladder for carrying water, a large shell that doubles as a basket and cradle, a pair of sandals, a skin to hold these things. Nomads, the Siriono live from day to day. When the hunt is successful, they gorge themselves (they cannot store meat for more than two or three days); when game elude them and foraging yields little, they go hungry. But feast or famine, food is distributed equally among all members of the band. The Siriono expect those who "have" to share with those who "have not"; they do not tolerate hoarding. As a result, no individual or family has the opportunity to accumulate food and buy the services or deference of another. Economically, all are equals. But the Siriono *do* have a pecking order. Older people, those who exhibit magical talents, and skilled hunters occupy special positions in the band. And the respect and honour they earn through longevity or prowess spill over into political matters, where these individuals carry more than equal weight (Lenski, 1966, pp. 102 -12).

Social stratification is not simply a question of wealth, even in capitalist societies such as the United States. There are obvious social differences among people who earn $ 50,000 by drawing salary as a business executive, collecting interest from an estate ("clipping coupons"), selling heroin, winning a Nobel prize, holding public office, or "hitting on the lottery". When we say that people have "class," we mean we admire their style, the way they conduct themselves and spend what they have - not just that they are wealthy. The label "nouveau riche" gives expression to the belief that money, like wine, needs time to mellow. Money may be a prerequisite for status in this country, but it is not a guarantee. The bosses of organised crime, for example, are rich and powerful; they can and do buy politicians. But they cannot buy respect or prestige outside the underworld. On the other hand, ministers and professors enjoy high status in the United States, although their incomes are relatively small. In short, income alone does not determine status. Family name, ethnic and religious background, age, sex, education, occupation, life-style, club membership, neighbourhood - even grammar - all influence a person's social ranking.

Sensitive to such differences, Max Weber distinguished between classes, parties and status groups (in Gerth and Mills, 1946, pp. 180 - 95). By *class,* Weber meant people who occupy the same rung on the economic ladder; by *party,* people who share interests and seek to further them by gaining access to power. A *status group,* in Weber's scheme, is a group of people whose life-style or pattern of consumption gives them a similar social identity. Weber emphasised that while these three classifications often overlap (it takes money to support an upper-class life-style; poverty usually means powerlessness as well), they do not necessarily coincide. A very rich man, such as Franklin D. Roosevelt, can become a working man's hero and an enemy to his own class, for example. Weber's point was that in complex, modern societies, social stratification is multidimensional. It involves the unequal distribution of power and prestige, as well as wealth. In the pages that follow we will examine these three dimensions of stratification - property, power and prestige -in the United States.

Income and Wealth

Economic stratification depends on what people earn and what they own. The earnings are income and the "ownings" (property and assets) are wealth. Two people may have similar incomes, but one person's may come entirely from a salary and the other's may come from dividends on vast holdings of securities. The second person is wealthier than the first and ranks higher on the economic scale. Both income and wealth are distributed unevenly, but to different degrees.

Income - On April 15 every year, the Internal Revenue Service demands an accounting from all adult Americans of what they earn. The official records do not include all noncash income (expense accounts and other fringe benefits) or noncash social benefits that raise a person's standard of living (Medicaid, food stamps, school lunches, and the like). And there is undoubtedly a great deal of underreporting, deliberate and accidental (Rose, 1972, p. 162). Nevertheless, government statistics do give a clear picture of the range of incomes and the dimensions of inequality in this country.

In 1972 the medium family income was $11,120 per year -double that in 1960 {*Statistical Abstract*, 1973, p. 328). Approximately 16.6 per cent of American families earned $ 5,000 or less; 27.0 per cent between $ 5,000 and $10,000; 49.1 per cent between $10,000 and $25,000; 7.3 per cent over $ 25,000. Breaking the population down into fifths, we find that the poorest 20 per cent of Americans earned only 4.5 per cent of all personal income - about one-fourth what their share would be if income were distributed equally in the United States. The wealthiest 5 per cent of Americans earned over 17.0 per cent of all personal income, about three times their "share".

Education and occupational difference explain these gradations in part. While the median income of white family heads who had not gone beyond elementary school was $7,629 in 1972, the median income of high-school graduates was $12,426, and that of college graduates $17,497. For black family heads, the corresponding 1971 figures were $5,407, $ 8,814 and $14,063, respectively. These figures suggest that education is an excellent investment. In fact, statistics show that every year of college is worth roughly $ 70,000 in lifetime earnings. This figure is probably exaggerated, however, for many of the people who go to college usually come from middle- and upper-class, achievement-oriented families and would probably earn better than average incomes without advanced education. Still, the more education a person has, the better his or her chances of working in a high-paying occupation. Self-employed professionals receive the highest wages in this country (a $17,169 median income in 1971); nonfarm labourers earn the lowest ($ 4,847). Table 8.1 shows

Table 8.1
Median Earnings, by Occupation, Sex and Race, 1971
(For Year-round Full-time Workers)

	Male			*Female*		
Occupation[1]	*Total in dollars)*	*White*	*Black*	*Total (in dollars)*	*White*	*Black*
All workers	9,399	9,659	6,669	5,593	5,641	5,014
Profession and technical workers	12,518	12,629	10,046	8,312	8,294	8,298
Farmers and farm managers	4,308	4,356	(NA)	(NA)	(NA)	(NA)
Managers and administrators, except farm	12,721	12,781	9,867	6,738	6,690	(NA)
Clerical workers	9,124	9,257	7,742	5,696	5,685	5,779
Sales workers	10,650	10,769	(NA)	4,485	4,448	(NA)
Craftsmen, formen	9,627	9,749	7,556	5,425	5,511	(NA)
Operatives	7,915	8,198	6,188	4,789	4,825	4,448
Private household workers	(NA)	(NA)	(NA)	1,926	1,870	1,895
Service workers, except private household	7,111	7,560	5,556	4,159	4,169	4,039
Farm labourers	3,752	4,134	(NA)	(NA)	(NA)	(NA)
Nonfarm labourers	6,866	7,129	5,990	4,548	4,645	(NA)

(NA) Not available.
[1] 'Occupation of longest job.
Source: Bureau of the Census, *Current Population Reports,* series p-60, no. 85.

the percentage of white and black Americans working in different occupations, and the median incomes for males and females in each occupation. Clearly, race and sex influence a person's economic standing in the United States.

Wealth - The rich and soperrich derive only a small proportion of their incomes from wages and salaries. Whereas Americans who earned $ 20,000 or less in 1966 drew 87 per cent of their income in wages and salaries, those in the over $100,000 a-year bracket earned 15.2 per cent of their income from salaries, 13.3 per cent from small businesses they

Table 8.2
American Wealthholders,[1] 1969

Number of Wealthholders		
Male	5,643,000 (62.6 per cent)	
Female	3,370,000 (37.4 per cent)	
Total	9,013,000	
Size of Estate	*Number*	*Percentage*
$ 60,000 - 99,999	3,341,000	37.1
100,000 - 499,999	5,214,000	57.9
500,000 - 999,999	311,000	3.4
1,000,000 - 9,999,999	113,000	1.6
10,000,000 + 4,000	(less than 0.05)	
Assets	*Amoung (in Billions of Dollars)*	*Percentage*
Total	1,625.8	
Real estate	428.3	26.3
Bonds	85.4	5.3
Corporate stock	551.5	33.9
Cash	189.9	11.7
Notes and mortgages	59.4	3.7
Insurance equity	31.0	1.9
Other	280.0	17.2
Debts	203.7	12.6
Net worth (less deficit)	1,422,2	

[1]People whose tax returns showed gross assets of $ 60,000 or more.
Source: *Statistical Abstract of the United States*, 1973 (Washington, D.C.: Government Printing Office, 1973), p. 342.

owned, and 66.8 per cent from stocks, bonds, real estate, and other capital (Tumin, 1973, p. 55). The government's profile of American "wealthholders" is shown in Table 8.2.

Wealth - especially stocks and bonds - is concentrated even more than income. In principle, any person can "own a piece of America" by buying stocks or bonds. In reality, those who "own" the corporations by holding stocks are a small proportion of the population. According to Robert J. Lampman (1962), 1.6 per cent of the adult population owns 82.2 per cent of all stocks - plus 88.5 per cent of corporate bonds, 100 per cent of state and local bonds, and 38.2 per cent of federal bonds.

Taxes - The federal income tax is supposed to be a progressive tax, that is, the more money a person earns, the higher his or her rate of taxation. In 1973 the income tax rate for an income of $2,000 or less was 14 - 17 per cent; for $ 20,000-22,000, 38 per cent; for $100,000 or more, 70 per cent. Progressive taxes are designed to distribute the cost of public goods and services according to people's ability to pay, and to deprive the rich of some luxuries in order to provide the poor with necessities (Fried *et al.*, 1973, p. 45).

But does our tax system actually reduce income inequalities? To some extent, yes. The poor pay proportionately lower federal taxes than do middle- and high-income people, and they benefit more from "transfer payments" (welfare, Medicaid, workmen's compensation, unemployment insurance, and other subsidies that are not drawn from a person's salary, as Social Security is). The federal government allocated $28.3 billion to poverty programmes in 1972 alone.

But in many ways the tax laws favour the well-off. Interest earned from state and local bonds is tax exempt; so is 22 per cent of income earned from the production of oil, gas, and other minerals, and 50 per cent of income earned through capital gains (profits on stocks, real estate, and other property). According to one estimate, if all earnings were taxed at federal income tax rates, the government would have collected an additional $ 77 billion in 1972 (Fried *et al.*, 1973,

p. 51). In addition, many of the taxes Americans pay are regressive; for example, when everyone is taxed at the same rate, regardless of income, the poor actually contribute a higher proportion of their income than middle- and high-income people do. The federal payroll (or Social Security) tax, state and local taxes (including sales tax), and property taxes are all regressive. In 1965 people who earned $ 2,000 or less paid about 25 per cent of their income in state and local taxes; people who earned $15,000 or more, only 7 per cent (Miller, 1971, p. 16).

Box 8.1

Subsidies to the Rich

According to government figures released in the late sixties:

- 381 people with incomes of $100,000 a year or more did not pay one penny in federal income taxes in 1968.
- Over 1,000 people who earned $ 200,000 or more paid the same proportion of their incomes in taxes as did people earning $15,000 - $ 20,000.
- Most taxpayers in the $ 500,000 - $1,000,000 group paid the same proportion of their incomes in taxes as did people earning $20,000 - $ 50,000.
- The super-rich, with incomes over $ 5 million, paid the same proportion of their incomes in taxes as people who earned $500,000.

Mr. G., for example, earned $1,284,718, primarily through capital gains, only half of which are taxable. Mr. G. would have paid income tax on $ 600,000 if he had not taken out a loan for $10 million. Interest payments on the loan came to $ 588,000, and interest payments are tax deductible. Mr. G. paid exactly $383 in income taxes. Mr. I., whose income was $1,313,000, didn't pay any income tax. Why? He listed $125,000 for "intangible drilling expenses" (a legal deduction), claimed a spectacular loss of $ 828,000 on his farm, and received a $865,000 deduction under the oil depletion allowance. In effect, the U.S. Treasury underwrites these gentlemen's business ventures.

Source: Philip M. Stem, "How 381 super-rich Americans managed not to pay a cent in taxes last year, 'in Jerome H. Skolnick and Elliott Currie, eds., *Crisis in American Institutions,* Boston: Little, Brown, 1970

Regressive taxes and tax loopholes shift a substantial part of the tax burden *back* to poor and middle-income families.

Benjamin Okner, a Fellow at the Brookings Institution, calculates that federal taxes (income and pay-roll) reduced income inequality in the United States by only 4 per cent in 1966 (Rose, 1972, p. 162). Does this figure represent progress? Has poverty decreased?

The War on Poverty-Victory or Defeat? - The government's definition of poverty is based on the Department of Agriculture's estimate of the minimal cost of living for a family of four. In 1972 a nonfarm family with an annual income of less than $ 4,275 was considered officially poor. About 12 per cent of Americans fell into this category. Poverty is most prevalent among female-headed households and black Americans. In 1972, 33 per cent of black Americans earned less than $ 4,275 compared to about 9 per cent of white Americans; 38 per cent of female-headed households were

Table 8.3
Poverty in the United States, 1960 -1973

Year	*Number in Millions*	*Percentage of Population*	*Poverty Line*	*Per cent of Madian Income*	*National Median Income*
			The Poor		
1960	39.9	22.2	$ 3,022	53.8	$ 5,620
1963	36.4	19.5	3,128	50.0	6,249
1966	28.5	14.7	3,117	44.2	7,500
1969	24.1	12.1	3,743	39.7	9,433
1971	25.6	12.5	4,137	40.2	10,285
1972	24.5	12.0	4,275	38.4	11,120
	The Near-Poor[1]				
1960	54.6	30.4	$ 3,778	67.2	
1963	**50.8**	**27.1**	3,910	62.6	
1966	41.3	21.3	4,146	55.3	
1969	**34.7**	17.4	4,679	49.6	
1971	36.5	17.8	5,171	50.3	
1972	34.7	16.8	5,344	47.9	

[1]People earning less than 125 per cent of the poverty-level income.

Source: Adapted from Edward Fried *et. al. Setting National Priorities: The 1974 Budget* (Washington, D.C.: Brookings Institution, 1973), p. 42. (Updated from "Characteristics of the Low Income Population: 1972," *Current Population Reports,* series p-60, no. 88, June 1973.)

poor, compared to 8 per cent of male-headed households. However, almost 75 per cent of America's poor are white, and over 55 per cent live in male-headed households.

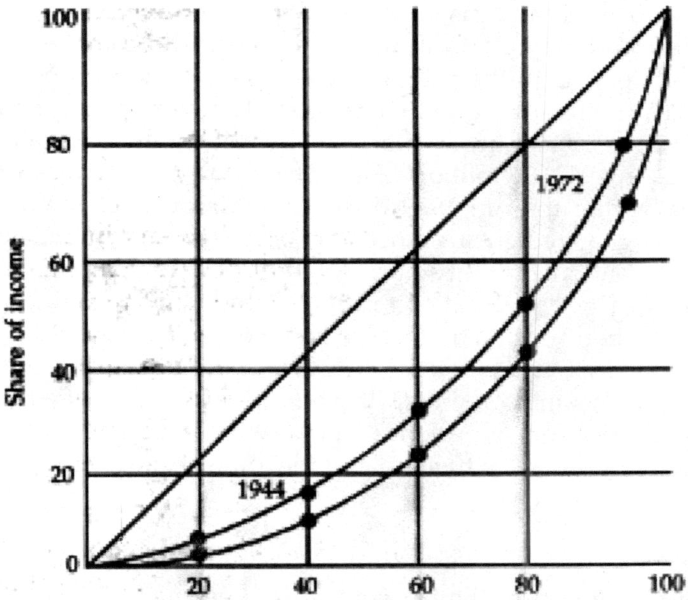

Figure 8.1: Measuring income inequality - the Lorenz curve.

The Lorenz curve is a simple method for portraying economic inequality in a graph. The straight diagonal line in the graph represents absolute equality with each percentage of the population earning exactly that proportion of all income. Thus, the lowest 20% would earn 20% of all income, the lowest 40% would earn 40% and so on. The curve represents the actual distribution of income at the lowest point, the poorest 20% of the population earned 5% of the income. The second point stands for the bottom 40%, the third point for the lowest 60% and so on. The space between the line and curve shows the degree to which income distribution deviates from absolute equality. The farther away the curve is from the line the greater the inequality of income. The curves for 1970 and 1944 show similar distributions of income, but the curve for 1929 shows far greater inequality.

Table 8.3 shows that the number of poor Americans dropped from 40 million in 1960 (before the War on Poverty) to 24 million in 1969. The figure then rose slightly in 1970. As Edward Fried and his colleagues (1973, p. 45) suggest, more Americans are able to purchase the necessities of life today than was true in the past. But the *gap* between the poor and other Americans has not changed. The number of people earning only half the median income was the same in 1971 as it was in 1963, 36 million. The distribution of income is more equal today than in 1929 during the Great Depression, but has not changed greatly since 1944 (see Figure 8.1). But despite this deviation from absolute equality, America is one of the most nearly equal nations in the world. The distribution of income here is similar to that in Great Britain, Canada and Japan; only Denmark, the Netherlands and Israel are closer to absolute income equality (Miller, 1971). This degree of equality is small comfort to America's poor, who still acutely feel the differences between their lot and the affluence they see around them.

Power

The presidency of the United States is generally conceded to be the most powerful office in the world. The trappings of the office alone show this: the White House and Camp David, the planes ready to fly the president anywhere at a moment's notice, the access to prime-time television to address the nation whenever he wants. The president never has to pay rent at the White House, wait for a haircut, or be put on "hold" by a secretary. The decisions the president makes are not like other people's either. Few of us think in billions of dollars, in millions of people, of the risk of triggering a nuclear war. The view from the top of the American power structure is very different from the one gained at the bottom.

Basically, power is the ability to mobilise collective energies, commitments and efforts. Personal power is the freedom to choose, to design one's own destiny. Social power is the ability to affect public affairs, even if others oppose you. Social power may be formal or informal. By formal power or *authority,* we mean the prerogatives that legitimately go with an office, such as the presidency of a nation or company. By informal power, we mean *influence,* the know-how and know-who to put the strings behind the scene. The president of this country has a great deal of formal power; Martin Luther King, Jr., had enormous informal power. But how many others share this power in our society?

Not surprisingly, this is one of the most hotly debated questions in sociology. C Wright Mills argued that the heads of government, the military and business in this country constitute a "power elite".

> [T]hey are in command of the major hierarchies and organizations of modern society. They rule the big corporations. They run the machinery of state and claim its prerogatives. They direct the military establishment. They occupy the strategic command posts of the social structure, in which are now centered the effective means of the power and the wealth and the celebrity which they enjoy. (1956, p. 4)

These are the men who make the decisions that determine how the rest of us will live. They move back and forth between the private and public sectors, never for a moment forgetting who they are, who their friends are, or where their interests lie. They are accountable only to themselves, and relatively immune to public pressure and the public interest.

David Riesman (1953), among others, disagreed with Mills. Where Mills saw one solitary elite, Riesman saw many competing elites whose varied goals and interests prevent them from pooling their resources. As a result, social power is widely dispersed; no one group commands. While this pluralistic system protects us from any kind of dictatorship, in Riesman's view it also deprives us of effective leadership. Decisions made through bargaining and compromise are not always the best decisions, however democratic their origins.

One point on which Mills and Riesman definitely agree is that the vast majority of Americans - the masses - have little power to speak of, personal or social. In Mills's words:

> The powers of ordinary men are circumscribed by the everyday worlds in which they live, yet even in these rounds of job, family and neighbourhood, they often seem driven by forces they can neither

> understand nor govern. "Great changes" are beyond their control, but affect their conduct and outlook nonetheless. The very framework of modern society confines them to project not their own, but from every side, such changes now press upon the men and women of the mass society, who accordingly feel that they are without purpose in an epoch in which they are without power. (1956, p. 3)

Mills's and Riesman's theories can neither be proved nor disproved unless power can be measured in some way. How do you calculate a person's or group's way over events? One measure of power is the *offices people hold*. We can reasonably assume that the president of a big corporation or the mayor of a large city has more power than ordinary people. But what about the people who work behind the scenes, who do not appear on official rosters? Another measure of power is *reputation*. We can ask people to identify the influential members of their community and conclude that individuals listed over and over belong to the local elite. But how do we verify the judges' opinions? A third measure of power is *participation in key decisions*. Who attends the crucial meetings? Who speaks for what groups? Who has lunch with whom? Who seems to have the final world? While this may seem the best method, in-depth analyses of key decisions require almost unlimited time and effort, and the combined skills of a psychologist and detective (Dahl, 1963). How many people admit to bribing, blackmailing, strong-arming, or even just pulling strings to get their way? As John Kenneth Galbraith once said, "Power obviously presents awkward problems for a community which abhors its existence, disavows its possession, but values its exercise" {in Domhoff and Ballard, 1968, p. 103).

An equally important question in this context is whether people *feel* they are able to influence the decisions that affect them (regardless of whether they do in fact exercise power). This is what is meant by "political efficacy." Robert Dahl (1963) found that the subjective sense of power rises with income, education, social status and political participation. The more influential a person feels the more likely he or she is to vote, to join organisations and attend meetings; and the more a person participates in political and community activities, the more likely he or she is to feel influential. Participation or whithdrawal is self-reinforcing. Like wealth and power, political efficacy is cumulative; the more you have, the more you get (Mills, 1956, p. 10). The same can be said of prestige.

Prestige

Consider the following advertisement:

> We don't think anyone in the city can rival our assortment of chic wares from the world famous House of Dior, each bearing the inimitable stamp of his renowned good taste.
>
> Christian Dior was a national asset to France and a by-word for taste. In fact, upon his arrival in New York (just after he launched his New Look), he received more publicity than did Winston Churchill on his trip. Ah, fashion!
>
> What intrigues us, of course, is that even though Monsieur Dior is no more, his vitality and zest, his unexpected and highly *civilised* mode of fashion still zips around the world, touching all kinds of fashion. Today, there is no more well-known name anywhere on our planet than Dior.
>
> Here is a random sampling of the exquisite *vendibles* you can find all around our store bearing the Dior label. We'll start with his signature luggage. Delectable, Noticeable at any airport. Woven in a tough, *take-it-on-the-chin* fabric, the pattern suddenly dawns on you. It's design of C's and D's (Christian Dior, of course). (Trahey Agency)

After all, what good is carrying Dior luggage if nobody knows that it's Dior luggage? Dior luggage, like designer-initialed scarves, shirts, dresses and underwear, is a status symbol. It shows that the individual has money and, more important, good taste.

Trivial as this example may seem, prestige is obviously one of the important dimensions of social stratification. People rank one another according to how they earn their money (their occupation), how they spend it (their "consumptive class"), who they are (their ancestry), who they know, how successful and well known they are, and how respectable.

For example, being listed in *The Social Register* or in *Who's Who in America* is definitely a status symbol. These publications have long reigned as the guides to who counts in this country. *The Social Register* describes itself as a list of "distinguished" people - by which it means people who come from the right families, attend the right schools, belong to the right clubs, and live in the right neighbourhoods. Applicants to *The Social Register* are only considered if they bring recommendations from several people already on the list. You cannot pull strings to get into *Who's Who in America,* however - a fact of which its editors are inordinately proud. *Who's Who* lists, in its own words, "the best known men and women" who have achieved "special prominence" by virtue of "reputable achievements" or "official positions" in government or religious and educational establishment. Coincidentally, perhaps, about 80 per cent of the people in *Who's Who* are also in their local *Social Register* - most of them bankers, lawyers, engineers, businessmen, architects, doctors, artists, public officials, educators, clergymen and social workers (Baltzell, 1966). Of course, neither listing is prepared in a scientific way, and both publications exclude (deliberately) the vast majority of Americans, who are only moderately distinguished or definitely undistinguished.

***Occupation Ratings* -** Probably the best measure we have of prestige in America is the Hatt-North scale of occupational prestige, which was designed for the National Opinion Research Center (NORC) in the 1940s. Paul Hatt and Cecil North (1947) compiled a list of ninety occupations and asked a cross section of Americans which term expressed their own personal opinion of each occupation's standing: excellent, good, average, somewhat below average, or poor. They then assigned a numerical value to each rating (100 for excellent, 80 for good, and so on), calculated the average rating for each occupation, and listed them accordingly. The job hierarchy shown in Table 8.4 is what one might have expected. Supreme Court justices, doctors, scientists, governors and cabinet members are at the top; garbage collectors, street sweepers and shoe shiners at the bottom; school teachers, builders, farmers and policemen in between. But there are some surprises. Americans are not as anti-intellectual as many intellectuals think: college professors rank eighth (well ahead of bankers). Oddly, movie stars and athletes were awarded no more prestige than welfare workers, farm owners and undertakers!

These occupational rankings have proven to be highly stable. The NORC study was repeated in 1963 and in an expanded form in 1964 and 1965. Although blue-collar occupations gained prestige and three categories of white-collar work (managerial, clerical and sales) dropped somewhat, there were very few changes over the twenty years. In another study, inspired by the NORC survey, Joseph Gusfield and Michael Schwartz (1963, pp. 265 - 71) tried to

Table 8.4

Prestige Ranking of Occupations in the United States, 1963

1	2
U.S. Supreme Ct. Justice	Priest
Physician	Head of a dept. in a state government
Nuclear physicist	Civil engineer
Scientist	Airline pilot
Government scientist	Banker
State governor	Biologist
Cabinet member in the federal government	Sociologist
College professor	Instructor in public schools
U.S. Representative in Congress	Captain in the regular army
Chemist	Accountant for a large business
Lawyer	Public school teacher
Diplomat in the U.S. Foreign Service	Owner of a factory that employs about 100 people
Dentist	Building contractor
Architect	Artist who paints pictures that are exhibited in galleries
County judge	Musician in a symphony orchestra
Psychologist	Author of novels
Minister	Economist
Member of the board of directors of a large corporation	Official of an international labour union
Mayor of a large city	

1	2
Railroad engineer	Owner-operator of a lunch stand
Electrician	Corporal in the regular army
County agricultural agent	Garage mechanic
Owner-operator of a printing shop	Truck driver
Trained machinist	Fisherman who owns his own boat
Farm owner and operator	Clerk in a store
Undertaker	Milk route man
Welfare worker for a city government	Streetcar motorman
Newspaper columnist	Lumberjeck
Policeman	Restaurant cook
Reporter on a daily newspaper	Singer in a nightclub
Radio announcer	Filling station attendant
Bookkeeper	Dockworker
Tenant farmer - one who owns livestock and machinery and manages the farm	Railroad section hand
Insurance agent	Night watchman
Carpenter	Coal miner
Manager of a small store in a city	Restaurant waiter
A local offickal of a labour union	Taxi driver
Mail carrier	Farm hand
Railroad conductor	Janitor
Travelling salesman for a wholesale concern	Bartender
Plumber	Clothes presser in a laundry
Automobile repairman	Soda fountain clerk
Playground director	Share-cropper - one who owns no livestock or equipment and does not manage farm
Barber	Garbage collector
Vlachine operator in a factory	Street sweeper
	Shoe shiner

Source: Adapted from Robert W. Hodge *et. al.*, "Occupational Prestige in the United States," in Seymour Lipset and Reinhard Bendix, eds., *Class, States and Power,* 2nd ed., (New York: Free Press, 1966), pp. 324-25.

learn why people consider some occupations highly prestigious and others degrading. Is it because they consider some jobs more important than others? more desirable? cleaner? stronger? Is it because some jobs seem more secure, a route to success? because they believe the occupants of certain jobs are honest? because they associate some occupations with rich, white Americans (wasps) and others with foreign-born or black or poor people? The authors found that people use different criteria to rate different occupations, but the overall ranking was very close to that in the NORC study. Indeed, parallel research in other countries, industrialised and underdeveloped, revealed striking uniformity in job ranking (Hodge, Trieman and Rossi, 1966). Summarising these studies, Hodge, Siegel and Rossi (1966) conclude that people rank occupations according to their importance for society, the power and influence that accompany them, educational, requirements, income, the nature of the work and dress (white vs. blue collar), and the characteristics of the people who fill each occupation.

The Hatt-North scale is a limited tool. It does not tell us anything about how family names, connections, life-style, or other intangibles affect a person's social standing. But it does show quite clearly that Americans award prestige unequally, that we are conscious of prestige differences, and that there is some degree of consensus about who counts in this country.

Classes in America

When asked, most Americans identify themselves as middle-class. This is part of our reverse snobbism. American culture glorifies the common man, "the average Joe"; the idea that no one is any better than anyone else is a central part of our national creed. Yet we have seen that there are startling inequalities in this country. Can "aristocracy cohabit with democracy" (Baltzell, 1966, p. 266)? Mrs. Marietta Endicott Peabody Tree's grandmother, a wealthy lady and a member of one of this country's most "distinguished" families, thought not. Mrs. Tree recalled:

> [T]he "first and only" time her grandmother ever slapped her was when, as a young girl, Marietta referred to an acquaintance as "very middle class". After the slap came these stem, grandmotherly words: "There are no classes in America - Upper, lower or middle. You are never to use that term again." (Birmingham, 1968, p. 340)

Only a person of unshakeable position could insist on this view. There are obvious inequalities in the distribution of wealth, power and prestige in America. To deny this would be foolish. Even a child knows how to distinguish between her "own kind" and families that are above a beneath hers socially.

Still, it is extremely difficult to identify distinct classes or social strata in America. The Lynds (1929,1937), pioneers in the study of stratification in this country, believed that power and prestige are a function of wealth. W. Lloyd Warner and Paul S. Lunt (1941) believed the Lynds had overemphasised economic differentials. An anthropologist by training, Warner was acutely sensitive to the rituals of class and differences in life-style. "Something more than a large income is necessary for high social position," he wrote. "Money must be translated intc socially approved behaviour and possessions, and they in turn must be translated into intimate participation with, and acceptance by, members of a superior class" (Warner *et. al.*, 1949).

In the Yankee City studies, Warner and his colleagues used two measures of stratification. First, they asked selected members of the community to explain their own personal view of stratification (how did they measure status?) and to rank individuals and groups (the subjective approach to measuring class). Then Warner devised on objective "Index of Status Characteristics" based on occupation (a measure of level of education and income), source of income, type of home and neighbourhood. Putting the two together, Warner concluded that there were six classes in Yankee City: upper-upper (1.4 per cent), lower-upper (1.6 per cent), upper-middle (10 per cent), lower-middle (28 per cent), upper-lower (33 per cent) and lower-lower (25 per cent). But how many people could say whether they themselves belong to the upper-middle or lower-middle or perhaps upper-lower class? Very few.

Over the years since Warner's study, rising wages and salaries for workers have acted as an economic leveller. The unionised worker has steadily improved his or her economic position and now may earn more than many white-collar workers. This, plus the belief that America is the land of opportunity and the feeling that no people are any better than anyone else even if they are better off, tends to retard the development of class consciousness in this country. In addition, racial, ethnic, and religious affiliations cut across economic lines. As a result Americans have multiple social identities that interfere with the development of a coherent class of rank consciousness (see Wrong, 1972).

LIFE CHANCES: THE CONSEQUENCES OF POVERTY

Nelson Rockefeller's secretary cannot afford to eat in the same restaurants as her employer, visit the same doctors, or own several lavish homes. But she can expect to live as long as, or even longer than her boss; she can afford nutritious meals, good medical care and pleasant housing. The life chances of the working, middle and upper classes are about the same. But the poor die earlier than other Americans. They are more susceptible to chronic and debilitating illnesses, physical and mental. They inhabit housing long since abandoned by others or "projects," and receive medical care from overcrowded and often substandard clinics. They are victimised by criminals on the one hand, the police and courts on the other. And they pay more than working, middle- and upper-class Americans for what they buy. In short, poverty is not only uncomfortable and degrading, it is a health hazard.

Nutrition

In the late sixties, Senators, Joseph S. Clerk and Robert Kennedy visited a neighbourhood just blocks from the Capital building, Clark reported:

> Gloria Palmer, a round-eyed, solemn-faced little girl of ten stood shyly outside her slum home in Washington, D.C., and shifted her six-months-old baby brother from one arm to another, while two other tots leaned against her and stared up at the two United States Senators....

> I asked Gloria - one of eleven children of Wilhelmina Palmer -what she had eaten for lunch. "We didn't have any lunch," said Gloria quietly, and added, "But we have blackeyed peas for supper a lot." I asked her little brother, George, age seven, "What did you have for lunch yesterday?" George replied, "Soup," "And what did you have for breakfast?" "Soup," George said. (Clark, 1971, p. 10)

Hard as it is to believe, millions of Americans (mostly children) live on beans, rice, peanut butter, grits, biscuits, corn bread, powdered milk, Kool-Aid, and one can of meat a month. From 30 per cent to 50 per cent of poor children suffer from protein, iron and vitamin deficiencies. Malnutrition stunts growth and makes a child more vulnerable to disease, but this is not all. There is a growing body of evidence to suggest that severe protein deficiency in the first twelve to eighteen months of life causes irreparable damage to the brain and nervous system. In addition, undernourished children are apathetic, lethargic, unable to pay attention for more than very brief spells, and often irritable and agitated (Reed, 1971). In short, hunger interferes with learning.

Medical Care and Mental Health

> "I went there at 9 o'clock like they said," recalled the young New York Negro mother. "About 12:30, I saw the doctor and he said I was in the wrong clinic. I went to the other clinic and waited until 2 o'clock and there were still people in front of me. The kids get out of school at 2:30, so I had to leave. That's just the way it is if you're poor." (*Newsweek*, July 7,1969).

Clinics in low-income neighbourhoods are understaffed and overcrowded. Clients rarely see the same doctor more than once, making it impossible to establish rapport and trust. Doctors, themselves middle class, find it hard to relate to lower-class people and to the conditions that make the poor disease-prone. Often, the poor feel intimidated by the staff, the red tape, and the possibility of costly fees and medicine (only 34 per cent of people with incomes under $ 2,000 have health insurance). As a result, most will try old remedies, over-the-counter drugs and simple stoicism, visiting a clinic only as a last resort and in emergencies (Rainwater, 1968).

And even then they may not be able to follow the regimen the doctor prescribes.

E. Pavenstedt (1965) is one of many psychiatrists who associates severe psychiatric disorders with disorganised, calamity-stricken homes. He writes of the "very low-lower class":

> Consistency was totally absent. . . . The mother might stay in bed until noon [one day] and get up at 6 A.M. [the next]. ... As the children outgrew babyhood, the parents differentiated very little between the parent and the child role. The parents' needs were as pressing and as often indulged as were those of the children, with strong competition for the attention of helpful adults. . . . The overwhelming demands of adults [produced! constant crises ... for every recurring frustration is experienced as crisis.... Abandonment and neglect of children is commonplace, (pp. 94 - 95).

While not all social scientists would agree with this characterisation, numerous studies have shown that the incidence of some severe psychiatric disorders increase as one moves down the socioeconomic ladder (Hollingshead and Redlich, 1958). Whereas middle- and upper-class people seek therapy with private doctors, the poor are most often treated with drugs, shock, psychosurgery, and custodial hospitalisation - which is no treatment at all in most cases (Coles, 1964).

Housing

The streets of Kenwood-Oakland, a poor section of Chicago, are lined with garbage. The sidewalks are crumbling; many of the buildings are condemned and abandoned. One woman told Senate investigators she was afraid to go to sleep, there had been so many fires because of faulty wiring. Her roof leaked whenever it rained, and the sewage was backed up in her toilet. The winter before, she and her seven children had had no water for two weeks (U.S. Senate Select Committee on Nutrition and Human Needs, November 1969).

Conditions in housing projects are batter, But Lee Rainwater (1971) found that 20 per cent of the apartments in Pruitt-Igoe, a highrise, low-income project in St. Louis, were vacant, and most tenants (half of them fatherless families, half living on public assistance) wanted to move. They complained of broken glass, dangerous and broken elevators, people urinating in the halls, and outsiders drinking in the stairwells and laundry rooms. Most were afraid of being held up or robbed, which they said were frequent occurrences. Rainwater characterised Pruitt-Igoe as "a world of trouble". Since then officials have written off the project as a disaster, evacuated the tenants, and dynamited the buildings!

The Urban League estimates that there were 6.7 million occupied substandard housing units in this country in the late 1960s, 4 million of them without indoor plumbing. About 6 million homes were overcrowded (more than one person per room). As with many things, the poor pay more (25 - 35 per cent of their income) for less (Ficker and Graves, 1971, pp. 91 - 102).

Criminal Justice

A redevelopment administrator in New Haven, Connecticut, told a group of people who were protesting the city's failure to enforce housing codes in that city's slums, "there are law violations and there are law violations" (Ryan, 1971, p. 187).

The courts, if not the law, favour white-collar offenders -slumlords who fail to repair housing-code violations, businessmen who use deceit in advertising or fraud, individuals or companies who violate price-fixing codes, embezzlers, and the like. More often than not, white-collar criminals are fined and given suspended sentences (Lundberg, 1969, pp. 124 - 28). In contrast, residents of low-income neighbourhoods are frequently arrested for drunkenness, gambling, and such ambiguous crimes as vagrancy, which together account for about 60 per cent of all arrests. Why? In William Ryan's view (1971), the police see their role as keeping order, not enforcing the law.

Poor people are more likely to be arrested than to receive a summons (as the nonpoor do); less likely to be released on their own recognisance (although they are the least able to afford bail); more likely to be sent to jail following conviction

(Cratsley, 1972, p. 192). Many poor people spend months, even years, in jail waiting for trial - if their court-appointed lawyers and the district attorney's office do not convince them to plead guilty to a lesser charge (to save "the people" the expense of a trial). The poor are also more likely to be the victims of crime than affluent Americans (see Table 8.5).

Table 8.5
Victimisation by Income (Rates per 100,000 Population)

		Income		
Offenses	*Under $3,000*	*$3,000-5,999*	*$6,000-9,999*	*Over $10,000*
Total	2,369	2,331	1,820	2,237
Rape	76	49	10	17
Robbery	172	121	48	34
Aggravated assault	229	316	144	252
Burglary	1,319	1,020	867	790
Larceny ($50 +)	420	619	549	925
Car theft	153	206	202	219

Source: *The Challenge of Crime in a Free Society* (Washington, D.C.: Government Printing Office, 1967), Tables 11 and 12.

The Poor Pay More

Merchants who locate in low-income neighbourhoods have a captive audience. Most of their customers do not have the cash to pay for television sets, sewing machines, and other appliances America seems to promise its citizens, and they do not qualify for credit at stores in higher-income areas. Ghetto merchants lure potential customers into the store with promises of easy credit, on the "dollar down, dollar a week" model. Small weekly payments create the illusion of low prices. In reality, a television marked $ 220 may cost as much as $300 when paid for on an instalment plan. Once the customer signs the papers, he has no choice but to pay. Should he default, the merchant can place a lien on the person's salary, reposess the goods, or sell the contract to a credit agency that will take the individual to court. In addition, such merchants often substitute inferior or slightly used goods for the items a customer saw in the id or selected in the store. Marking goods up 100 per cent or even 200 - 300 per cent is common practice. Door-to-door salesmen use the same tactics on a small scale. The following story is typical:

> "A salesman came by soon after we moved in told him. 'We don't want to buy anything because we moved and still owe a lot of money on the furniture.' The salesman said he would leave that ever we bought for two weeks and we wouldn't have to pay: 'After that, pay me one or two dollars a week/ he said." The couple took a spread and two pairs of curtains; they didn't sign anything. ... "A month later, the salesman returned with a Marshall and two policemen. The salesman said 'We came to get $ 52.' I told him I didn't have it. ... They took a T.V., radio and two-wheeled bike." (Caplovitz, 1963, p. 164).

The poor are frequent victims of business fraud and deceit. They even pay more for groceries.

The unequal distribution of life chances seems less formidable to correct when reduced \o simple numbers. In 1972 it would have taken $12 billion to raise every family in America above the poverty level. This is about what Americans spend yearly on cigarettes ($11.7 billion). Why, then, do millions of Americans go hungry and sick?

TWO THEORIES OF SOCIAL STRATIFICATION

Why do societies distribute wealth, power and prestige unequally? There are essentially two answers to this question. According to one school of thought, stratification is functional and inevitable; without it, people would have no incentive to perform socially necessary work. Another school holds that inequality is neither inevitable nor functional; it is simply a question of people who *have* exploiting people who *have not,* Kingsley Davis and Wilbert E. Moore (1945,1953) debated this issue with Melvin M. Tumin (1953) in the pages of the *American Sociological Review,* a debate which lasted for seven years.

The Functionalist Theory of Stratification

Davis and Moore reasoned as follows: If all the jobs that need to be filled in a society were equally important and equally pleasant, and if all members of society were equally capable of filling these jobs,, there would be no need for stratification. But the fact is, they are not. Some tasks are clearly more essential than others, and some require a great deal more talent and training. For example, almost anyone can learn to dig ditches in a matter of hours, but it takes years of schooling to become a physician. Medical school is tedious and demanding. For a year or more, medical students devote themselves full-time to the business of memorising the facts of human anatomy. As interns they are expected to work long hours, sacrificing their nights and weekends and social life. They earn very little for their efforts; many go into debt to finance their education. And the job of physician itself is not very pleasant. How many people would choose to spend their lives around the sick and dying if they did not know they would be amply rewarded in money and respect?

This is the key to Davis and Moore's argument. Societies must motivate people to seek socially important positions and to fill these positions conscientiously by awarding their occupants *more* of those things that contribute to sustenance and comfort, humor and diversion, self-respect and ego expansion than they would otherwise receive. In other words, societies have to entice people into essential jobs that are difficult to fill by rewarding them unequally. Otherwise, many essential tasks would not get done. Thus, social inequality is both necessary and functional. In the long run, the entire society benefits.

One Critique **-** Melvin Tumin (1953) could not disagree more. Tumin argues that stratification does not facilitate but rather limits competition for socially important positions to those who can afford training, eliminating people who may be equally or better qualified for the job. Perhaps a few poor people make their way into satisfying and important careers, but the vast majority do not. Nearly 20 per cent of physicians in this country and over 40 per cent of all professionals followed in their fathers' footsteps. There is no way to calculate the number of potentially brilliant doctors, statesmen, teachers, and so on who were too poor to attend college. The lower class's talents, energy and potential are lost in a stratified society. Davis and Moore seem to overlook the role inheritance plays in recruitment to important positions.

These authors do not consider the motivation of "the masses," other than to suggest that most members of society accept the stratification system and believe they get what they deserve. But as the riots of the sixties demonstrated so clearly, marked inequalities create distrust, hostility and suspicion among different segments of the population - a condition that can hardly be called "functional". People who are struggling to survive in a society that boasts hundreds of millionaires have little motivation to abide by society's norms, to respect the dictates of culture. And how many of the millionaires are actually performing socially useful work? Tumin drives his point home by criticising the notion that doctors receive high incomes because their jobs are both important and hard to fill. Doctors are scarce, not because the long years of training discourage people from pursuing a career in medicine, but because medical schools turn down thousands of qualified applicants every year. Physicians, who operate one of the most powerful lobbies in the country - the American Medical Association - protect their incomes by limiting their numbers. Again, society as a whole loses.

Tumin concludes that even if some economic incentive is necessary to motivate people to fill certain essential roles, it is hard to see how extreme inequality such as exists in this country is either functional or inevitable. He suggests that the functionalist theory of stratification is little more than a rationalisation of the *status quo*. Stratification exists because the rich and powerful use their considerable resources to hold onto what they have.

The Conflict Theory of Stratification

According to the second school of thought then, the rich are rich because they hold a monopoly over society's scare and valued assets and use their monopoly to dominate the poor. In effect, the poor subsidise the affluent, as Herbert Gans suggests (1973). Poverty creates a pool of labourers who are willing ("or at least unable to be unwilling") to perform menial, dirty jobs for low wages, creating surplus capital that can be used to support the arts and other lofty pursuits. The poor buy the things that other people do not want, for example, day-old bread and secondhand clothes. They remind other people that they are fortunate, and give those who help them the opportunity to feel righteous and altruistic (Gans, 1973, pp. 105 - 14). And without poor people the social scientists who study poverty, the journalists who write about it, the welfare and public health officials who run programmes to alleviate it would all be out of work - not to mention thousands of numbers runners, heroin dealers, manufacturers of cheap wine, faith healers, pawnbrokers and radicals. In short, the rich could not be rich (or "cultured" or charitable) if they did not exploit the poor so successfully.

The chief spokesman for this view was, of course, Karl Marx. Although Marx recognised the many dimensions of stratification, he believed that a person's social position ultimately depends on his or her relationship to the means of production (land, factories, and so on). These relationships constitute the objective class structure. Throughout history, the propertied class has exploited the non-propertied masses; the development of capitalism merely accentuated the gap between the powerful and the powerless, the rulers and the ruled. Marx argued that the capitalist class imposed poverty, ignorance, and powerlessness on the workers through a combination of coercion and deception, fostering a false class consciousness among the workers to obscure objective class structure. He saw the nation state as an instrument of oppression, religion as a method of diverting and controlling the masses, the family as a device for keeping wealth and education in the hands of the few. However, in crowding workers into factories and cities, capitalists had planted the seeds of their own destruction. Marx believed it was only a matter of time before the workers would realise that they were being exploited, that they outnumbered the owners, and that they "had only their chains to lose" in attempting to overthrow their oppressors. The result would be revolution and the creation of a classless society.

Marxist theory offers only one set of possible consequences of stratification: economic classes, capitalist dominance, working-class exploitation until the development of class consciousness, class conflict, and ultimately, a classless society. In the United States workers have not remained impoverished as in Marx's day, nor are economic interests always the determining factor in politics. Marx underestimated the power of other social dimensions both in creating special interests and in other cases for promoting social cohesion. The postcapitalist society he envisioned has yet to be achieved even in avpwedly communist nations. Marx's contribution, then, has been less in social prediction than in pointing out the importance of social class as a crucial variable in the social sciences.

THE LAND OF OPPORTUNITY: AN EVALUATION

The belief that any person who gets an education, works hard, and takes advantage of opportunities can "get ahead" is a central theme in the American dream (and one reason why Marxism has never attracted American workers). But is this country truly a land of opportunity? Have we moved any closer to the ideal of equal opportunity in the last decade? Can we?

Social Mobility

The first step toward answering these questions is to determine the degree of social mobility in this country. By *social mobility* we mean the movement of people from one social position to another. The term *vertical mobility* refers to changes in status, upward or downward. A living example of upward mobility is Leonard Stern, whose father came to this country from Germany several decades ago. The elder Stern and a friend decided to import canaries when their textile business got into trouble. They were moderately successful but then the canary business, too, fell into debt. Meanwhile, Leonard had gone to college and acquired an M.B.A. at record speed. He took over the business in 1959. The younger Stern built the family's Hartz Mountain Company into a $150-million-a-year enterprise, and by the time he was thirty-five he had amassed over half a billion dollars *(Fortune,* September 1973, pp. 172-73). There are fewer stories in *Fortune* magazine of people slipping down the socio-economic ladder (downward mobility), perhaps because readers do not like to be reminded that this is the opposite side of the coin. The term *horizontal mobility* refers to changes in position that do not appreciably alter a person's status, as when an oil company executive becomes the secretary of transportation.

The amount of mobility depends on how rigid and how unequal the strata are. In a classless society, where everyone is equal, there is no mobility. In a society with unequal strata, mobility may or may not be possible.

Open and Closed Systems - In a truly *open class system* (if such existed; this is an ideal type), there are inequalities but few impediments to social mobility: positions are awarded on the basis of merit, and status is tied to individual achievement. Family origins, race, creed, colour, sex, and other ascribed (or inherited) characteristics do not matter. Anyone with talent and ambition can advance. Class lines are blurred in open systems, and there is little class consciousness (in the sense of political solidarity among people in similar economic situations). This is not to say that an open society is an equal society; there is a difference between equality of opportunity and equality of situation (when all members of a society have the same standard of living). Open systems provide the opportunity to succeed or fail.

A closed or *caste system* (also an ideal type) is the opposite: status is determined at birth; people are locked into their parents' social position, and their opportunities are limited accordingly. In caste systems, ascribed characteristics outweigh achievements. Caste lines are clearly defined, and legal and religious sanctions are applied to those who attempt to cross them. The South African apartheid system (which is euphemistically described as "separate development") exemplifies a rigid caste system. In South Africa, blacks, Asians and whites live in separate neighbourhoods, attend separate schools, obey separate laws, suffer different punishments. It was in South Africa that Gandhi began his crusade against caste systems, first attacking discrimination against overseas Indians, later his own people's attitudes toward untouchables as well as British colonialism. Although the caste system has been legally abolished in India, attitudes about caste members remain. (See the Box 8.2.)

Box 8.2

In the News
Life as an Untouchable

India - Legally, castes no longer exist in India. But a stratification system centuries old does not disappear by mere edict, and the effects of caste linger. At the bottom of the caste system are the harijan, or untouchables. Barriers to their mobility are still strong.

Laxmi Rani is terrified to leave her mud hut in the morning and climb on her bicycle to pedal to school four miles away.

"I will be beaten," the 16-year-old girl said, "I will be abused. I think the people are displeased. I think they do not want anybody of low caste to get an education."

Laxmi, the only untouchable in the mango-shaded village of 3,000 to attend high school - she is in the 12th grade - added: "I am missing my examinations now. What will, happen to me?"

This girl has already been beaten by relatives of a high-caste, or Brahman, landlord. Her fears are that the intimidation will continue.

> "In this case they were trying to intimidate Laxmi Rani because she is the smartest girl in the village - smarter than the landowner's daughter - and they didn't want a harijan who was smarter than a Brahman. By shaming her, by harassing her, they wanted the girl to stop going to school or leave the village" [said Chedi Lai Sathi, a Congress parry official who works with untouchables].

Complaints to the police about the boating were of no avail. When her father tried to report the incident to local police, he, too, was threatened. Travelling to a nearby city, be complained to police there,

Box 8.2 - *(Contd.)*

but they simply asked the local police to investigate and the matter was dropped.

As in numerous cases involving untouchables - at least 200 die each year in caste murders and there are frequent reports that others are burned or maimed - the police were unsympathetic.

"In villages and towns a harijan who wants a higher education is a threat to the landlords and upper castes," said Mr. Sathi. . . . "If harijans leam their rights, if they become literate, then exploitation will have to stop. If they become educated, then who will do the mental jobs, the servants' work? Who will accept the conditions and wages that harijans tolerate?"

The actions of the upper castes are not simply a matter of vanity or the attempt to enforce custom. The stratification system is based on certain realities of economics and power, as well as prestige.

Source: Bernard Weinrauo, "Low-Caste Indians Still Know Terror," *The New York Times* (October 1973): 3.

Most societies fall between the two extremes of open and closed stratification systems, including the United States. Forty or fifty years ago, the social structure of the South was more castelike than it is today. Jim Crow laws prevented blacks from crossing racial lines, and many preachers taught that black skin was an emblem of the Hamitic curse. Today the law explicitly forbids racial discrimination, and there are signs that the Civil Rights Act of 1964 has worked to some extent. Surveying the most recent data, Richard Freeman (1973) concludes that black women and young black college graduates are earning as much as their white counterparts today, whereas twenty years ago, they earned substantially less (perhaps 30 - 40 per cent less) than whites with equivalent education. Despite the progress, blacks remain an "outgroup" in American society, if not an "outcaste".

Horatio Alger: Myth or Reality? - As a whole, Americans today are better off than their parents and grandparents were. In 1950 the median family income was $ 5,601; by 1972 it had risen to over $11,000. More than 50 per cent of American families had incomes of $11,000 or more in 1971, compared to 14 per cent in 1950. This "success story" is partly an illusion: the dollar does not buy nearly as much today as it did in 1950 because of inflation. Still, Americans as a whole are somewhat better off. *Structural mobility* - changes in the number and kind of jobs and in the number of people available to fill them - accounts for some of the rise in incomes.

The labour market has grown dramatically since the turn of the century, with the total number of jobs more than doubling. Perhaps most important, the number of white-collar jobs has skyrocketed (and white-collar workers earn more than blue-collar, service, or farm workers). These changes can be traced to industrialisation on the one hand and to massive migration from farms in this country and abroad to American cities on the other. In the short run mechanisation eliminates jobs, but in the long run it opens up whole new fields of employment (mechanics to fix the machines, for example). These new jobs require specialised skills, and the demand for educated workers increases. Employers who need highly trained personnel cannot afford to hire brothers and cousins first. As a result, the job market becomes more and more open - that is, more people are hired for *what* they know, not *who* they know.

Technology also contributes to geographic mobility: it becomes easier for people to move to areas where jobs are plentiful. An influx of unskilled and semiskilled labourers, such as occurred here in the late nineteenth and early twentieth centuries, frees experienced workers to move up the occupational ladder. (A man who did all the work in his shop can hire assistants-use his own time to expand operations, don a white collar, and so on.) The fact that white-collar workers tend to have fewer children than workers in other categories further stimulates upward mobility. Quite simply, they do not "produce" enough children to refill their ranks, which gives other groups a chance to move up. Thus, changes in the birth rate, improved technology, the demand for more and more education, and migration have acted to expand and change the American labour market.

Sociologists measure mobility by comparing fathers' jobs to sons' (intergradational mobility). Using this measure. Peter M. Blad and Otis Dudley Duncan (1967) conclude that Americans as a whole are upwardly mobile, but that most advance only a step or two. (See Figure 8.2 in the following section.) Inheritance plays an important role in determining occupational status. As noted earlier, about 40 per cent of professionals in this country are the sons and daughters of professionals. This is nearly five times as many as would be expected in a perfectly open society. (If society were perfectly open or mobile, there would be no correlation between fathers' and sons' occupations, ascribed characteristics, and status. See Tumin, 1973, p. 127.)

Even though ours is not a perfectly open society, Americans have always believed the opportunities for advancement are greater here than in any other nation. Is this true? Seymour Lipset and "Reinhard Bendix (1959) think not. Comparing the number of people who move across the manual-nonmanual line, they found relatively little difference in mobility rates for the United States, Europe, Scandinavia and Japan - despite the fact that some cultures encourage mobility and others discourage it. The mobility rate in this country is about 34 per cent, compared to 32 per cent in Sweden; 31 per cent in Great Britain; 29 per cent in France; 25 per cent in West Germany and Japan (Lenski, 1966, p. 41). Lipset and Bendix conclude that industrialisation creates high social mobility rates in a culture, and that there is nothing special or distinctive about America.

S.M. Miller and others have questioned both Lipset and Bendix's data and their interpretation. Is the fact that sons of blue-collar workers become clerks really evidence of great opportunities? Miller argues that statistics on the number of working-class people who rise to the elite are more significant. About 10 per cent of working-class people obtain elite status in this country, compared to 7 per cent in Japan, less than 4 per cent in France and Sweden, and 1.5 per cent in West Germany (Fox and Miller, 1965; Blau and Duncan, 1967, pp. 432 - 35). By this measure, the United States is considerably more open than other industrialised nations.

Reducing Inequality

The available data on social mobility suggest that most Americans can look back on and forward to slow but more or less steady improvement in their standard of living and occupational status. This improvement leaves the nation's poor farther and farther behind. As indicated earlier, the gap between the median income and the poverty line has doubled in the last ten years (from $2,600 in 1960 to over $ 6,000 in 1971). Thus, the poor are relatively worse off. What can be done to reduce this inequality?

Education — For years most Americans have believed that the principal way to break the cycle of poverty is to close the education gap. In the 1960s the government spent massive amounts on preschool programmes and job training, the courts began to attack *de facto* school segregation, and a number of colleges instituted open enrolment of all high-school graduates. But as Charles Silberman (1971) suggests, these programmes were overly optimistic. Americans tend to romanticise the role education plays in social mobility. Politicians, for example, are extremely fond of reminiscing about how they climbed out of poverty on their diplomas. But history suggests otherwise. Many immigrant groups "did not begin to view education as important, either in itself or as a means of mobility, until *after* they had become middle-class" (Silberman, 1971, p. 56).

This is not to say that education has no effect on mobility. As Figure 8.2 shows, 76 per cent of those who continue their education beyond college and 70 per cent of college graduates are upwardly mobile. And college graduates earn about $ 6,000 more a year than high-school graduates. Income thus *seems* to be directly related to education. However, if we trace these data back one generation, we find that parents' education, occupation and income have a decisive impact on the amount of education their children obtain. Thus, education may merely reflect family background and *its* impact on economic success.

Blau and Duncan (1967) devised the diagram shown in Figure 8.3 to depict the complexities of occupational

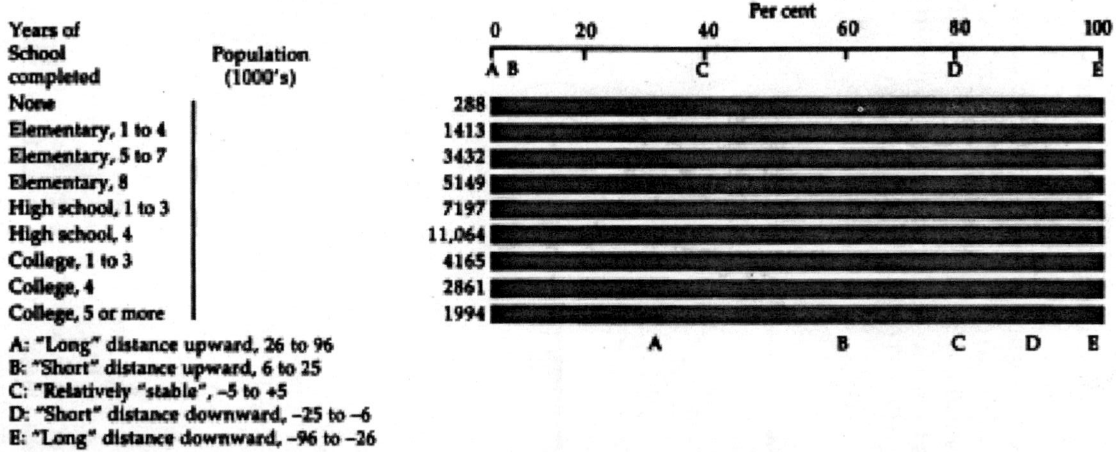

Figure 8.2: Education and intergenerational mobility.

Although education helps an individual up the social ladder, most people remain relatively close to their father's status. The changes of a long jump (A) increase with education. Less than a fifth of those who complete elementary sschool rise far above their father's position, but a half of those who go beyond four years of college do so. The majority of Americans however either rise only a few steps (B) remain at the same level (C) or fall only a few steps (D). The lower the education, the greater the relative stability; people with no education are least likely to gain or lose status presumably because they cannot easily rise without some education, but cannot fall very far because they are already at the bottom. Although rapid ascent and relative stability correlate with differences in education large drops in status do not indicating that factors other than education are involved in downward mobility.

inheritance. The diagram is based on correlations between fathers' educations and occupations and sons' educations, first jobs and current occupations. Each arrow represents a direct influence; the wider the arrow, the stronger the influence. The arrows with no source indicate other factors not accounted for by the model. As these arrows, show, sons do not inherit their occupational status directly. Rather, their fathers' occupation influences their level of education, and this in turn influences their occupation. Thus, a young person whose

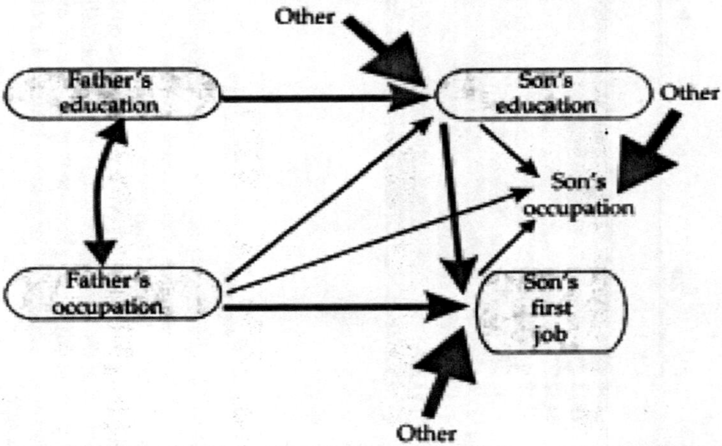

Figure 8.3: Education, background and social mobility.

Both education and social background are used to explain a person's social status, but neither education nor occupational inheritance alone determines a person's occupation. This path diagram was devised by Blau and Duncan to show the influence of background and education on men. The heavien the line, the greater the influence. The son's education strongly affects his first and subsequent jobs. Bu this education is determined in part by his fathers education and occupation. This link is stronger than the one between the father's occupation and the son's. Occupational inheritance, then, is indirect and works through the father's influence on his son's education. The chain of causanon among the father s and son s educations and occupations is even more complex but these chains are less important note than the fact that many of the determinants lie outside these paths entirely. The heavy arrows marked other designate these unaccounted for influences.

parents work in low-income, low-prestige jobs is the least likely to pursue the education that might enable him or her to escape poverty.

Christopher Jencks (1972) interprets these same data in another way. Looking at the large amount of unexplained variance, he writes: "Anyone who thinks that a man's family background, test scores, and educational credentials are the only things that determine the kind of work he can do in America (and what he will earn) is fooling himself. A most, these characteristics explain about half the variations in men's occupational statuses" (p. 192). Pointing to the fact that people working in the same occupation do not necessarily earn the same amount of money. Jencks suggests that policy-makers and theorists have overlooked some of the crucial variables - namely, how much an individual cares about money and how much he is willing to sacrifice for it; such immeasurable talents as being able to persuade people to buy bigger cars than they want; and luck, the accidents that cause a person to pick one job instead of another (pp. 226-27). Jencks concludes:

> Despite much popular rhetoric, there is little evidence that academic competence is critically important to adults in most walks of life. If you ask employers why they won't hire dropouts . . . they seldom complain that dropouts can't read. Instead, they complain that dropouts don't get to work on time, can't be counted on to do a careful job, don't get alongwith others in the plant or office, can't be trusted to keep their hands out of the till, and so on. *(The New York Times,* August 10,1969).

In short, Jencks believes that it is unrealistic to expect the schools to work miracles. Isn't it possible that all the attention public officials have given to education - all the ads warning young people about the dire consequences of dropping out of school - have done little more than convince employers not to hire dropouts? Jencks calls attention to the Coleman Report, a government-sponsored study of school desegregation in the South, published in 1966. The authors found, to their surprise, that neither integration nor better schools (better facilities and higher expenditures per pupil) had a significant effect on student achievement. The evidence indicated that students' backgrounds - their family and neighbourhoods, what they learned on the streets, from television, and from their friends - had far more impact on their development than schooling. None of these researchers is suggesting we abandon the educational system. Integrating and improving schools are worthy goals, in and of themselves. But we cannot expect educational reform alone to close the poverty gap.

Income Redistribution - If Americans are serious about reducing inequality, Jencks argues, they will not focus on schools or even individual mobility but on reducing overall inequality through income redistribution. This could be done by closing tax loopholes, providing an income floor below which no one will fall, and keeping the rich from passing on their wealth. America already makes a modest effort with programmes that redistribute some money to the poor. The government is spending over $86 billion a year in cash transfers, to rich and poor alike (Friend *et. al.,* 1973, p. 69), and this figure does not include various services the government provides to the poor. Where does this money go?

Social Security accounts for $54 billion. Payments are based on the amount of money a person earned before he or she retired (with the poor receiving proportionately more than more affluent people). In 1973 the average payment to an elderly couple was $3,500 a year. Recipients are allowed to earn up to $ 65 a month without losing benefits; thereafter, the government deducts $1 for every $2 they earn. Another $20 billion goes to the blind and disabled and to retired veterans, government employees and railroad workers.

Cash transfers to people who are neither disabled nor old account for less than $10 billion a year. The government pays out about $ 5.2 billion a year in unemployment insurance. To be eligible, a person must have worked for a certain number of weeks before being laid off. He or she must register with an employment office and accept a suitable job. Benefits are paid for a maximum on twenty-six weeks (or thirty-nine weeks if the national unemployment rate is above 4.5 per cent for three consecutive months). This income is tax exempt.

By far the most controversial programme is Aid For Dependent Children, or welfare, which costs the government $ 4.3 billion a year. The typical welfare family is a mother with three children. (About 55 per cent of welfare recipients are children, 19 per cent mothers, only 0.9 per cent "able-bodied fathers.") Contrary to popular myths, nearly half the families receiving welfare are white, and most stay on the welfare rolls for less than two years ("Welfare Myths, vs. Facts," 1972, pp. 14 - 16).

Thus, cash transfers are administered through a hodgepodge of uncoordinated programmes, developed piecemeal over the years. There is no provision for the working poor - that is, adults who work part or full time but do not earn enough to support their families. In effect the law discourages many from seeking employment. For example, in many states a single mother looses all benefits if she takes a job. By the time she deducts a babysitter from her salary, her earnings may well fall below the welfare payment. Until quite recently-a mother could not obtain assistance for herself or her children if their father was living with them, whether or not he had a job - a policy that encouraged families to break up or fake separation. In addition to these problems, welfare payments vary tremendously from state to state. Monthly benefits per person range from $14.41 in Mississippi to $ 95.01 in Massachusetts. There startling differences encourage migration to such places as New York and California, where payments are relatively high. In 1970 the number of people on welfare in New York exceeded the entire population of Baltimore. Even so, there are perhaps as many as 4 million poor families who receive no assistance whatever.

Corruption compounds these problems. Before an investigation of New York's Human Resources Administration in 1968, a group of city workers who called themselves "the Durham mob" managed to send themselves over $1 million in phony paychecks. One former official attempted to buy a house in Los Angeles with a check intended for the poor; the money withheld from paychecks to Youth Corps workers for Social Security had disappeared (*The New York Times*, January 12,1969).

Most damaging is the humiliation that accompanies welfare. In Detroit, for example, welfare workers have conducted "special investigations" at 3 A.M.; some threaten clients with loss of payments for "faulty housekeeping" (*Newszveek,* February 8,1971, p. 103). In the words of Daniel P. Moynihan:

> This is the heart of it. The issue of welfare involves a stigmatised class of persons. The recipient knows this.... It cannot be stated too often that the issue of welfare is not what it costs those who provide it, but what it costs those who receive it. (1973, p. 18).

What can be done to "clean up the welfare mess"? The central problem is how to provide poor families with an income that would guarantee a minimum standard of living without destroying the incentive to work. Under the current system families lose all financial assistance (and sometimes public housing, Medicaid, and the like as well) if the parents go to work. The negative income tax would change this. All families would be guaranteed a minimum amount, say $1,600 a year, by the federal government (plus whatever allotment states chose to provide). For every $ 2 earned, the guarantee would be reduced by $1. Thus, a family that earned $1,000 would lose $ 500 in federal payments, but its total income would be $ 2,100 ($1,600 - $ 500 + $1,000 = $ 2,100). The chief advantages of a negative tax are that it provides work incentive; it sets national standards; it would be less cumbersome and expensive to administer than existing programmes; and it would eliminate the humiliations of welfare. President Nixon sent a variant of this proposal containing stiff provisions requiring registration for work or job training to Congress in 1970, but the Family Assistance Plan, as it was called, did not pass the Senate (conservatives balked at the idea of a guaranteed income; liberals thought the income guaranteed was too low). But even if the national allotment were raised, is money enough to break the cycle of poverty?

The Culture of Poverty

Is it possible that the poor themselves may thwart attempts to reduce inequality? that second-and third-generation poverty may make people unsuited for life in the working or middle class?

Oscar Lewis introduced the term *culture of poverty* in *Five Families: Mexican Case Studies in the Culture of Poverty* (1971). An anthropologist, Lewis spent much of his career living with and studying the very poor in Latin America and the United States. After a time he began to notice surprising similarities in the way people in different societies cope with chronic poverty on the one hand, and a culture that stresses individuality and upward mobility on the other.

Lewis found that the very poor generally do not participate in society's major institutions. Often they fear and mistrust government, avoid when possible the public and private agencies that are designed for them, and develop a cynical attitude toward the church. Nor do they create organisations of their own (with the exception of youth gangs). The families Lewis studied knew little about the world outside. This low level of organisation carries over into the family. Most believe in marriage. But for men who are never steadily employed and have almost nothing in the way of property to pass on to their children, marriage makes little sense. Many women, too, opt for living with a man without the legal ties that would bind them to a man who may prove unreliable. As a result, "illegitimacy" rates are high in all slums, and many families are mother-centered. "The absence of childhood as a specially prolonged and protected state in the life cycle" combined with an early initiation into sex make growing up in poverty different from growing up in more affluent and stable homes. Lewis notes particularly the present-time orientation, lack of impulse control, and fatalism that develop among very poor people. He concludes:

> By the time slum children are six or seven years old, they usually have absorbed [these] basic values and attitudes of their subculture and are not psychologically geared to take full advantage of changing conditions or increased opportunities which may occur in their lifetime. (1970, p. 69).

If, as Lewis says, the poor have a life-style that prevents success, then simply providing more money or education cannot break the cycle of poverty. Are the failures of the American poverty programmes due to the incapabilities of the poor themselves, as Edward Banfield suggests in *The Unheavenly City* (1970).

Not all of those who recognise the differences in behaviour between the poor and the rest of society accept that this difference is cultural and therefore quite difficult to change. To sociologists like Elliot Liebow (1967) the conditions of poverty are sufficient to explain the responses of the poor. No unique culture is involved. The poor are trying to achieve the same goals as the rest of society, but they cannot, and so they try to hide this failure from others and themselves.

> Many similarities between the lower-class Negro father and son (or mother and daughter) do not result from "cultural transmission" but from the fact that the son goes out and independently experiences the same failures, in the same areas, and for much the same reasons as his father. What appears as a dynamic, self-sustaining cultural process is, in part at least, a relatively simple piece of social machinery which turns out, in rather mechanical fashion, independently produced look-alikes. (Liebow, 1967, p. 223).

To Liebow, the basic problem is that a black man hasn't the skills to obtain a job that pays enough to support a family. From this comes the instability of family life, the contempt for work that the rest of society also scorns, the search for thrills, and other characteristics of the poor. The solution is not to change values but the conditions of neglect, exploitation and outright racism. Changing the poor means changing the larger society. Lewis himself agrees with the necessity of taking the social structure into account:

> There is nothing in the concept [of the culture of poverty] that puts the onus of poverty on the poor. Nor does the concept in any way play down the exploitation and neglect suffered by the poor. Indeed, the subculture of poverty is part of the larger culture of capitalism, whose social and economic system channels wealth into the hands of a relatively small group and thereby makes for the growth of sharp class distinctions, (p. 79).

9

RACIAL AND ETHNIC MINORITIES

ETHNIC DIVERSITY IN AMERICA

Sunday is still the most important business day on Delancey Street on New York City's largely Jewish Lower East Side (Saturday being the Jewish Sabbath). Next door lies Chinatown, with its own language and customs, temples and grocery stores. Little Italy is just across Canal Street, its streets lined with social clubs and funeral parlors and on saints' days, with booths selling sausage and pastry from old-country recipes (and perhaps buttons reading "Kiss me, I'm Italian"). These are but three of the many ethnic groups that make up America.

An *ethnic group* is "any group that is defined or set off by race, religion, or national origin, or some combination of these categories." This is not to say that race, religion and national origin are equivalent. They are not. Race refers to inherited physical characteristics, which have no connection to religion or nationality, both of which are cultural institutions. But these classifications are similar "in that all of them serve to create, through historical circumstances, a sense of peoplehood" (Gordon, 1964, p. 28). In other words, an ethnic group is a group of people whose ancestry and heritage make a difference" - to them, and to the society in which they live. Customs, language, religion, family names, social ties, food, dress and appearance all play a part in denning ethnic groups.

For some Americans ethnic identity is only marginally important - something to march and sing and drink about on special holidays. For others, such as the Amish, maintaining ethnic integrity is a constant struggle against school officials and other intruders. The Amish, of course, choose to isolate themselves from mainstream America. In contrast, blacks, Indians, and others have historically had little choice about their isolation. And then there are the so-called "white ethnics," who seem to have gotten lost in the recent flood of interest in Afro-American, Indian and Spanish-American cultures.

How do these very different groups relate to one another? Why have they not disappeared into the "melting pot"? In part because established Americans have usually treated newcomers (and Indians, Mexican-Americans and blacks) as foreigners and avoided them; in part because the groups themselves have an emotional investment in their ethnic communities and identities and have resisted enculturation. Portraits of the largest ethnic communities in this country follow.

Black Americans

The self-transformation of "Negroes" and "coloured people" into blacks is one of the most dramatic chapters in recent American history. In the space of twenty years, blacks have successfully challenged the traditional "lily white" version of American history, which portrayed blacks as docile and willing slaves and Indians as blood-thirsty savages and said nothing about the way Irish, Italian and Jewish immigrants literally thought for acceptance and success in this country. It is blacks, more than any other group, who are responsible for a reawakening in recent years of ethnic consciousness and pride.

The 25 million Americans who trace their ancestry back through 300 years of poverty, exploitation and violence to Africa are this country's largest racial minority. As late as World War II, 80 per cent of black Americans lived in the South, where they functioned in large part as farm workers.

Today, 50 per cent live in the North and 52 per cent in metropolitan areas. These city dwellers are young. (The average age in the black community is twenty-one to twenty-two years, compared with twenty-eight to twenty-nine years in the population as a whole.) And they are proud.

To understand black pride, white Americans will have to learn black history, its joys as well as its sorrows. The African roots of this history are obscure. (Slave-owners made a concerted effort to separate members of the same tribe and to wipe out African customs.) As a result, little is known about the specific origins of black Americans. We do know that the first African immigrants settled in Virginia as indentured servants in 1619, and that by the end of the century nearly all blacks and their descendants had been relegated to perpetual servitude under the law. Slavery was a barbaric institution, but it was not always insurmountable.

> My mother was the smartest black woman in Eden. She was as quick as a flash of lightning, and whatever she did could not be done better. She could do anything. She cooked, washed, ironed, spun, nursed and laboured in the field ....
>
> My mother certainly had her faults as a slave. ... She was too high spirited and independent. I tell you, she was a captain.
>
> The one doctrine of my mother's teaching which was branded upon my senses was that I should never let anyone abuse me. "I'll kill you, gal, if you don't stand up for yourself," she would say. "Fight, and if you can't fight, kick; and if you can't kick, bite." Ma was generally willing to work, but if she didn't like doing something, no one could make her do it. At least, the Jennings [the masters] couldn't make, or didn't make her, (in Lerner, 1972, pp. 34-35)

Slavery was abolished in 1865, but white terrorism and discrimination were not. Jim Crow laws, which barred blacks from public facilities, and when these failed, lynchings kept blacks "in their place". For example, in July 1919 a mob took seventy-two-year-old Berry Washington from jail and lynched him from a tree near his house. Why? He had defended himself against two white men who were threatening a widow and her daughters (Lerner, 1972, pp. 188-89). During Jim Crow, blacks worked in fields, on river boats and trains, as domestics, as "boys". They went to school (sometimes only when it rained) and built schools; they formed their own baseball leagues and vaudeville circuit (whose blues singers began to attract white attention in the twenties). The black church was perhaps the most important institution in the black community throughout this time; it was both a tranquiliser (promising freedom in the new world) and a stimulant (creating solidarity reinforcing indignation).

As World War I approached, blacks began leaving the South in increasing numbers some as soldiers in all-black regiments, others in search of work at factories in Chicago Detroit, and other big cities. Harlem, Roxbury Chicago's South Side became cities within cities. Many of their residents were as poor at they had been in the South. But in the North-blacks fought back when they were attacked. The urban riots in the early part of this century were interracial.

However, the decisive battle against segregation began in the South, with boycotts and nonviolent demonstrations. Blacks marched, picketed, and sat-in at "white only" restaurants.

> At noon, students from a nearby white high school started pouring into Woolworth's. When they first saw us they were sort of surprised. They didn't know how to react. . . We just kept our eyes straight forward and did not look at the crowd except for occasional glances to see what was going on....
>
> The mob started smearing us with ketchup, mustard, sugar, pies, and everything on the counter. [We] were joined by John Salter, but the moment he sat down he was hit on the jaw with what appeared to be brass knuckles. Blood gashed from his face and someone threw salt into the open wound. .. .
>
> About ninety policemen were standing outside the store: they had been watching the whole thing through the windows, but had not come in to stop the mob or do anything. . . . After the sit-in, all I could think of was how sick Mississippi whites were. (Anne Moody, in Lerner, 1972, pp. 428 - 31).

The black migration north continued, and the ghettos grew, largely untouched by civil rights victories in the courts and in Congress. A new generation of leaders, street wise and uncompromising, began to attract attention. Black children started asking: Who is Frederick Douglass? Nat Turner?

Sojourner Truth? Touissant L'Overture? The Black Panthers among others, responded with classes in black history and self-defense and with free breakfast programmes. Given the long-standing belief that blacks were "culturally deprived" that the ways of the black community were nothing more than adaptations to discrimination, the fact that blacks stopped asking white America for answers in the late 1960s was nothing short of revolutionary.

Although too brief to do justice to the full history of blacks in America, this account gives some idea of the roots of black culture, which today is a mixture of southern and city tunes, of revolutionary rhetoric and Biblical intonations, of combativeness and cool.

Jews

> As the children of immigrants my brothers were aware of the fact that they represented the "undesirables," the "foreigners," as others had been "undesirables" in previous decades. They realised, too, that the only way to rise above undesirability was not merely to become desirable, but to become indispensable. This would require equal amounts of education and sacrifice. They filled every hour not devoted to study with part-time jobs as truant officers, book salesmen, teachers of English to foreigners - wearing out their eyes, their pants and their books, drinking black coffee to stay awake, postponing marriage, sharing clothes, colds, money and dreams. (Sam Levenson, in Freedman and Banks, 1972, pp. 194 - 97).

Like Sam Levenson, thousands of contemporary American Jews grew up on the streets of New York, under the watchful eyes of parents who believed that, by becoming educated, their children would "get ahead". Today, although only 23 per cent of all Americans are college educated, 42 per cent of Jews hold college degrees (Gallup, 1972, no. 70).

The first Jews came to America from Brazil in 1654, but it was not until the 1840s that Jews began arriving in the thousands, fleeing pogrammes (periodic massacres of Jews) in Europe. Today there are more Jews in America - about 6 million - than in any country in the world (the Soviet Union is second, Israel a close third). Nearly half live in or around

New York City. The Jewish community in this country is characterised by high levels of education, above-average income, a tradition of family-owned businesses, and a group-identity stemming from 2,000 years of political insecurity.

It is this sense of peoplehood that sets Jews apart. Jews are not a race; physically, they are indistinguishable from other peoples of European and/or Semitic descent. And their religious beliefs and practices are as varied as those of the different Christian denominations. They come from Germany, Russia and Poland; from France, England, Spain, Syria and Morocco. Many are as Americanised as any immigrant group, and many are not religious. What sustains the Jewish community, here and elsewhere, is a strong sense of peoplehood, a deep emotional identification with Jewish history and with one another.

Urbanites and entrepreneurs through much of their past, Jews adapted to America with relative ease. Not that they did not encounter discrimination - time and again they have been accused of disloyalty (because of their association with Israel), of participation in international conspiracies, of unscrupulous business practices. Traditionally, many corporations, major law firms, banks and private clubs did not admit Jews (some still do not), and until World War II many universities maintained strict quota systems. Jews prospered nonetheless - in part by using old-world skills to start businesses (the garment industry, for example), in part by taking advantage of public education, and in part by continuing to some extent to see themselves as the "chosen people," whatever their circumstances - a doctrine Jews share with Black Muslims. Of course, most Jews are not wealthy, and many are poor, but as a group, Jews have prospered and are highly represented in business and professions: 30 per cent of Jews earn $15,000 and over, compared with 14 per cent of the total population, and 40 per cent are in business and professions, compared with 22 per cent nationally (Gallup, 1972, no. 70).

Chicanos

The third largest minority in this country are the 5 million Catholic, Spanish-speaking Americans of Mexican descent, or Chicanos. The Spanish settled in what is now the American Southwest before New England was colonised, but not until 1848 did they and their land become part of the United States. Soon after, English-speaking settlers were edging them out: if all else failed, they were "sent back" to Mexico. Except in New Mexico, where Hispanos were able to hold their ground, most withdrew to rural towns and mining camps that were soon forgotten. When they went into Anglo areas to work as migrant labourers, they were housed in segregated camps; when they moved to big cities, they lived apart. The English-speakers called them "greasers" and "spies"; they called the English-speakers "anglos," "gringos" "gabachos". Many did not want to send their children to schools where they were slapped for speaking Spanish and often renamed {from Jesus to Jesse, for example).

Hostilities between Chicanos and Anglos reached a peak in Los Angeles in 1943, when police and restless sailors stormed the *barrio* (or neighbourhood), beating and then arresting some 600 of their victims in what came to be called the "zoot suit riots". In the fifties, however, an influx of Cold War related industries brought jobs to the Southwest, and by 1960 nearly half the Chicanos owned their own homes. (Still the median income for Chicanos remained about two-thirds that for the nation as a whole.) At about the same time, Chicanos began to exercise their voting power, supporting John Kennedy and later George McGovern. Cesar Chavez, a man appropriately compared to Martin Luther King, Jr., succeeded in organising grape pickers and other agricultural workers for a struggle that continues today. And a new pride and militancy began to grow among the young: *Is Raza Unida* was born.

Puerto Ricans

The United States acquired Puerto Rico in 1898, and in 1917 all Puerto Ricans were declared American citizens. Mainland companies began to open branches on the island, but were met with violent, nationalist resistance. A compromise was reached, granting Puerto Rico aid in modernisation and economic development as well as commonwealth status. The majority of Puerto Ricans did not benefit from economic expansion, however, and when the airlines introduced low fares after World War II, increasing numbers left the island to seek their fortune in New York. Today there are about 1.7 million Puerto Ricans on the United States mainland, most in and around New York City.

In city ghettos Puerto Ricans often suffer double discrimination - for their language and for their colour (which actually ranges from black to white, but Puerto Ricans are usually labelled nonwhite). What makes the Puerto Rican situation unique is that immigration is a two-way street: the island is close enough for immigrants to return home, and most do, temporarily or permanently. As a result, there is less incentive to learn English, and American ways. Moreover, the Puerto Rican community here is divided - between those who practice traditions (the authoritarian, father; strict surveillance of daughters) and those who think modern; between those who seek Americanisation and those~who do not (Simpson and Yinger, 1972, pp. 478 - 80). A nine-year-old girl told Oscar Lewis: "I have been here for a long time already so I am forgetting Spanish. English is what comes to my head. In school, I want to say *'ven ace'* and what comes out is "Come on". *Mami* says that if I learn to talk English she'll beat me" (1965, pp. 256-57).

American Indians

Indians are the poorest of the poor in America. Their past and present are stories of lies and abuse. The wars against the American Indians reached a peak toward the middle of the nineteenth century, when the eastern United States was becoming crowded, and the transcontinental railroad made travel easier. During this period gold was discovered in the sacred Black Hills of Dakota and in other Indian lands, and adventurers could still make a profit from buffalo hides. Over

500,000 Indians died before the century was over. The 300,000 who survived war, disease, hunger and bounties ($ 25 to $100 per scalp in many places) were forced onto inhospitable reservations that were administered by the notoriously corrupt Bureau of Indian Affairs (BIA).

Today, about two-thirds of the 790,000 American Indians live on reservations, under the trusteeship of the BIA. Many of the reservations are more like Third World countries than like part of the richest nation in the world. Only one out of five adults on the 25,000-square-mile Navajo reservation, for example, has a high-school diploma; the median educational level is 5.3 years (compared to 12.1 years nationally). The Navajo nation today numbers 137,000 and over half the adults are either unemployed or work only part time. The per capita income is $1,000 (compared to $ 4,000 nationally). Outsiders own 80 per cent of the general stores on the reservation. Housing, built by outsiders, is substandard. Many Navajo rent one- or two-room houses, 80 per cent of which have no running water or plumbing and 60 per cent of which have no electricity.

Although the government no longer pursues a policy of termination (breaking tribal properties into individual holdings and thereby "terminating" the tribe), it maintains a patronising attitude toward tribal organisation. Indian leaders are advisers at best; the BIA still holds a veto power over all plans. (In the words of anthropologist David Aberle, "The Navajo Government is treated in a style I recognise from having served on the student council of my high school.") Nor does the government recognise the Navajo language and culture. Classes at BIA schools are taught in English only, and Navajo history is an elective or extracurricular activity - if it is taught at all. Forty-nine of sixty schools are boarding schools, designed earlier in this century to forcibly separate Indian children from their family and customs - "for their own good". Alcoholism is a serious problem on reservations, even in grade school, and the suicide rate among Indians is ten times the national average (*The New York Times,* October 29,1973, p. 69C).

In the early 1970s the rise of ethnic consciousness among other minorities, such as blacks and Chicanos, was beginning to affect Indians as well. In 1973, the newly organised American Indian Movement (AIM) returned to the scene of the 1890 massacre at Wounded Knee and occupied reservation headquarters. This was not simply theater. Once again the government had reneged on extravagant promises; once again it had subverted Indian efforts to achieve self-determination and reform the BIA (Collier, 1973).

Chinese- and Japanese-Americans

The Chinese began immigrating to the West Coast in the middle of the eighteenth century. Labouring on the railroad, washing and cooking (women were scarce in the Old West), they earned a reputation as hard workers. However, when the railroad was finished and unemployment began to rise, Occidental settlers turned on the Chinese. The Chinese Exclusion Act of 1882 halted further immigration, and in most places the Chinese were denied schooling, jobs and horsing. They withdrew to ethnic enclaves in coastal cities, keeping largely to themselves until anti-Chinese feelings subsided. The border was reopened to the Chinese in the early fifties, and today there are about 435,000 people of Chinese ancestry in the country.

The Japanese came somewhat later, spreading out on farms all along the West Coast. But anti-Oriental sentiments ran high, and in 1924 Japanese immigration was halted. Then, in 1942 110,000 Japanese, including 70,000 who were American citizens, were rounded up and placed in "relocation centers" even though most had become American citizens and supported the Allies. During their internment, Japanese families lost an average of $10,000 each (Simpson and Yinger, 1972, p. 121). Despite this, the Japanese have prospered in America. Like the Jews, they emphasised the value of education and specialised in middle-level professions such as engineering, accounting and management. They also practiced the middle-class values of hard work, thrift and self-control. Although the Japanese have kept their language and cuisine alive, the traditional Japanese family has largely disappeared (arranged marriages are a thing of the past, for example), and the 591,000 people of Japanese ancestry in this country today are thoroughly Americanised.

White Ethnics

White ethnics have been called by many names - "the silent majority" (by Richard Nixon), "The little man" (by George Wallace), "the man in the middle" (by sociologist David Riesrnan). These are the policemen, truck drivers, lathe operators, and office workers who earn between $ 5,000 and $10,000 a year and own their own homes in areas such as Boston's Charlestown or Cleveland's West Side (Binzen, 1970, p. 5). They are the children and grandchildren of eastern and southern Europeans, who themselves had been free of serfdom for barely a hundred years.

Although they are very fiercely loyal to America, white ethnics have never quite felt at home in this Protestant, Anglo-Saxon dominated country. They do not take to the culture of "quantity, homogeneity, replaceability and mobility" that characterises America today (Novak, 1971). "This alienation is reflected in distrust of most politicians, in contempt for white rich and black poor, in a bristling defensiveness and a yearning for the recent past when life was simpler and loyalties less complex, when children were reared by the Bible and the beltstrap, when the schools stuck to the three R's, and when patriotism meant 'My country, right or wrong'" (Binzen, 1970, p. 11). They believe in paying their own way, in respect for authority, in taking care of their own, and in living with their own. They resent the "breaks" they believe blacks and other nonwhite minorities are getting. It isn't so much that they are racists as that they are loyalists, from cultures where anyone not from your village was a foreigner (Binzen, 1970, p. 9).

RACE, PREJUDICE AND DISCRIMINATION

The presence of varied ethnic and racial groups in the same society creates problems as well as opportunities. Diverse styles, languages and traditions do enrich a culture, but they may also accentuate in-group/out-group tensions. In America race has always served as a dividing line between "us" and "them".

Table 9.1
The Five Largest Ethnic Groups in the United States

Origin	*Population (in Millions)*	*Per cent of Total Population*
English, Welch	29.5	14.4
German	25.5	12.5
Irish	16.4	8.0
Spanish	9.2	4.5
Italian	8.8	4.3

Source: Current Population Reports, series p-20. no. 249,1973, pp. 1 and 19.

What is Race?

Biologically a *race* is a population that through generations of inbreeding has developed several distinctive physical characteristics that are transmitted genetically. In principle it should be relatively simple to divide the human species into distinct categories and assign each individual a racial identity. In reality it is not.

Suppose we begin with the three groups most people identify as races - the white or Caucasian race, the yellow or Mongoloid race, and the black or Negroid race. Few of us have any difficulty telling Africans from Orientals or Europeans. But where do we put the peoples of southern India who have black skin but straight hair and "Caucasian" features? Do we classify the Bushmen of southern Africa, who have yellowish skin and epicanthic folds (which make the eyes appear slanted), Mongoloid?

In an effort to define racial categories, physical anthropologists have long studied physical differences among groups of people, including skin colour, hair texture, facial features, head size and shape, body build and blood types.

They have found that some characteristics are adaptive. Dark skin, for example, with its high concentration of the pigment melanin, protects Africans and other equatorial peoples from harmful ultraviolet sun rays. The light skin of people in northern regions is also adaptive. Ultraviolet rays facilitate the body's production of Vitamin D, necessary for bone growth. Too much Vitamin D, however, may be harmful. It seems, then, that dark skin protects people in southern latitudes from producing too much Vitamin D, while light skin maximises its synthesis (Loomis, in Ember and Ember, 1973, pp. 179-80).

But studies of physical differences have not led to clear and distinct definitions of racial categories. William Boyd, for example, attempted to classify people according to blood types. He found, among other things, that the cDe gene is very common among people who live in sub-Saharan Africa. However, the gene is also found in Europeans, Asians, even Navajo Indians. Moreover, blood types do not correlate with outward appearance. The Papuans of New Guinea look very much, like Africans; they could easily disappear into the streets of Nairobi or New York's Harlem. But the "negroid gene," cDe, is exceedingly rare in New Guinea. In short, it is impossible to say where one race stops and another begins. As Theodosius Dobzhansky suggests, the number of races you find depends on the criteria you use:

> Boyd has recognised five, and Coon, Garn, and Birdsell nine of thirty or thirty-two races. Does it follow that some of these classifications are wrong? No, all may be right; it should always be kept in mind that while race differences are objectively ascertainable facts, the number of races we choose to recognise is a matter of convenience. (1962, p. 266)

Dobzhansky himself identifies thirty-four races, including such "emerging races" as North American blacks and Neo-Hawaiians, but he cautions that races are not clear and distinct like breeds of dogs (1973, chapter 2). The human species is the product of over 2 million years and 100,000 generations of adaptation, migration, sexual selection and cultural conditioning. There is as much variation *within* races as there is among them.

Nevertheless, people perceive and react to racial differences, and this is why sociologists study them - not because skin colour, hair texture, or other physical characteristics are intrinsically significant. A sociological definition of race is a group of people whom others believe to be genetically distinct and treat accordingly.

Racial Myths

Numerous myths about racial and ethnic differences circulate in American society - for example, the notion that blacks have natural mythm, the belief that Jews have a talent for finance. And while there is no biological basis for these stereotypes, there are social explanations. As slaves, blacks were forced to perform the most menial jobs; they were not allowed to form organisations of any kind. But slaves *were* allowed to make music. When slavery ended blacks were still in demand as entertainers. After all, no respectable white family would allow their children to enter the theater. The field was relatively open. Blacks cultivated the talents they had opportunities to use. Similarly, Jews became traders and moneylenders because for centuries they were not allowed to own land anywhere in the world. Like black Americans, they took advantage of the one field open to them, a field respectable Christians shunned.

Still, many people, noting certain differences in achievement by race, conclude that the biology of race is responsible. As a result, there is a long list of writing affirming or denying racial predisposition to cultural achievements, athletic ability and intelligence. What is the truth about such claims?

Race and I.Q. — In 1969 Arthur Jensen, a respected educational psychologist at the University of California at Berkeley, published an article on race, heredity, and intelligence in the *Harvard Educational Review.* The average score for black Americans on I.Q. tests, he reported, is ten to fifteen points lower than the average of whites. Reviewing the literature on this subject, Jensen concluded, "It [is] a not unreasonable hypothesis that genetic factors are strongly implicated in the average Negro-white intelligence difference" (1969).

Not surprisingly, Jensen was immediately labelled a white supremacist. Students at Berkeley invaded his classes and prevented him from teaching; spokesmen for the American Psychological Association issued a press release that characterised his findings as "unwarranted"; the *Harvard Educational Review* hastily collected a series of rebuttals, which were attached to reprints of the article. In Jensen's own words, "Almost overnight I became a *cause celebre,* at least on college campuses. I had spoken what [columnist] Joseph Alsop called the 'unspeakable'. To many Americans, I had thought the unthinkable" (1973, p. 80). For some years now, any implication that one race is innately superior to another has been socially and academically taboo. Yet the suspicion that this is true lingers on. What are the facts?

Few researchers dispute the fact that there is a ten- to fifteen-point difference in average I.Q. for whites and blacks. The controversey centers rather on the *interpretation* of this finding, and few scientists agree with Jensen. If blacks are innately "slow," how do we account for the fact that about 25 per cent have higher than average I.Q.'s (Simpson and Yinger, 1972, p. 56); that blacks living in the North score higher on I.Q. tests than either blacks *or whites* living in the South (Klineberg, 1944)? Numerous studies indicate that schooling, teacher expectations, and the test situation itself influence I.Q. scores. For example, black youngsters do better on intelligence tests when the examiner is black (which is not usually the case) and when they are told that they are being tested for coordination rather than intelligence, coordination being something that blacks feel more confident about (Katz, 1964).

Melvin Tumin (1973, pp. 164 - 67) attacks Jensen's conclusions on four grounds. First, he argues that racial comparisons would be meaningful only if we were able to assign every individual a clear racial identity, but we can't do this. Approximately 70 per cent of black Americans have some white ancestry (and 20 per cent of whites have some black ancestry; Hunt and Walker, 1974, p. 12). How can we assume that "black genes" are creating an I.Q. difference? Second, the idea that I.Q. differences reflect *biological* differences is based on the assumption that I.Q. tests measure innate intelligence. This is not the case. The I.Q. test measures performance of certain cultural skills, and while it has proven to be a relatively accurate predictor of school achievement, there is no conclusive evidence that it measures a person's inborn abilities. Third, research indicates that environment has a substantial effect on

Box 9.1

The Politics of Intelligence Testing

Eugenics - the "science" of improving the quality of the human race through selective breeding - first became popular in this country at the turn of the century. Interestingly, the three men who were responsible for translating and importing the first intelligence tests - Lewis Terman, Robert Yerkes and Henry Goddard - were all active in the eugenics movement. Terman was gravely concerned about the genetic consequences of charity. He wrote, "[O]nly recently have we begun to recognise what a menace [feeble-mindedness] is to the social, economic and moral welfare of the state. . . . [O]rganised charities. . . often contribute to the survival of individuals who would not otherwise be able to live and reproduce.... If we would preserve our state for a class of people worthy to possess it, we must prevent, as far as possible, the propagation of mental degenerates. . . . the increasing spawn of degeneracy." As chairman of the Committee on inheritance of Mental Traits of the Eugsaics Research Association, Yerkes was responsible for "discovering" that Poles were only slightly more intelligent than blacks. Goddard, who set up a testing center for the United States Public Health Service on Ellis Island, labelled 83 per cent of Jewish immigrants, 80 per cent of Hungarians, 79 per cent of Italians and 87 per cent of Russians as feeble-minded. The overtly racist Immigration Act of 1924, which established national quotas, was based on these findings. Thus, from the very beginning, intelligence tests have been used to rationalise discrimination.

Source: Leon J. Kamin, "Heredity, Intelligence Politics and Psychology," Princeton University, Unpublished paper, 1973.

intelligence, perhaps more than heredity. Jensen downplays the differences between black and white schools, neighbourhoods, jobs and experiences. He assumes that blacks and whites from similar socioeconomic backgrounds are alike in all respects but heredity.

Tumin argues that the level of prejudice and discrimination in this country makes it impossible to equate blacks and whites, even if their incomes and educations were alike. If we were able to find people whose experiences were identical, only then could we make valid racial comparisons, concluding that whatever differences we found were innate. But we cannot. Tumin concludes that there is no substantial evidence that the difference in I.Q. averages has anything whatever to do with genetic endowment.

Race and Culture **-** Another racial myth, that whites are culturally superior to other peoples, is based on an ignorance of history. The great civilisations of China, Africa and South America - the Shang dynasty, the Sonniki Kingdom of Ghana, the Mayan civilisation - predate the birth of Western civilisation by centuries. Nor is there any evidence that one race is more or less temperamental, healthy, or moral than any other (see Simpson and Yinger, 1972, pp. 56 - 59).

For example, the relatively high rate of broken homes among black Americans can, in part, be traced to welfare laws. Until the late 1960s, a family could receive assistance for children only if the father were absent. In short, if there are differences between blacks and whites, Jews and Gentiles, they exist largely because these groups have not enjoyed and **do** not enjoy the same opportunities. The significant differences are social, not biological.

Prejudice and Discrimination

The word *prejudice* comes from the Latin *prejudicum,* a pretrial that determined a defendent's social status in ancient Rome. The results decided how the court would treat the accused. In contemporary usage, prejudice still means a prejudgment. It is an irrational and categorical like or dislike of a group of people because of characteristics associated with their race, religion, ethnic group, sexual orientation, or perhaps occupation. When a person is so convinced that all members of a group are immoral, violent, and backward (or moral brilliant and creative), that he or she cannot see them as individuals and ignores evidence that refutes his or her other convictions, he or she is prejudiced. Prejudice justifies the fear and hostility people feel toward out-groups and provides a rationale for maintaining intergroup boundaries. Often, it becomes a self-fulfilling prophecy. If you start by saying that women are not qualified to be anything but secretaries, and then use this as an excuse to exclude them from executive training programmes, you prove the original assumption correct by creating and enforcing unpreparedness among women (Simpson and Yinger, 1972, p. 156).

Prejudice is an attitude; *discrimination,* an act. Ordinarily we use this word to describe the act of disqualifying or mistreating people on grounds rationally irrelevant to the situation (Antonovsky, 1960). But granting people privileges on the basis of imagined characteristics that attach to race, religion, or sex is also discrimination. Discrimination is not necessarily an expression of prejudice. For example, a black store owner may decide not to hire Jews, not because he himself is prejudiced against Jews, but because he believes his customers are. A white woman who has many black friends may refrain from dating blacks because she thinks, rightly or wrongly, that this would alienate all of her friends, black and white. However, discrimination tends to create and support prejudice by keeping people apart and limiting opportunities to disprove rumours and stereotypes.

Why are people prejudiced, and why are some people more prejudiced than others? Prejudice exists on three levels. It is a *psychological* phenomenon that seems to fulfil certain needs in people. It is also a *cultural* phenomenon, reflecting the traditions and history of a people. And it is part of the system of *stratification,* reinforcing the way power is distributed in a society.

The Psychology of Prejudice - Suppose a man works six or seven days a week in a factory, trying to support his family in the way he thinks they expect, but never seems able to make ends meet and is perennially in debt. If he analyses his situation rationally, he would probably blame the upper classes generally and his employers specifically for failing to pay him an adequate wage. But these people have the power to cut off his income; to oppose them openly would be selfdestructive. He might also blame himself for his financial problems, but this too makes him uncomfortable. Instead, he looks to the Mexican immigrants who have begun working in his factory. He doesn't really know them, but he suspects they are willing to work for low wages and that many other Mexicans are eager to take his job. By a process of twisted logic, he blames the Mexicans for his poverty. Soon he is exchanging rumours about "them" with his cronies and supporting efforts to close the border. Hating Mexicans makes the man and his friends feel a little better. When they forcibly eject a group of Mexicans from the local tavern, they feel at last they've accomplished something. "That'll show 'em".

This psychological portrait of prejudice is based on frustration-aggression theory. According to this view, people are goal-directed creatures who become angry and hostile when their desires are frustrated. If they do not know who or what is blocking their ambitions or believe the obstacle is too threatening and powerful to attack, they displace their hostility to a substitute target or scapegoat who is more accessible and, conveniently, too weak to retaliate.

Once a scapegoat is found people justify their irrational feelings and behaviour by "discovering" evidence that the out-group is indeed wicked and inferior. In this way people can maintain some feeling that they are reasonable and kind. The catch is that in verbally or physically attacking Mexicans Jews, or any other group; prejudiced people avoid confronting the true enemy. Their situation does not change, and frustration and hostility grow.

The stereotypes that develop about minority groups serve a similar psychological function. In the old South, for example, many whites believed blacks were violent by nature, and that black men were "over-sexed" and hence a chronic threat to the purity of white women. In reality, it was the whites who were most violent, and white men who were sexually exploiting black women. But it is easier, psychologically, to condemn unacceptable feelings and behaviour in others than to admit to them oneself. That is called *projection:* seeing qualities in others that you do not like in yourself, and condemning them for it. Projection explains the curious combination of guilt and license, aversion and fascination that often characterises minority majority relations.

In the aftermath of World War II, T.W. Adorno and co-workers (1950) undertook a study of prejudice in an effort to understand why the German people had condoned burtal atrocities against Jews. They also hoped to establish some way of identifying "potentially fascistic" individuals. Adorno concluded that racism is an expression of a particular psychological make-up that he called the *authoritarian personality.* This is a second theory of the psychology of prejudice. The authoritarian personality is motivated by deep feelings of insecurity. According to Adorno prejudiced people are also rigidly conventional, moralistic (with a tendency to see people as good *or* bad), enamoured of pseudoscientific theories (for example, about racial superiority), unrealistic in their goals and expectations (and therefore continually frustrated), and preoccupied with power and status (they are prejudiced *toward* the upper classes). They cannot tolerate ambiguity or weakness. Although Adorno's study has been criticised methodologically, it has proved to be a rich source of new ideas for research into the psychology of prejudice. Is prejudice related to age? education? intelligence? (And if so, why?) Do people who score high in ethnocentrism on psychological tests act in a prejudiced way? These areas are being researched today (Simpson and Yinger, 1972, pp. 77 - 93).

Prejudice and Culture **-** In many societies prejudice is part of the culture, a social habit handed down from generation to generation. Children, learn to value their whiteness or blackness and to avoid or defer to members of different races and ethnic groups, much as they learn their gender identity and sex role. Learning prejudice (including sex prejudice) is part of socialisation in some societies; it is not an isolated phenomenon.

Allport found many youngsters were confused about whom they were supposed to hate and shun. But despite this initial confusion, children do learn what groups of people to like or dislike and why. They learn from parents, siblings, friends, and of course television, which until recently "taught" young Americans that black people are like Amos and Andy, and Indians are hostile, ignorant savages. Eugene Horowitz (1947) found that children develop antiblack feelings as early as kindergarten: white four- and five-year-olds showed a distinct preference for white playmates. A Southerner describes his socialisation for racial and religious prejudice as follows:

> I grew up just 19 miles from Appomattox. The teaching I received both in school and from my parents was hard core South, with no chance of insight into the thinking and ways of other peoples. I was taught to look down upon Negroes, tolerate Jews (because we had to do business with them) and ignore Catholics.
>
> We celebrated Jefferson Davis's birthday, but ignored Lincoln's; the name Robert E. Lee was spoken with reverence and Appomattox was a shrine. The Golden Rule only applied to others who were either Methodist or Baptist, white and without a foreign-sounding name. (Letter to the Editor, *The New York Times,* May 16,1963).

Cultural stereotypes can and do change. Forty years ago a survey of Princeton students found that most thought blacks were lazy, superstitious and ignorant - the classic Steppin' Fetchit. Table 9.2 shows that attitudes have changed at Princeton (although, interestingly, the percentage who think blacks are musical has increased). Tragically, studies conducted in the 1940s and 1950s suggested that black children had the same derogatory image of blacks as white children had (Clark and Clark, 1947). But this has changed. A poll conducted in 1969 revealed that 74 per cent of blacks believe "brack is beautiful" *(Newsweek,* June 30,1969).

Table 9.2
Characteristics Princeton Students Assigned to Blacks: Stereotypes are Fading

	1933 *(Per cent)*	*1951* *(Per cent)*	1967 *(Per cent)*
Superstitious	84	41	13
Lazy	75	31	26
Happy-go-lucky	38	17	27
Ignorant	38	24	11
Musical	26	33	47

Source: Marvin Karlins, Thomas Coffman and Gary Walters, "On the Fading of Social Stereotypes: Studies in Three Generations of College Students," *Journal of Personality and Social Psychology* (September 1969): 4-5.

Still, Americans are highly conscious of racial and ethnic identities, and stereotypes persist, even if they are couched in humour. One wonders whether the television show *All in the Family* is popular because members of minority groups nearly always come out on top in the show, or because Archie Bunker has made bigotry respectable (Rose, 1974, p. 139). In fact, two researchers who studied viewers of *All in the Family* concluded that "nonprejudiced viewers and minority group viewers may perceive and enjoy [the programme] as satire, whereas prejudiced viewers may perceive and enjoy the show as 'telling it like it is.' . . . By making Archie a 'lovable bigot' the programme encourages bigots to excuse and rationalise their own prejudices" (Vidmar and Rokeach, 1974).

Prejudice and Stratification - Flare-ups of bigotry often can be traced to economic conditions that make it profitable for one group to exclude and stigmatise another. Oliver Cox may have exaggerated when he wrote, "Race prejudice in the United States is ... a calculated and determined effort of a white ruling class to keep some people or peoples of colour and their resources exploitable" (1948, p. 475). But there is some truth in what he says. In the words of one unusually candid nineteenth-century Southerner, "[H]aving learned to make cotton and sugar (we) find slavery useful and profitable, and think it a most excellent institution. We of the South advocate slavery, no doubt, from just as selfish motives as induce the Yankees and English to oppose it" (in Simpson and Yinger, 1972, p. 114). Antiblack feelings climbed with the price of cotton.

Similarly, in the early 1870s, when the Gold Boom faded and the Central Pacific Railroad began to bring thousands of settlers to California to compete for a declining number of jobs, the once-welcome Chinese (who had helped build the railroad) became villains almost overnight. By 1880 it was nearly as safe politically to oppose Orientals is it was to oppose sin (Simpson and Yinger, 1972, p. 118). Thus, economic competition transformed a trickle of Oriental immigrants into "the yellow hordes" by igniting prejudices that laid dormant in the culture.

Prejudice justifies social rank - both low and high, as, for example, when some people argue that members of minorities are poor because they don't want to work or because they aren't capable of learning skilled trades. In conclusion, prejudice stems from a combination of psychological and social predispositions. It is most likely to occur in a culture that supports this kind of thinking and among people who have to defend or justify their social status.

PATTERNS OF ETHNIC RELATIONS

Relationships between racial and ethnic groups in a heterogeneous society range from full integration to the absolute intolerance that motivates extermination. Both of these extremes are rare, however, and intergroup relations are usually more complex than the everyday definitions of such words as *integration* and *segregation* imply. Nevertheless, it is possible to identify certain basic patterns.

Patterns of Acceptance

In a fully integrated society, race, religion and national origins would not influence a person's access to society's rewards. Being born a Lopez or an O'Reilly or a Goldberg would be neither an asset nor a liability; it simply wouldn't matter. The society would be structured to protect individual rights and to ignore ethnic identity. Perhaps the best way to illustrate this is to call attention to the "armed truce" between people of British and French descent in Canada. In the United States this distinction is insignificant: people of British and French descent are fully integrated.

There are essentially two routes to integration: amalgamation and assimilation. *Amalgamation* occurs when members of different ethnic and racial groups mix indiscriminately: a new hybrid culture emerges (cultural amalgamation), and perhaps a new "race" as well? Ethnic differences disappear. This is what Israel Zangwill had in mind when he described America as a melting pot: "There she lies, the great melting pot - listen! Can't you hear the roaring and bubbling? Ah, what a stirring and seething - Celt and Latin, Slav and Teuton, Greek and Syrian, Black and Yellow -Jew and Gentile" (1909, pp. 198-99).

Assimilation means that immigrants give up their old ways and adopt the language, customs, religion and dress of the country to which they've moved. For example, the American public school system was specifically designed to teach the waves of immigrants that began coming here in the nineteenth century the English language and English customs, to enforce what Stewart and Mildred Cole (1954, pp. 135 - 40) call "Anglo-conformity." (Later, public education was extended to blacks, Indians and Chicanos - for the same purpose.)

Amalgamation and assimilation are most likely to occur if (1) the immigrants' appearance and customs resemble those of the dominant group, (2) they arrive in small numbers, (3) they are, too far from their homeland to return for visits, and (4) they possess skills that the dominant group admire and need (Warner and Srole 1945; Silvers, 1965). Yet the fact that an immigrant group is able to fill some economic need (as the Jews did in Europe and the overseas Indians did in East Africa) does not guarantee their acceptance (Hunt and Walker, 1974, p. 20). To the contrary. If members of a group fill the need for menial and domestic workers, they may be stigmatised; if they are conspicuously successful, they may inspire envy.

In America the melting pot of Zangwill's dream? No, according to Milton Gordon (1964). Gordon makes the important distinction between behavioural assimilation (immigrants adopting the language and behavioural patterns of the host culture) and structural assimilation (immigrants gaining admission to the host's government, businesses, schools, churches, clubs and ultimately its families). While most ethnic groups have undergone behavioural assimilation and structural integration into secondary relationships in America, relatively little integration has taken place on the levejr of primary relationships. In part this is because Americans of northern European descent integrated only with themselves, in part because later immigrants resisted complete assimilation to Anglo-Saxon, Protestant culture?

When people migrate to a strange country, they usually huddle together for comfort and support, recreating as many of their old-country institutions as they can. Their children may succumb to the lure of democracy and equality, assuming that if they act American they will be fully accepted as Americans. However, when they see that the doors to private clubs are not open to them and the sons and daughters of established Americans not available to them, they return "to the homelier but dependable comfort" of their ethnic communities. Gordon notes that integration has taken place within religions (German, Russian and Sephardic Jews have intermarried, for example), but for the most part not between religions. Of course, the invitation to participate in the American mainstream has never been extended to blacks, Indians, Chicanos, and other racial and quasi-racial groups.

An alternative to integration is *cultural pluralism,* wherein different ethnic groups maintain their cultural identities and distinct ways, but no one group enjoys special privileges or suffers discrimination. Cultural pluralism is based on the belief that ethnic diversity strengthens a society. Horace Kallen (1965, p. 220) compared a pluralistic society to a symphony: each instrument (each ethnic group) contributes distinct themes and melodies, harmonies and dissonances. In Switzerland, for example, Protestants and Catholics of German, French and Italian descent coexist peacefully and equally. Each group has its own language and customs. This diversity is viable because all consider themselves Swiss as well as German or French, because the religious differences cross-cut national differences (preventing the formation of solid political blocks), and because members of all groups can easily visit their ancestral country.

An analogy might be drawn between the ethnic mix in Switzerland and the sometimes uneasy pluralism of America's large cities, with their Little Italies, Chinatowns, Germantowns, and other ethnic enclaves. Nowhere is this better illustrated than in New York City. But Americans as a whole have never found the heterogeneity of New York very attractive. "The only New York image that has permanently impressed itself on the national mind is that of Wall Street - a street on which nobody lives. Paris may be France, London may be England, but New York, we continue to reassure ourselves, is *not* America" (Glazer and Moynihan, 1970, p. 2). The only area in which we do tolerate and indeed protect pluralism in this country is religion.

Patterns of Rejection

In a *segregated* society, contacts between different groups are restricted by law and/or custom. Segregation is based on the premise that ethnic and racial groups are inherently unequal, and that the differences between them are permanent (hence the myths of racial inferiority). An individual's ethnic identity determines his or her social status; members of minorities are denied full participation in social institutions and relegated to activities that benefit the majority (Hunt and Walker, 1974, pp

6-7). Clearly, segregation is an imposed arrangement, designed and enforced by the majority.

Segregation is a matter of law in South Africa, where blacks (the native Bantu) and to a lesser extent coloureds (people of mixed ancestry and overseas Asians) are not allowed to live in white neighbourhoods, use white facilities, or participate in white government. Blacks are required to carry passbooks at all times, and may be arrested and jailed merely for being in a white district without authorisation. In many ways, South Africa is unique. Unlike British, French and Portuguese colonials, 3 million *Afrikaners* have no home to return to should the 15 million blacks demand independence.

The history of racial segregation in the United States goes back hundreds of years. It began when the new Americans started to distinguish between white indentured servants, who were released at the end of their contracts, and black servants, who were not. Gradually slavery was written into law, and black people were reduced to the legal status of two-thirds of a person. The Emancipation Proclamation abolished slavery, but not servitude. Except for the small number who prospered during Reconstruction blacks became sharecroppers, working white-owned land for very low wages. When Union troops withdrew from the South, states, counties, and towns began to pass the legislative programmes that came to be known as Jim Crow. Lacks were disenfranchised (through property qualifications, literacy tests, and "grandfather clauses"); public facilities such as restaurants and trains were segregated; interracial marriages outlawed; lynchings ignored.

By World War I, large numbers of blacks were moving north, urged on by industrialists who desperately needed workers. Riots broke out in New York, Chicago and elsewhere, as blacks competed with European immigrants for space. But racism was still considered a southern problem. Congressional attempts to knock down Jim Crow failed. Then, in 1954, the Supreme Court overturned the separate-but-equal doctrine in its decision on *Brown vs. the Board of Education of Topeka,* citing evidence gathered by social scientists that segregated schools affected the "hearts and minds [of black children] in a way unlikely ever to be undone." Soon after, the young Reverend Martin Luther King, Jr., was organising a boycott in Montgomery, Alabama.

The Civil Rights Movement succeeded dramatically in some respects. Today, the United States is desegregated, in the sense that *legal* barriers to interracial contacts have been removed. As Martin Luther King, Jr., once remarked, "The law may not make a man love me, but it can restrain him from lynching me, and I think that's pretty important" (in Rose, 1974, p. 103). But this is not yet a racially integrated society; there is no "easy and fluid mixture of peoples of diverse racial, religious and nationality backgrounds in social cliques, families (*i.e.*, intermarriage), private organisations and intimate friendships" (Gordon, 1964, p. 246). Moreover, the white exodus to the suburbs has made most of America's big cities minority enclaves, indeed *de facto* segregation may be increasing.

Expulsion is another form of minority rejection. In 1972, for example, Uganda's General Amin deported 27,000 Indians, many of whom were second- and third-generation Ugandans, with only a few months' warning, appropriating their homes, businesses and savings (see Kramer, 1974). This country, too, has expelled minorities. In the 1830s the Cherokee Indians were forced to march from their homelanos in Georgia to an arid reservation in Oklahoma. As many as 4,000 died on what came to be known as the Trail of Tears. As we mentioned earlier, during World War II the American government forcibly sent over 100,000 Japanese to "relocation centers" for the duration of the war. Both the Soviet Union and Germany deported millions of minority citizens during that war.

The severest response to minority groups is *extermination*. The Nazis murdered 6 million Jews between 1933 and 1945 - as well as countless gypsies, communists, and other ethnic and political minorities. A century before, Americans slaughtered the Indians (a story that has been "whitewashed" for years). American Indians fought the European invaders, but to little avail. About two-third of the Indian population was wiped out. Some died in battle, but just as many died from the white man's diseases, from which they had no immunity, and from starvation, after white hunters killed off the buffalo.

Minority Responses

How do minorities respond to discrimination and abuse? How do people cope with a society that defines them as undesirable? *Acceptance* of the majority culture is one response. Some members of a minority will try to "pass"-change their name, their appearance (with hair straighteners or skin bleaches), and their way of life, thus shedding their minority identity. Passing means rejecting one's family and origins, and may leave a person stranded between two worlds, neither of which accepts him or her entirely. And there is always the possibility of "discovery".

For sheer survival, psychological as well as physical, others play the role the majority assigns to them, obeying the etiquette of racism, deferring in most interracial contexts. The classic example of this response to segregation is Uncle Tom, who smiled and shuffled and "Yes Mam'd" his way through Harriet Beecher Stowe's novel. Simpson and Yinger tell a revealing story about Uncle Toms:

> A Negro drives through a red light in a Mississippi town. The sheriff yells, "Where you think you going?" The Negro thinks fast and answers, "Weil, boss, when I see that green light come on an' all them white folks' cars goin' through, I says to myself, 'That's the white folks' light!' So I don' move. Then when that ol' red light comes on, I jus' steps on the gas. I says, 'That mus' be the niggers' light!" The sheriff replies, "You're a good boy, Sam, but the next time you kin go on the white foils' light." (1972, p. 224).

It's obvious who had the last laugh here. Flattery, deference and feigned stupidity can be effective forms of passive aggression - as when a slave pretended he was so simple-minded he couldn't understand a job he didn't want to do.

Psychological theory suggests, however, that if people are abused day after day, their anger will build until they find some way to vent it. Sociologists have speculated that the relatively high crime rate in black ghettos is evidence of displaced aggression (see Simpson and Yinger, 1972, pp. 224-25). Hitting back at whites is too dangerous, so blacks take out their hostility on one another - or so the argument goes. It is difficult to prove or disprove this theory, but we should point out that when racial tension runs high, the majority may interpret any effort by minorities to climb the economic and social ladder as aggression. For example, thirty or forty years ago a black person who obtained advanced education or bought fine clothes and cars was labelled "uppity," a troublemaker. More recently, Black Panthers organised patrols to follow police around black communities with the aim of preventing brutality. They were policing the police. But was this aggression or self-defense?

The alternative to acceptance (real or feigned) and aggression (direct or indirect) is *avoidance*. For example, when anti-Chinese sentiments began to increase in the American West, Chinese families withdrew to cities on the West and East coasts, shutting themselves off from the hostile society around them (Yuan, 1963). Self-segregation not only provides insulation from aggression and slurs; it also enables minorities to maintain close family ties, to assist one another, to practice their own way of life and keep their culture alive. Separatist movements such as the Black Muslim movement have always played an important role in the black community in this country. The Muslims have no plan to go to war with white society; rather, they want as little to do with white society as possible.

The Psychological Consequences of Racism - What does living in a society that preaches black inferiority do to a black person, inside? In *Dark Ghetto* (1965), psychologist Kenneth B. Clark argues that chronic social injustices "corrode and damage the human personality, thereby robbing it of its effectiveness, of its creativity, if not its actual humanity. . . . Human beings who are forced to live under ghetto conditions and whose daily experience tells them that almost nowhere in society are they respected and granted the ordinary dignity and courtesy accorded to others, will, as a matter of course, begin to doubt their self worth' (pp. 63-64). Clark notes that black children often describe black dolls as ugly, dirty, or bad. Similarly, the preoccupation with hair straighteners and skin bleaches among the black bourgeosie in the fifties and early sixties suggests that they accepted the white dislike of black physical traits.

Recent investigations, however, show that blacks have as much self-esteem as anyone else - perhaps more. For example, Morris Rosenberg and Roberta G. Simmons (1971) interviewed black and white children in predominantly black and racially mixed schools in Baltimore. Many of the children were not conscious of the low status assigned to blacks in society at large, living as they did in nearly all-black worlds. Others more or less accepted the white stereotype of blacks as

Box 9.2

Self-esteem and Social Ranking

Many sociologists have long taken for granted the idea that children internalise their society's values and standards in the process of growing up. From this it logically follows that black children who see a negative image of their group in the social looking glass must experience some ambivalence about themselves, perhaps even a degree of "ethnic self-hatred". (The Supreme Court school desegregation decision of 1954 was based on this premise.) Rosenberg and Simmons (1971) found, however, that most black children rank blacks *high* on the social ladder, just as white children, except for Jews, rank their own religion high (see Tables 9.3 and 9.4). The authors conclude that children do accept society's evaluations of most groups (their evaluations of other groops mirror those of adults), but pull their own group out of order to protect feelings of group pride and self-esteem. By the time they are fifteen or over, however, black youngsters have more social experience, and recognise that most Americans do not rank blacks very high (see Table 9.3).

Source: Morris Rosenberg and Roberta G, Simmons, *Black and White Self-esteem: The Urban School Child,* Washington, D.C.: American Sociological Association, 1971.

Table 9.3
Children's Opinions of "Most People's" Ranking of Blacks, By Race and Age

Of four racial-religious groups "Most people" Rank Blacks	*8-11 years* *Blacks*	*Whites*	*12 -14 Years* *Blacks*	*Whites*	*15 + Years* *Blacks*	*Whites*
	(Per cent)		*(Per cent)*		*(Per cent)*	
First	63	1	32	1	15	—
Second	17	6	26	4	14	1
Third	9	24	20	24	26	17
Last	11	69	23	71	44	81
Difference in per cent ranking blacks "Last"	58		48		37	

Source: Morris Rosenberg and Roberta G. Simmons, *Black and White Self-esteem: The Urban School Child,* Washington, D.C.: American Sociological Association, 1971, p. 34.

slow and lazy, but did not feel this image applied to them personally. And some attributed the negative evaluation of blacks to white irrationality. As for their feelings about themselves, Rosenberg and Simmons found black children were *less* likely to consider poor grades or test scores evidence of personal inadequacy than were white youngsters. Thus, prejudice may insulate a person from self-criticism. When a black child or adult fails, he or she can blame white society.

Most studies of the consequences of discrimination have focused on the victims rather than on the victimisers. We do not know how to calculate the psychological and social costs of treating a whole group of people as less than human. What research there is in this area suggests that members of the dominant group in a segregated society suffer from insecurity and fear, particularly if that society respects rationality and democratic values. In South Africa, whites fear the possibility of a black revolution. Whites in small towns in the American South often own more than one firearm, and New Yorkers avoid the streets at night, closing themselves in with three and four locks. "Thus, a pattern of discrimination is supported

Table 9.4
White Children's Opinions of "Most People's" Ranking of Religious Groups, by Religious Affiliation

Of four Religious Groups, "Most People" Rank Protestants	*Protestant Respondents (Per cent)*	*Non-Protestant Respondents (Per cent)*
First	55	32
Second	38	56
Third	6	10
Last	1	2

Of four Religious Groups, "Most People" Rank Protestants	*Catholic Respondents (Per cent)*	*Non-Catholic Respondents (Per cent)*
First	80	45
Second	19	43
Third	1	5
Last	—	2

Of four Religious Groups, "Most People" Rank Jews	*Jewish Respondents (Per cent)*	*Non-Jezvish Respondents (Per cent)*
First	5	2
Second	21	8
Third	72	65
Last	2	25

Source: Morris Rosenberg and Roberta Simmons, *Black and White Self-esteem: The Urban School Child,* Washington, D.C., American Sociological Association, 1971, p. 34.

only at the cost of much irrationality, moral confusion, arrogance and fear" (Simpson and Yinger, 1972, p. 242).

PROTEST AND PROGRESS

On August 28,1963, about 200,000 black and white Americans, gathered jubilantly at the steps of the Lincoln Memorial in Washington, listened raptly as Martin Luther King. Jr., told the nation, "I have a dream.........."

The euphoria of that sunny afternoon was short lived. Just a month later a bomb exploded in the basement of a black church in Birmingham, Alabama, killing four small girls. Congress began to move. The public Accommodations Act was passed in 1964, the Voting Rights Act a year later. The legal obstacles to integration had been destroyed, but relations between blacks and whites became increasingly abrasive over the years. The Student Nonviolent Coordinating Committee (SNCC) expelled its white members, and its leaders began talking of Black Power. Roy Innis, a charismatic nationalist, became the director of the Congress on Racial Equality (CORE). Confused by the new militancy in the black community, startled to find Dr. King marching in Chicago, white liberals began to pull back. It was one thing to fight segregation in the South; another to discover discrimination in your own back yard.

Meanwhile, the black exodus from the South continued: over a million blacks moved north between 1960 and 1970. But the Civil Rights Movement had barely touched the North. The church-born rhetoric of freedom, dignity and equality seemed strangely out of tune on the hot, crowded streets of the ghetto. The Watts riot of August 1965 set the pattern for the next three summers. Dr. King's assassination in April 1968 sparked a new round of destruction, a grim memorial to a man who had dedicated his life to nonviolence and brotherhood. The Kerner Commission, appointed to explain the riots to a bewildered and frightened white America, issued an unexpected indictment that same year:

> What white Americans have never fully understood - but what the Negro can never forget - is that white society is deeply implicated in the ghetto. White institutions created it, white institutions maintain it, and white society condones it.

The Commission went on to Prophesy

> Our nation is moving toward two societies, one black, one white -separate and unequal. ... To pursue our present course will involve the continuing polarisation of the American community and ultimately, the destruction of basic democratic values.

When the riots stopped, an uneasy quiet settled on the race issue. The leadership of the Civil Rights Movement dispersed to such issues as welfare and prison reform, and to local political and economic campaigns. The gap between those blacks who were able to take advantage of newly opened opportunities and those whose lives are encircled by poverty widened. But despite the erosion of black leadership and unity, despite setbacks and phantom hopes, much has changed since August 28, 1963.

One of the most significant achievements of the Civil Rights effort was the development of black pride. A number of studies have found that feelings of racial pride are "widespread throughout the Negro community. Ninety-six per cent of [one] sample agreed that 'Negroes should take more pride in Negro history'" (Campbell and Schuman, 1968). Also four out of ten of the respondents thought that "Negro school children should study an *African* language" (Caplan, 1970, pp. 66-67).

The awakening of black pride has touched all corners of American society. In a sense, blacks made ethnicity respectable. And they gave hope to other groups - to Chicanos. Indians, peace demonstrators, women, homosexuals, even the "white ethnics" who don't want their children bused to schools in black districts - all of whom adopted the tactics and slogans of the Civil Rights Movement. In short, the spirit of togetherness that motivated the March on Washington has given way to a new pattern of race and ethnic relations based on ethnic pride.

Where Do We Stand?

The picture of America that emerges in the seventies is uneven and contradictory. Blacks have gained in some areas and fallen behind in others. Ten years ago, half as many blacks as whites completed high school; today a black student is almost as likely to obtain a diploma as a white student. There are twice as many blacks in college today as there were in 1960, and twice as many blacks hold professional, technical and related white-coller jobs. However, the median income of black male *college* graduates is only $100 more a year than the median income of white male *high-school* graduates. A black person's chances of holding a white collar job are only half as good as a white person's, and the unemployment rate for blacks is twice that for whites. The median income for black families is still substantially lower than the white median income (see Table 9.5). Only 34 per cent of black families have intermediate or comfortable incomes, compared to 59.2 per cent of white families, and over a third of the nation's 25 million blacks live in poverty (25 per cent receive some kind of public assistance). The most concrete gains for black Americans over the last ten years have been in politics. In Mississippi, for example, black voter registration leaped from 5.2 per cent in 1960 to 59.4 per cent in 1970; in Alabama it soared from 13.7 per cent to 54.7 per cent. As of 1974 there were 16 black Congresspersons (15 Representatives and 1 Senator), 108 black mayors, and a total of 2,991 elected black

Table 9.5
A Measure of Change Since 1960

Per cent of Age Group who are High School Graduates 25 - 29 years	*White*	*Black*
1960	63.7	38.6
1972	81.5	64.0

Per cent of Age Group who are College Graduates 25 - 29 years	*White*	*Black*
1960	11.8	5.4
1972	19.9	8.3

Median Income of Families (in 1972 Constant Dollars)	*White*	*Black*
1964[1]	6,858	3,724
1972	11,549	6,864

[1]1060 data are not available.

Source: Bureau of the Census, *Current Population Reports,* series p. 23, no. 46.

officials. This is an increase of *152 per cent* over the number of blacks in elective offices during just a five-year period. In part the number of black mayors reflects the fact that whites have more or less abandoned inner cities to blacks, who are nearly a majority in most big cities.

Neighbourhood racial isolation has not declined since 1960. On the contrary, it may have increased, particularly in the North. Indeed, things have changed more in the South than in the North and West. Twenty years after the Supreme Court ruling on school desegregation, 9 per cent of black students in the South attend all-black schools (compared to 98 per cent ten years ago) and 54 per cent attend schools where blacks are a majority. Desegregation in the North seems to be a greater problem than it is in the South. (See Box 9.3)

The employment picture is mixed too. Whereas 50 per cent of whites hold white-collar jobs, only 29.8 per cent of blacks do. And although 10.6 per cent of whites are in managerial positions, only 3.7 per cent of nonwhites are (Department of Labour Statistics for 1972). Blacks are conspicuously underrepresented in securities, insurance, restaurants and bars, food processing, utilities and retail stores. And while some of the black middle class has benefited from newly opened opportunities in the last decade, those who do not have white-collar skills have been left behind.

Box 9.3

In the News

Twenty Years After the Brown* vs. *Topeka Decision

Once, liberals considered segregation a southern problem and scorned the South for its bigotry. Today, however, the South seems to be pulling ahead of the North, at least in school integration. As of 1972, 70 per cent of black students attended predominantly black schools outside the South; compared to 54 per cent of black students in the South. New York and Chicago schools are more racially segregated now than ever before. And unless the courts resolve the issue of busing students across city/suburban lines, this trend is likely to continue. Twenty years after the Supreme Court ordered public schools to integrate, a reporter surveys the situation.

Box 9.3 - *(Contd.)*

According to interviews with education specialists and a survey of a number of large cities, the meager - some say "disastrous" - record of the North in creating biracial classrooms results from antipathy to busing for purposes of integration, the complacency and timidity of school boards and other units of government, protracted litigation, the exodus of whites to the suburbs and segregated housing patterns.

None of these developments is new.... What is relatively new, however, is the widespread recognition by ordinary politicians, school officials and lower court judges that so-called *de facto* segregation - that is, school segregation caused by housing patterns rather than overt political decisions about the placement of pupils -presents what might well be the *most painful and ambiguous question facing the nation* (italics added).

On one side are millions of black children trapped in schools that remain, for the most part, separate but unequal. On the other are millions of white parents who do not regard themselves as racist but who look with evident dismay on the idea of returning their children to the cities and school systems they fled.

The complexity of the question is illustrated by random comments from those most affected:

A black mother in Philadelphia, Mrs. Shirley Waites: "I'm in favour of busing to achieve integration. Obviously, you can't achieve it any other way." A black mother in Detroit, Mrs. Doris McCrary: "1 don't'discuss busing. As far as I'm concerned I've always been against busing. I have built my kids where they have self-confidence in themselves. If you take them out to Grosse Pointe where they would be looked down on, that would do something to their self-image." A white mother in Pontiae, Mich.: "I'd go to jail first. We moved here to get good schools."

Dr. [Kenneth] Clark, whose psychological findings were cited in the 1954 Supreme Court decision outlawing school segregation said that "the major problem now in the desegregation of the schools is clearly the Northern urban problem. There is no question of this."

He asserted that the major stumbling block to effective integration of Northern schools "is the intransigence of the Northern school boards - their *refusal to obey law.*"... Spot checks of a number of large cities showed [growing resistance to school busing in June 1973].

Source: Excerpt from William E. Farrell, "School Integration Resisted in Cities of North," *The New York Times,* May 13, 1974, p. 24.

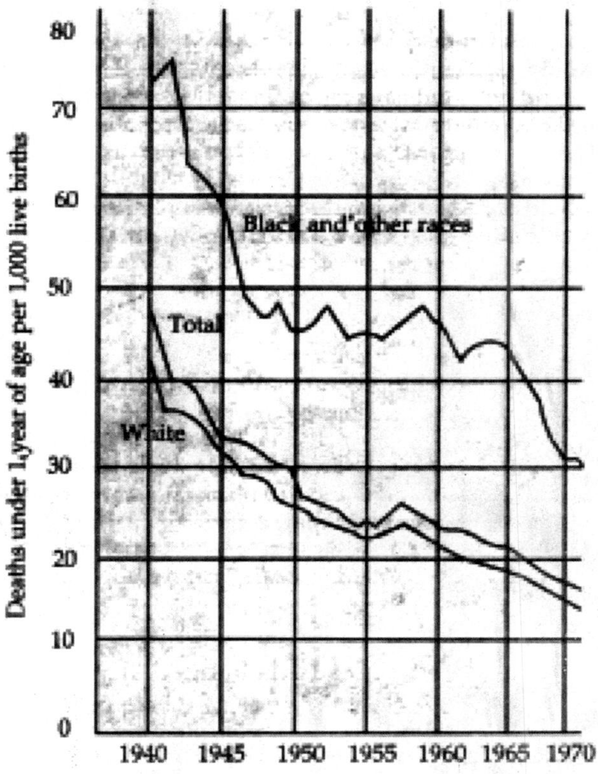

Figure 9.1 : Infant mortally rates : 1940-1971 (by race).

In 1940, the infant mortality rate for blacks and other nonwhites was about 75 per cent higher than it was for whites. By 1971, both rates had dropped dramatically yet the nonwhite rate was still about 75 per cent higher than the white rate.

Attitudes of Whites - In 1963, the year of the March on Washington, the majority of white people still believed blacks had fewer ambitions and looser morals than whites, and over one-third thought blacks were innately inferior to whites (Brink and Harris, 1963, p. 148).

Table 9.6
Attitudes of Whites Toward Blacks, 1968

86% - would not mind having a qualified black person as a supervisor.
89% - believe orderly protests against racial discrimination are justified.
68% - believe landlords and real estate agents discriminate against blacks.
67% - favour laws to prevent discrimination in hiring and promotions.
49% - would not mind at all if a black family with the same education and income moved in next door.

At the same time:

67% - believe blacks are pushing too fast.
56% - believe blacks are responsible for their disadvantages in education, jobs and housing.
51% - oppose laws to prevent discrimination in housing.
33% - would rather their children had only white friends.
24% - would not vote for a qualified black mayoral candidate, even if their party nominated him.

Source : Angus Campbell, *White Attitudes Toward Black People*. Ann Arbor, Mich.: Institute for Social Research, 1971, pp. 4-5.

By 1968 white attitudes had changed (Table 9.6). Angus Campbell who conducted a survey of white people in fifteen major cities suggests that the most significant changes are that whites attribute the problems of blacks to lack of motivation rather than to innate, biological differences; and that although most whites feel blacks are pushing too fast and that violent rhetoric and acts are not justified, only a few condone violent reprisals against blacks (Campbell, 1971, pp. 4-5).

Campbell also analyses data collected in 1964 (after the March on Washington but before the riots), 1968 (at the peak of civil disorders), and 1970 (after two years of relative quiet). Over these years more and more white people reported meeting blacks at work, in school, in their neighbourhoods, and in public places. Thirty-one per cent had black friends in 1970 (compared to 17 per cent in 1964). Campbell attributes these changes in large part to the upward mobility of blacks in the last decade, which reduces class differences and thereby weakens the basis for prejudice. He concludes:

> It cannot be doubted that since World War II there has been a massive shift in the racial attitudes of white Americans [But] despite the changes we have noted and the trends we foresee, the white population of this country is far from a general acceptance of this principle and practice of racial equality— We are at present at a point of uneasy confrontation. The black demands for change in th-e status of black people in this country are insistent and sometimes abusive. Most white people agree that change should occur but they want to move gradually and they are repelled by the violent aspects of black rhetoric and action. Change is taking place but black expectations rise as achievements rise. American society is developing a new pattern of relationships between white and black and the period of change is a time a tension for both faces (pp. 150 - 62),

Attitudes of Blacks - How do blacks assess their situation in America? A survey conducted for CBS by the Opinion Research Corporation of Princeton in the spring of 1968, just a month after Martin Luther King, Jr., was assassinated, found both satisfaction and restlessness in the black community (Chandler, 1972 pp. 17 - 35). The overwhelming majority (78 per cent) said black progress was too slow (68 per cent of whites in Campbell's survey said black progress was too fast), and most believed white America was indifferent to black problems (see Table 9.7).

Table 9.7
Attitudes of Black in 1968

78% -	blacks are not making enough progress
45% -	blacks have not made more progress because of discrimination
22% -	blacks have not made more progress because they haven't worked hard enough
59% -	whites in America are not sympathetic toward the problems of black people
67% -	whites do not want complete racial equality[1]
80% -	blacks have played an important part in American history
86% -	schools should teach subjects that will enhance black children's pride in their race
59% -	in general, police have been too brutal in their treatment of blacks

[1] '54% of whites surveyed ageed.

Source : Robert Chandler, *Public Opinion*, New York: Bowker, 1972, pp. 17 - 35; © 1968,1972 by Columbia Broadcasting System, Inc.

The subject on which blacks strongly disagreed with whites was tactics. Two-thirds of blacks thought peaceful demonstrations were a good way for people "to get what they want," but only one-third of whites favoured, this tactic. And while a strong majority of blacks favoured boycotts and pickets, less than one-third of whites approved of these measures. Less than 10 per cent of both races, however, favoured demonstrations that might lead to violence (Chandler, 1972, p. 27). In most areas, however, there was much agreement between blacks and whites, and both groups were quite moderate despite the turmoil of those months. For example, although 42 per cent of blacks blamed racial tension on whites (compared to 9 per cent of whites) and 31 per cent of whites blamed racial tension on blacks (compared to 1 per cent of blacks), 48 per cent of blacks and 54 per cent of whites thought *both* races were responsible for the problem.

A survey conducted by *Newsweek* in June 1969 suggested that more and more black Americans were becoming disillusioned. Only a small minority (25 per cent) thought the federal government was helping blacks in 1969 and most (69 per cent) believed white Americans were either hostile or indifferent toward blacks. [See Box 9.4 for a summary of the attitudes of nonwhite (mostly black) youth.] Kenneth Clark describes these changes as an "end of innocence" in the black community, which passionately believed the Civil Rights Movement would succeed in the early sixties. Initial bitterness over the fact that white liberals walked out before the struggle was over has, in Clark's view, given way to a new realism and self-reliance. Increasingly, blacks are shedding the illusions they had about white America helping them. More and more they are working to gain political and economic control of their neighbourhoods, their schools, their lives. In the words of Richard Hatcher, the first black mayor of Gary, Indiana, "That's not separatism - That's good old Americanism" (*Newsweek,* June 30,1969, p. 17).

Box 9.4

Minority Youth and the "New Values"

In his 1973 survey, Daniel Yankelovich found minority youth disheartened by blatant discrimination, cynical about American society, and doubtful about their futures. The overwhelming impression was one of frustration. Fifty-five per cent of minority youth described America as a "sick society" (compared to less than a third of white youth); 76 per cent did not consider this a democratic society (compared to 56 per cent of young whites); only 56 per cent expressed positive feelings about their futures (while 79 per cent of whites were optimistic).

More minority than white youth labelled themselves radical (one-third vs. one-fifth), and they were generally more liberal about such issues as amnesty for draft evaders and legalisation of marijuana. A majority of nonwhite young people endorsed the "new value". For example, two out of three non-whites believed in sexual freedom, but only two out of five whites did. At the same time, however, minority youth were more concerned about education, work and money than other young people, and in some ways more traditional. Fifty-five per cent thought a woman's place is in the home (45 per cent of whites agreed), and half believed it is important for a man to be strong physically (compared to a quarter of white young people).

Source: Yankelovich Youth Survey © 1974 by the JDR 3rd Fund.

Obstacles to Full Equality: Institutionalised Racism

In the last decade blacks have made some gains, and in the future, Chicanos, Puerto Ricans, and Indians may follow the same path. But unless we eliminate *institutionalised racism,* a true pluralism of ethnic groups will remain a dream. This term refers to a social phenomenon: over time, habits of discrimination have become crystallised into the social structure, in institutional patterns of employment, schooling, housing, government, and so on. Once this happens, these institutions need not be "prejudiced" to discriminate - just by continuing to operate the way they always have, they perpetuate lines of discrimination.

As Stokely Carmichael and Charles V. Hamilton wrote in *Black Power* (1967), institutionalised racism "originates in the operation of established and *respected* forces in society" (italics added). For example, if a suburban community zones against low-or even middle-income housing, it automatically excludes most black families, without ever mentioning the word *race*. A tanker will refuse loans to black would-be businessmen if he simply applies existing guidelines (credit standards, collateral requirements, and so on), without regard to race. The custom of neighbourhood schools, a cherished tradition in this country, is as effective in segregating schools as a law that prohibits "mixed education" (Knowles and Prewitt, 1969, chapter 1). These practices in turn perpetuate the disadvantages of race in the next generation.

10

ORGANISATIONS AND BUREAUCRACY

FORMAL ORGANISATIONS

An *organisation* is a group that has been consciously designed to seek specific goals. People organise to pursue collective aims for the simple reason that if they did not - if seven, eight, or more individuals each did whatever he or she thought best, without consulting the others - they might end up working at cross-purposes. So they form a committee or a business firm, a union or a religious council. The members decide who will have responsibility and authority over what areas, and establish procedures for communicating with one another. Procedures are also devised for making decisions, coordinating activities, reviewing policy and strategies, resolving conflicts among members and keeping them in line, and filling and refilling the organisation's ranks (see Blau and Scott, 1963, pp. 1-2).

Once established, organisations tend to become self-perpetuating—that is, they develop an existence apart from the specific people who founded them. This is one of the primary differences between organisations and other kinds of social groups. Family members are not replaceable; relationships among members are *expressive,* that is, they are centered on the emotional dimension of the relationship. In contrast, relationships in an organisation are *instrumental;* they are built around the completion of specific tasks. Members of an organisation may come and go, but the offices and procedures and identity of the organisation remain more or less stable. The Roman Catholic church is a prime example of an enduring organisation. General Motors, A.T.&T., the League of Women Voters, the Scouts, all share these basic features of an organisation.

Of course, a business that cannot pay employees will fall apart (unless, like an acting or dance company, it provides other satisfactions). A political party, too, can collapse if its goals and tactics begin to seem unrealistic or dated. Similarly a union whose leadership sides more closely with management than with its members will be weakened. Organisations endure if they continue to provide the goods and services that originally motivated people to join them. By "goods and services" here we mean everything from job satisfaction to salaries (in business organisations), to the assurance of national defense (in armies), to the hope of influencing government (in special interest lobbies). Maintaining internal discipline by rewarding members who contribute to organisational goals and punishing or ostracising those who do not is also important. Organisations must be able to recruit members who accept and support their goals, or to inspire and perhaps coerce the uncommitted.

In summary, then, the major difference between organisations and other social groups is that organisations are formally established for the express purpose of pursuing a specific goal, whether it is practicing the true religion, making money, electing a candidate or keeping criminals off the streets (Blau and Scott, 1963, p. 3). A division of labour and authority into clearly defined roles, set channels of communication, explicit rules and procedures, and formal and informal sanctions are all part of the self-perpetuating design of organisations.

Types of Organisations

Although all organisations are alike in some respects, the differences between them can be highly significant. Some organisations are concerned with economic matters (for example, businesses), some with power (political organisations). Still others are designed to resolve intergroup conflicts in a society (the court system) or to teach and maintain social values (churches and schools). (See Parsons, 1960, chapter 1.)

People may or may not join an organisation of their own free will, as Amitai Etzioni points out (1961, pp. *55 - 67).* Social clubs, churches, political parties, professional associations and pressure groups are all *voluntary organisations.* People join them out of personal interest, because they share the organisation's goals and norms. They can withdraw at any time. At the opposite extreme are the organisations people are forced to join, such as prisons, the military (when soldiers are drafted), and schools (education being compulsory between the ages of six and sixteen). Etzioni calls these *coercive organisations:* they depend on force. Between these two extremes lie a great number of *utilitarian organisations* that people join for practical reasons. The clearest example of this type is the business firm. Although no one actually forces people to take specific jobs in this country, most adults do have to work, and their choice of careers and employers is limited (more limited for some than for others). People devote time and energy to utilitarian organisations, and abide by their rules and regulations because they expect to benefit personally, not because they are emotionally committed to the organisation.

Knowing why people join an organisation does not necessarily tell us who benefits from it. Business organisations, for example, are run for the benefit of the owners, whose goal is to maximise efficiency and profit. Peter Blau and W. Richard Scott (1963, pp. 40 - 58) identify three other types according to who benefits most. Unions and religious sects are specifically designed to further the interests of their members. Blau and Scott call these *mutual benefit organisations,* and suggest that ideally they are characterised by a high degree of member participation. *Client-centered organisations,* such as hospitals, schools, and most social agencies, are designed to serve a particular group of people (patients, students, etc.). The main problem in these service organisations is to maintain a balance between client interests and administrative necessity. Finally, there are *commonweal organisations,* which are operated for the benefit of the public-at-large. Examples are the Internal Revenue Service, the Food and Drug Administration, police departments, and other organisations that the public controls (at least in theory).

The importance of these distinctions becomes clear if you think about whether prisons are service organisations, whose primary responsibility is to rehabilitate inmates, or commonweal organisations, responsible for keeping convicts off the streets. The kinds of facilities we build and the kinds of people we staff them with reflect society's view of what prisons should be. The same kind of analysis can be made of universities. From the student's point of view the university is a student-centered service organisation, whose primary purpose is to stimulate and educate people. Faculty tend to see universities as communities of scholars and students, or mutual benefit associations. Adding to this confusion, legislators and other government officials consider universities commonweal organisations that should lend their talents and resources to the solution of community and social problems. Much of the controversy on campuses in the 1960s revolved around the question of whether it was ethical for universities to accept research grants from the Defense Department, or to allow the military and corporations manufacturing war materials to recruit on campus. These questions were not widely raised during the 1940s, when the commonweal nature of the university "in the nation's service" was assumed.

Similar questions can be asked about associations that seem to be voluntary. Do people join social clubs or professional associations because they want to, or because they feel they might lose important friends or a promotion if they did not? The categories suggested here are no more than models or ideal types against which the realities of specific organisations may be measured. Organisations have complex social structures.

Box 10.1

In the News

Lordstoivn: Informal Structure on the Assembly Line

It is hard to imagine any work more routine, more non-negotiable than assembly line work. But men at the General Motors Vega plant in Lordstown, Ohio, have found a way to regain control of their working hours through a system they call "doubling up". Management claims that doubling up seriously lowers the quality of work, and the United Auto Workers' Union refuses to acknowledge the practice. But workers are proud of the system they've improvised and intend to fight for it. The following excerpts are taken from an interview of Lordstown workers.

Q: What's doubling up and how did it start?

McGEE: Now what happens is that the guys who have their operations side by side, they're relating together.... In other words, they all worked in the same area. They started saying, "Go ahead, take off." It started like an 'E' break - you asked for emergency bathroom call. The utility man might be tied up.

I'd say, "Go ahead, man, I think I can handle it." I'd run to the front of the car and I'd stick in the ring we used to have, and I'd run to the back then. I mean, I'm not running, really running, but I'm moving. I put the gas in, I go up to the front of the car again.... go back again. I'm getting it done, and I'm not having any recovery time. I'm going right back again.

Well, the guys started doing this on a larger scale.

McGARVEY: You have to double up and break the boredom to get an immediate feedback from your job, because the only gratification you get is a paycheck once a week, and that's too long to go without any kind of gratification from the job.

Q: So there's a philosophy behind doubling up?

GENERAL: Definitely.

McGEE: Sure, if you're on the damned line here and you've found a way to double up and you've found a way to shuck and jive - all day long, have a good time, help each other and get out the work. I don't have to take these pain pills any more. My ulcer's gone.

Q: Has it - and your doubling up - come from laziness or inventiveness?

DICKERSON: Inventiveness. One way to explain the thing is that anytime there's a human need, there's always an invention, or a way to get around it.

Box 10.1 - *(Contd.)*

The men feel strongly that, because doubling up gave them added responsibility - for two jobs rather than one - the quality of their work actually improves. By bending the formal rules of the company to fit their own needs, the workers at Lordstown feel they have improved not only their own morale, but the company's product as well.
Source: Sennet Kremen, "Lordstown - Searching for a Better Way of Work," *The New York Times* (September 9,1973): III, 1 - 4.

Formal and Informal Structure - Whatever their orientation and whoever benefits most from them, all organisations seek to define members' responsibilities and regulate their activities. This is an organisation's *formal structure:* explicit rules that define each person's duties: written or unwritten organisational charts, that describe relationships among members (who has authority over whom); and a system of rewards and punishments (for example, promotions and demotions). In principle, this formal structure governs all members' activities. However, any time people join forces to accomplish a task, friendships and power relationships develop, and with them come cliques, grapevines, and the like. Some people wield more influence than their job title indicates; others less.

In addition, an organisation's rules may not keep pace with problems. For these reasons, members improvise an *informal structure:* procedures that enable people to solve problems not covered by the formal regulations, to eliminate unpleasant or unnecessary work, and to protect their own interests. (See Box 10.1) All organisations have both an official, formal structure, and an unofficial, informal structure of relationships among members. In the pages that follow we will discuss both the formal and informal structures of a wide variety of organisations.

MODERN BUREAUCRACIES

Giant bureaucratic organisations are not a modern invention. The pyramids of Egypt are monuments to organisation; the

Roman Empire could never have existed without a vast administrative structure. But never before in history have bureaucracies been so pervasive or so powerful. The "Age of Bureaucracy" was launched in the nineteenth century when Western nations began to industrialise.

"The Mighty Machine"

The Greeks understood the principles of the steam engine and probably could have produced one had they so desired. They didn't, presumably because they had an abundant supply of labour in the form of slaves. The practical application of mechanics to production did not interest them. Rather, they aimed their technical inventiveness at surprises and miracles -temple gates that opened by themselves when a priest lit the fire on an altar, for example. This nonutilitarian attitude toward mechanisation persisted for centuries. As late as 1870, the French were talking and writing not about Jacques de Vaucanson's silk factory (probably the first industrial plant in Europe), but about his marvellous mechanical duck, which waddled, swam, wagged its head, quacked, and even pecked, digested, and expelled grain (Giedion, 1948, pp. 31 - 36).

However, by the end of the nineteenth century this dilettantish fascination with machines had blossomed into a full-fledged love affair. It was the wedding of rationality and this worldliness to the miraculous, sanctified by the creed of Progress. The cotton gin, the steam engine, and the iron horse all made their appearance. Rather suddenly, Europeans recognised the enormous power of mechanisation.

Soon, writers on two continents were heralding the dawn of a new age. With machines, humankind would transform the world. "We remove mountains, and make seas our smooth highway; and nothing can resist us," wrote Carlyle. "We make war with rude Nature; and, by our resistless engines, come off always-victorious, and loaded with spoils" (Carlyle, in Marx, 1964, p. 171). Machines would wipe drudgery and menial labour off the list of human complaints, freeing people to follow more uplifting pursuits. The forefather of sociology, Saint-Simon, was one of the first, but *not* the last, to see industrialisation as the route to peace and social justice: mechanisation would eliminate poverty and want; nationalism and militarism would disappear; no longer would the powerful exploit the weak (Giedion, 1948, p. 30). Machines became a favoured metaphor in this period. "What is the heart but a spring, and the nerves so many springs, and the joints but so many wheels, giving motion to the whole body," wrote Hobbes.

Looking back, we can imagine the enthusiasm for mechanisation in this earlier time, the sense of unlimited possibilities, the faith people had in reason and progress. By any measure, the standard of living has risen dramatically since the advent of mechanisation: we have minimised distances in the jet age; we do have the capacity (if not the will) to feed, clothe, and provide medical care for every person on earth. It is doubtful that these developments would have occurred without the spread of bureaucracy.

Bureaucracy: Ideal and Real

> The fully developed bureaucratic mechanism compares with other organisations exactly as does the machine with non-mechanical modes of production. (Weber, in Gerth and Mills, 1946, p. 214).

A machine is "an apparatus consisting of interrelated parts with separate functions, used in the performance of some kind of work" *(Random House Dictionary of the English Language,* 1967). If we substitute the word *organisation* for *apparatus,* we have a basic definition of *bureaucracy:* an organisation consisting of interrelated parts with separate functions. The key terms here are *interrelated* and *separate functions.* Bureaucracy represents the application of mechanics to social organisation in the performance of some kind of work.

Weber's Model of Bureaucracy - Weber's analysis of bureaucratic structure, written long before red tape became a social problem and the word *bureaucrat* an epithet, remains the classic in the field. Weber traced the development and spread of bureaucracies to large-scale production and advances in technology coupled with the nineteenth-century belief in progress and reason. He believed bureaucracy to be *technically* superior to other forms of social organisation, despite its dehumanising side-effects (which he recognised fully and regretted). "Precision, speed, unambiguity, knowledge of files, continuity, discretion, strict subordination, reduction of friction and of material and personal costs -these are raised to the optimum point in the strictly bureaucratic administration" (Weber, in Gerth and Mills, 1946, p. 214). To dramatise the differences between bureaucracies and other organisations, Weber defined bureaucracy in terms of five characteristics. Together, these characteristics describe an ideal type or model, against which the realities of actual bureaucracies can be measured.

1. **Specialization:** Bureaucratic organisation is based on the belief that dividing production into small tasks and having people specialise in one of these tasks is the most efficient way to perform complex work. If you consider the impossibility of one person learning every step in the production of an airplane or all there is to know today about medicine, the reasoning behind this belief will be obvious. Specialisation is more efficient than "generalisation". Bureaucracies rely on a complex division of labour, with clearly defined areas of jurisdiction. The men and women in each area are familiar with and responsible for only one step in the production or administration of the bureaucracy's essential task. This arrangement encourages the development of special competence or expertise in limited areas. But no one person knows the entire process, which can be a terrible handicap if something goes wrong.

2. **A hierarchy of offices:** Once production is broken down into a number of separate activities performed by separate groups of people, the entire operation must be integrated **in** a workable fashion. If not, experts in one department might design a bolt that is one-eighth-inch larger than the nut designed by another department (Blau and Meyer, 1971, p. 8). In small organisations all the workers can call a meeting to talk about ideas and problems, but in large organisations it is

impossible for everyone to meet together. Nor can the boss supervise the activities of hundreds of employees, even if he or she knows their jobs, which is unlikely. To resolve this problem, workers are organised in a *hierarchy*. Each person is responsible to the person directly above him or her in the hierarchy and responsible *for* the actions of those who work under him or her.

Organisational hierarchies are defined in terms of positions or offices. Each office carries with it specific duties, responsibilities, and privileges, as well as a specific salary. Authority rests in the office, not in the person who occupies it. This individual may be promoted or fired, but the office remains the same. An office-holder's power over those beneath him or her in the hierarchy derives from the *position*, not from the individual qualities or "secred rights" (such as a parent's rights over a child). In addition to being depersonalised, the authority of bureaucratic officials is clearly defined and limited. While they have the power to recommend individuals for promotions or to fire them, supervisors have no authority over subordinates' personal lives, as was true when sons worked for their fathers in family businesses. (Remember, Weber was describing an ideal type. He was not oblivious to the pressures toward conformity in dress, political attitudes, outside activities, and the like in bureaucracies.)

Weber believed hierarchical organisation would minimise interpersonal friction. If subordinates accept the hierarchical division of responsibility and authority, and the supervisor's right to regulate their activities, it is no more degrading to accept orders from the boss than it is to obey orders from a policeman (Blau and Meyer, 1971, p. 67). Moreover, when a supervisor makes an unpopular decision, she can avoid subordinates' hostility and maintain good working relationships by blaming the people above her in the hierarchy.

3. **Rules and regulations:** Activities and relationships among officers in a bureaucracy are governed by explicit rules and regulations. In this way, each employee knows (at least in general terms) what is required of him and how his decisions

will be carried out. Rules make the workings of even the most complex bureaucracy orderly and predictable. They are the connecting rods in the bureaucratic engine.

4. **Impartiality:** Weber believed that personal emotions impede efficiency and therefore have no place in a bureaucracy. Impartiality toward both co-workers and those who do business with the organisation is essential. Ideally this assures that all people will be treated equitably and that personal considerations will be subordinated to organisational goals. If an official promotes a subordinate solely because he or she is a friend, or awards a contract to a company because his or her brother owns it, the organisation will suffer.

5. **Technical competence:** Finally, positions in a bureaucracy are awarded on the basis of technical qualifications (as measured by tests or other standardised procedures), and people are paid for their work. However, Weber believed that a salary was not enough to motivate people to work harder, faster, or more efficiently. People must be guaranteed a place, so long as they perform their official duties adequately. Promotions and raises, awarded on the basis of merit and or seniority, are essential to a bureaucracy's *esprit de corps*. In addition, Weber thought the more complicated and specialised work became, the more bureaucracies would need "personally detached and strictly objective' *experts*."

Does Weber's model of bureaucracy exist in reality? Not entirely. Studies of business firms in 150 societies and an analysis of ten organisations in this country suggest that the five bureaucratic traits don't always appear together (Udy, 1959; Hall, 1963 -1964). Wide variations were found in degree of specialisation, hierarchical organisation, and adherence to rules and regulations, both within and among companies. The fact that an organisation relied on specialisation did not mean that employees were arranged in a hierarchy or that their relationships were impersonal.

As we suggested earlier, Weber's model is an ideal type which calls attention to significant characteristics by emphasising, and perhaps overstating, trends. It was not meant to describe reality. "The ideal-type bureaucracy may be used much as a twelve-inch ruler is employed. We would not expect, for example, that all objects measured by the ruler would be exactly twelve inches - some would be more and some would be less" (Gouldner, 1950, pp. 53-54). Other critics have focused not on how accurate Weber's model is, but on how well bureaucracies function.

Ritualism - Do rules and regulations facilitate rational decision-making and maximise efficiency, as Weber suggested? Not always. In his classic study of the bureaucratic personality, Robert Merton (1968) suggests that when people become devoted to procedures, as bureaucrats tend to do, they lose sight of why those procedures were created in the first place. Following regulations becomes an end in itself. Rigid adherence to established procedures prevents people from recognising and adapting to new conditions and problems. They become inflexible. Organisational goals and efficiency may be lost in the shuffle. The bureaucrat Merton describes feels totally satisfied if he does everything just exactly as he is supposed to, regardless of the consequences. The phenomenon commonly known as "passing the buck" is simply a variation on this theme: unless the official is clear about which rules to follow in a given case, and unless he is certain that it falls within his jurisdiction, he may refuse to take any action at all (Blau and Meyer, 1971, pp. 104-5). Merton argues that bureaucracies encourage overconformity, or ritualism.

Harry Cohen cautions against regarding flexibility as an unqualified asset in bureaucrats (1970). He cites the example of an interviewer who filed the required complaint when an employer refused to hire an applicant because she was black. However, the bureaucrat then visited the employer and advised him to mention insufficient qualifications, not race, when rejecting applicants in the future. From one point of view, this action was highly adaptive: the interviewer avoided antagonising an employer who could provide jobs for his clients. But, in an indirect way, he broke the law, as well as the rules. Cohen's point is that flexibility as well as excessive rigidity can be harmful to the bureaucracy. Moreover, in many instances a bureaucrat finds he is damned if he does follow the rules (by discriminating employers in this case) and damned if he doesn't (by those who suffer from or disapprove of discrimination).

Protection of the Inept - Weber believed that bureaucratic organisations would make the best possible use of available talent. Recent research indicates that bureaucracies tend to protect the inept as well. Given the fact that the boss has the power to promote or fire subordinates, it is in employees' interest to conceal problems and withhold information from supervisors. In William Goode's words:

"Almost every inquiry into the productivity of workers has shown that the informal work group protects its members by setting a standard which everyone can meet, and they develop techniques for preventing a supervisor from measuring accurately the output of each [person]" (1967, p. 6). Goode also calls attention to the fact that companies are usually reluctant to demote or otherwise discredit incompetent employees. Thus, people who do not meet company standards in one position may be "kicked upstairs" to a less responsible but still prestigious job, or fired but , provided with glowing recommendations. Discrimination against blacks, women, Jews, or other minorities and the requirement that workers have at least a high-school diploma to perform work a child could master, also limit competition and thereby protect inept workers who already hold those jobs.

Weber also believed that regular promotions based on merit and or seniority would contribute to efficiency, but each of these criteria can prove inefficient. If granted solely on the basis of merit, some people will not advance, creating discontent in the lower ranks; if granted on the basis of seniority, inefficient people will be advanced as a matter of course (Goode, 1967).

The Peter Principle - Even if promotions are based solely on merit, this method of filling jobs can be disadvantageous. When supervisors need to fill positions, they choose persons who are particularly good at their current jobs. If these people prove capable in the new job, they will very likely be promoted again and again - until they reach their level of incompetence. For example, an outstanding teacher may be promoted to principal, a very different kind of job which she may perform poorly. However, if she is a good principal, she may be moved up to district superintendent. If she proves to be a poor superintendent, she will not be promoted but will *stay* in the job she cannot quite fill. This is the famous *Peter Principle:* "In a hierarchy every employee tends to rise to his [or her] level of incompetence" (Peter and Hull, 1969, p. 25). Knowing that your knowledge and ability are not quite up to your job can be a frightening experience, leading to poor performance. One way to alleviate the anxiety is to bury yourself in the rules and regulations, ignoring the consequences of your work (Blau and Meyer, 1971, p. 104).

Waste-making - Writing when he did, Weber could not have foreseen all the possible ramifications of ever-increasing size. In principle, people hire assistants when they feel they can no longer handle all of their work alone. In practice, however, people may request additional staff to increase their prestige in the organisation. Suppose a bureaucrat hires two assistants (two being safer than one, who might become a competitor). In all likelihood, he will reserve the power to make decisions for himself, thereby adding supervision to his original work load. If all goes well, however, in a year or two his assistants will need assistants, and there will be five or even seven people to do the work of one. But the ritual of shuffling paper back and forth among seven people - by itself - will keep them all *demonstrably busy*. This is the essence of *Parkinson's Law:* "Work expands to fill the time available for its completion" (Parkinson, 1957).

A. Ernest Fitzgerald (1972), who spent several years as an efficiency consultant for the Pentagon, found numerous examples of Parkinson's Law. Investigating the military and civilian firms working for the military, he invariably found overstaffed departments and bureaus - a condition the military thinly disguised under the code words, "maintaining capability". In most cases, when Fitzgerald recommended cutbacks, the official in charge would challenge the data in order to keep his staff. One manager, however, stood out. Fitzgerald recommended a 56 per cent cutback in his area. The manager praised Fitzgerald's methods and data, but claimed it was good to keep so many people employed but unproductive. Laying people off would be wrong.

> What if someone were to hire them and put them to work *producing* things, items which would compete in the commercial marketplace? That would never do, our manager said, because competition might set in, driving prices down, and some of the less efficient companies might go broke. This sort of thing could develop into a chain reaction and ruin the whole business climate. (Fitzgerald, 1972, p. 5)

Fitzgerald concludes that the military believes in "The Ape Theory of Engineering". This theory was proposed by a psychologist who calculated that, according to the laws of probability, if enough apes were set down at typewriters, they would eventually write *Hamlet*. Fitzgerald quotes one manager who, in all seriousness, described his approach as follows: "I just assign a thousand or so guys to the problem. One of them is bound to come up with a solution" (p. 7).

MEETING ORGANISATIONAL GOALS

Corporations, armies, churches, neighbourhood associations have one thing in common, as well indicated at the beginning of this chapter: they are conspicuously designed to achieve certain goals. Motivating people to support "the cause," establishing procedures for coordinating activities, making decisions, and dealing with outsiders are essential to any organisation. In this section we look at how organisations distribute power and elicit work from their members. We will also consider how workers shape the rules to meet their own needs.

Leadership and the Negotiated Order

Leaders or bosses play many roles in modern organisations. They are decision-makers, administrators who see that decisions are carried out and activities coordinated, and disciplinarians who enforce the rules. They represent the organisation to the outside world and to the rank-and-file below them, who do not participate directly in the organisation's policy councils.

Alvin W. Gouldner's *Patterns of Industrial Bureaucracy* (1954) is a case study in two different styles of leadership - democratic and authoritarian. The book is based on a three-year study of a gypsum plant located near the Great Lakes, which employed approximately 225 people - 75 in the mines, 150 in different "surface" operations - over the course of the study. Gouldner's arrival coincided with a change in management: Vincent Peele, an outsider with his own ideas about how to run a plant, was replacing "Old Doug," as the former boss was known.

In the old days management had been unusually "indulgent" (to use Couldner's term) toward employees. As long as a worker did his job, his free time while at work was his own. Supervision was minimal and working hours flexible. As a result, employees had considerable control over the working lives. No one was reprimanded for taking time off during the hunting season. In fact, management always gave employees the benefit of the doubt. One mechanic told Gouldner, "No body ever gets fired from this plant. Maybe Bill [a supervisor] fired one guy in all the time I've known him, and *he was given three or four warnings*" (p. 48). As a matter of policy, men injured on *or off the* job were given light work in the sampling room, which became known as "the hospital". In addition, officials allowed workers to borrow company tools and materials for private use. Gouldner found the majority thought this basically democratic company had the "proper attitude" and that they were being treated "humanly".

Peele was a stranger when he took over as manager, and knew little about the way things were done in the plant. Anxious to do his job well, he began to attack what he perceived as laxity. In a very short time, he fired one man for borrowing company-owned material (an acceptable practice in the old days); replaced a popular foreman with a college-educated outsider; formalised warnings with written notices; instituted regular, written work reports; and announced that workers who were absent without a valid excuse would be laid off for an equivalent number of days.

Workers did not take kindly to these changes. Their complaints centered around the implication that they had been goldbricking and required close supervision, which they deeply resented. Old Doug's inner circle, his "lieutenants," did not consider Peele a "legitimate heir" and grew pointedly recalcitrant, so that he had difficulty learning exactly what was going on.

Gouldner suggests that Peele became authoritarian almost as a last resort, because he lacked the informal social ties that would have enabled him to manage the employees with a lighter hand.

> Like all other solutions Peele adopted to handle the problems of his succession, the development of formal rules also had an anxiety-allaying function. The rules define the new situation into which the successor has entered, allowing him to make decisions with a minimum of uncertainty and personal responsibility .... The belief that he was only doing what he must, softened Peele's doubts about his own behaviour. As he remarked: "Some of the men probably think I'm a mean cuss, but I've got to follow our Company policy like everyone else. If I don't someone else will." (Gouldner, 1954, 95 - 96)

In time Peele was able to establish a bureaucratic system in surface operations, but not in the mines. The hazards of underground work strengthened the miners' feeling that they had a legitimate right to make their own decisions.

Gouldner's study raises an important point about leadership. The power to hire and fire and to impose rules through sanctions is of limited value without the support of an informal organisation. Peele discovered very quickly that he could not be all places at all times to see that regulations were being followed. Moreover, his authoritarian style generated a good deal of resentment and apathy. Before the rigid, bureaucratic rules were applied, workers had been largely self-regulating. Afterwards, they used the rules to justify and excuse minimal effort.

> "Well, if that's the way he wants it, that's the way he wants it. But I'll be damned if I put in any overtime when things get rough and they'd like us to."
>
> "O.K. I'll punch in just so, and I'll punch out on the nose. But you know you can lead a horse to water and you can lead him away, but it's awful hard to tell just how much water he drinks while he's at it." (Gouldner, 1954, p. 175).

As these quotations suggest, the effectiveness of leadership depends on the kinds of understandings which various people - the men in the mines, the workers on the surface, the office managers - work out among themselves. Anselm Strauss and others have called this the *negotiated order* (1964). Discovered when they studied how psychiatrists, nurses, social workers, psychologists and attendants work out their relationships when caring for mental patients, this term alerts us to the way in which organisational power becomes shaped and altered. It is not the same as the informal structure of an organisation, because the negotiated order will usually involve both informal and formal arrangements. For example, Mr. Peele relied heavily upon formal rules in an effort to renegotiate the organisation of the gypsum factory. Central to this process is *legitimacy* - who can persuade others that he or she has the right to a certain organisational power. While Mr. Peele had official power, he lacked legitimacy in the eyes of many employees. One reason he did so goes back to the exchange theory of social life. The old manager, Doug, had created social debts (by overlooking minor violations of the rules and by protecting subordinates from official sanctions) which the men repaid in extra effort (Blau and Meyer, 1971, pp. 63 - 68). The negotiated order is an example of social exchange, and Mr. Peele had trouble creating his new order because he did not realise this sociological truth.

Socialisation into Organisations

As the preceding discussion suggests, new members of an organisation experience a period of initiation, during which they learn the skills and vocabulary of their new position, the formal and informal pecking order of the organisation, and its written and unwritten rules. For the organisation, socialising new members means "breaking them in". For the boss, it is an opportunity to test neophytes (who might one day become competitors) and to reassert his or her own power. Newcomers learn that pursuing organisational goals is in their own best interests, and that the demands to be made on them are legitimate and meaningful - or at least, unavoidable. For recruits, socialisation into an organisation means adjusting expectations to reality, learning the "system," establishing new loyalties, and discovering their own strengths and countervailing power.

Anticipatory Socialisation **-** Socialisation into a new job or position builds on the new member's expectations and desire to convert, to conform, and to do things "the company way". William F. Whyte, Jr., demonstrated this point in *The Organisation Man* (1957). The people who interested Whyte "are not the workers, nor are they white-collar people in the usual, clerk sense of the word. These people only work for The Organisation. The ones I am talking about *belong* to it as well. They are the ones of our middle class who have left home, spiritually as well as physically to take the vows of organisation life, and it is they who are the mind and soul of our great self-perpetuating institutions" (p. 3).

Raised with visions of split-level houses, two-car garages, a wife and children, and summers at the lake, the executive aspirants of the fifties wanted *to work for somebody else* (unlike their fathers and grandfathers).

> Today (1957) it is a very rare young man who will allow himself to talk [of becoming president of a corporation, or building a bridge, or making a million dollars], let alone think that way.... The life that he looks ahead to will be a life in which he is the only one of hundreds of similarly able people and in which they will all be moved hither and yon and subject to so many forces outside their control that only a fool would expect to hew to a set course. (Whyte, 1957, p. 144)

Whyte tied the practicality of youth in the fifties to the optimistic belief that the system operated in their best interests, that their goals and the organisation's coincided. Far from wanting to change society, they actively sought ways to cooperate with the *status quo.*

Training and Socialisation - The demand for college and graduate degrees grew steadily in the fifties, so that by the time Whyte wrote *The Organisation Man,* a Bachelor's degree had become a prerequisite for most white-collar jobs. With some exceptions, however, formal schooling did not (and does not) prepare men and women for specific occupational roles. Rather, college offers a general orientation to a wide range of careers - as well as experience with an organisation, the university.

Recognising this, most large corporations conduct formal training programmes. "Come graduation," writes Whyte, seniors "do not go outside to a hostile world; they transfer". The locale shifts; the training continues, for at the same time that the colleges have been changing their curriculum to suit the corporation, the corporation has responded by setting up its own campuses and classrooms. By now the two have been so well molded that it's difficult to tell where one leaves off and the other begins (Whyte, 1957, p. 69).

Ostensibly, corporation training programmes are designed to teach newcomers the requisite skills of a manager, an accountant, or an engineer. However, all have a hidden agenda, namely, teaching "the company way". Whyte summarises the corporate litany as follows:

> Be loyal to the company and the company will be loyal to you. After all, if you do a good job for the organisation, it is only good sense for the organisation to be good to you, because that will be best for everybody. There are a bunch of real people around here. Tell them what you think and they will respect you for it. (p. 143)

As training proceeds, recruits realise that they are being evaluated for the way they conduct themselves and get along with others, as well as for their skills. Ideally, when trainees move from the programme to a formal position in the organisation, they have been sufficiently indoctrinated to fit in smoothly. A recent article on I.B.M. supports Whyte's view of corporate indoctrination.

> As [one observer noted] "I.B.M. is a religion, a very successful religion more so than most. It really indoctrinates people. ... Those who can't stand the discipline leave. -.. Ultimately, the vast majority of I.B.M.'ers stay put giving the company low turnover rate, a high *esprit de corps* and lots of people who will say they're "proud to be a small part of I.B.M." (Shapiro, 1973, p. 35)

Loss of Idealism and Role Conflict - Once managers settle into an organisation or professionals into a daily routine, they often find reality more complicated and disappointing than they had expected. Medical students, for example, typically enter school with the idea that all a doctor need do is make an accurate diagnosis, apply the correct treatment, and the problem will be solved - a decidedly Utopian view. In reality, there are many, many questions medical science cannot answer, and no doctor - no matter how conscientious or brilliant - can absorb all there is to know in the field. An important part of the physician's socialisation is learning to cope with doubt and uncertainty (Fox, in Merton *et al.*, 1957, pp. 207 - 41). The neophyte soldier, politician, teacher, or dental technician runs head on into contradictions between the organisation's or profession's avowed creed and actual practices. These revelations are particularly disturbing to those who believe in the ideal goals and values, yet find they are routinely expected to engage in "illegitimate" activities (Caplow, 1964, pp. 199-200).

In some cases, conflicts are built into a job or role. Doctors, for example, are supposed to be self-critical but to act decisively when the situation requires it. They should be emotionally detached but never callous; respect their colleagues, but put medical ethics first [Merton *et al.*, 1957, pp. 73 - 75). A military chaplain is expected to ease soldiers' anxieties about killing even though his religion teaches him to abhor violence.

Added to these problems is the fact that socialisation into an organisation does not occur in a vacuum. Taking on a new role often requires adjustments in other areas of a person's life. The college graduate who takes a job becomes financially independent of his or her parents, perhaps for the first time.

A person who enters a demanding occupation, or is moved up the corporate ladder, or takes a job of questionable respectability, may have to neglect family obligations or give up previous friendships and associations.

TOTAL INSTITUTIONS

At first glance, prisoners, mental patients, monks and soldiers may seem to have little in common besides their drab uniforms. But Erving Goffman, in *Asylums* (1961), argues that they all live in structurally similar institutions. A monk may take his orders voluntarily; he may wear a cassock instead of army drab or prison gray; he spends his hours in prayer or study, not drills or therapeutic arts and crafts. But the structure of his life in a monastery is much the same as a convict's in a prison, an inmate's in a mental hospital, a draftee's in the army - all of which are total institutions, or asylums in Goffman's terminology. Goffman defines an *asylum* as a place where "a large number of like-situated individuals, cut off from the wider society for an appreciable period of time, together lead an enclosed, formally administered round of life." In asylums, bureaucratic control is carried to its extreme.

Because they are extreme cases, asylums highlight certain features that are less visible in most other bureaucracies. First, the asylum's relation to inmates is *coercive,* even if they volunteered to join. All organisations are coercive to some degree: schools coerce though for fewer hours of the day, and corporations coerce employees to follow company rules. But in total institutions, people lose all control over and all responsibility for their lives.

Once admitted to a total institution, the process that Goffman calls *mortification* begins. Individuals are methodically stripped of the clothes, adornments, and personal possessions people use to define themselves in everyday life. In exchange, they receive standard, nondescript, and often ill fitting attire - a uniform or hospital robe. They may be disfigured as well, by a military or prison haircut, for example. The spirit is mortified too. The institution designs exercises to break the will: people are forced to perform meaningless acts, to submit to arbitrary and unreasonable commands as well as to personal abuse (verbal or physical). Finally, they are deprived of privacy, both physical (through a debasing physical examination) and social (they must sleep, shower and eat with a group). They are under constant surveillance, with every moment of every day being planned by others. All of these procedures disabuse people of their feelings of self-worth and train them for deference. Individuals in total institutions are forced into a kind of regression; they are made to feel helpless and therefore dependent on the organisation. At this point they are ready to be resocialised to a new role, one the organisation designs.

People may react to their confinement in one of three main ways. In hospitals, some actively work to sabotage routines, but their rebellion is generally short-lived because the institution can isolate or drug the rebel. Moreover, the staff can withhold privileges, fail to communicate messages to a doctor, and the like. Second, inmates can simply withdraw, detaching themselves from their surroundings as much as possible. Finally, they can accept their subjugation, as a high proportion do. For those individuals the asylum becomes a home that they do not want to leave. Indeed, some actively seek out these curtailments of the self, so that modification is complemented by self-mortification, restrictions by renunciations. Attached to the simple, predictable routines and the security of the asylum, they resist being discharged and, if this fails, many people find ways to be readmitted.

Goffman attributes the extremes of total institutions to the low status accorded inmates, to the fact that inmates greatly out-number staff, and to the tendency for means to become ends for the staff. Finishing the day's work becomes more important than meeting the institution's goals, which are themselves only poorly defined. "Keeping the lid on" mental hospitals, prisons, and the military occupies hundreds of thousands of bureaucracies.

BEYOND BUREAUCRACY

Cracks in prison walls make headlines. On September 13, 1971, National Guardsmen and state police moved into New York's Attica prison. When the tear gas and smoke cleared, 45 people had been killed (11 of them guards who had been held hostage) and more than 150 were wounded - by "peace officers," not by inmates. So ended one of the most highly publicised prison riots of recent times. But "Attica fever" spread in the following months. Prisoners in Vermont went on strike; a dozen or more were seriously wounded in a riot at an Illinois penitentiary; convicted soldiers burned down the disciplinary barracks at the army's Fort George in Georgia.

Prison riots are nothing new. What makes these uprisings different is that the prisoners of the seventies are younger, better educated, and more politically aware than prisoners were in the past. Well-versed in unfair bail procedures, interminable delays in court, inadequate legal counsel, arbitrary and ambiguous sentencing, and the impossibility of rehabilitating themselves in a brutal and perverse atmosphere, they see themselves as political prisoners. They rebel against enforced idleness in jails. They demand not only better living conditions and an end to brutality, but the right to due process in prison, the right to legal counsel in probation hearings, the right to practice their religion (which is often denied Muslims), and the abolition of mail censorship - all basic constitutional rights (Chaneles, 1973).

The prison riots are symptomatic of widespread changes, not only in asylums but in many other bureaucratic organisations. To cite just a few examples: approximately 100,000 employees of 700 -1,000 firms are working four days a week instead of five *(U.S. News and World Report,* March 20, 1972, p. 82); the Hewlitte-Packard Company, among others, allows workers to choose their own hours. In the words of one forty-eight-year-old employee, "It makes me feel that the company thinks I'm intelligent enough to keep my own hours. The company is treating us like adults" *(The Wall Street Journal,* July 12, 1973, pp. 1, 25). The new McDonald's headquarters outside of Chicago boasts a soundproof "think tank" with been bag chairs and adjustable work surfaces that any employee can reserve, and a meditation room complete with suedelike walls, a hi-fi system, and a waterbed. There are no walls and doors to emphasise hierarchical divisions on the three floors the company occupies *(Time,* February 28,1972).

Even the military is changing. The "Now Navy" allows well-kept beards, moustaches, and longer hair. In September 1973 West Point published a new manual that stresses *self-discipline* more than rules. The hated practice of confining cadets to their rooms during free hours has been abolished. These innovations reflect changes in both the nature of work and the nature of the worker.

The Future of Bureaucracy

Traditional bureaucratic organisations are based on what Douglas McGregor (in Bennis, 1970) called the X Theory of human behaviour.

1. The average human being dislikes work and will avoid it if he [or she] can.
2. Therefore, most people must be coerced, controlled, directed and threatened with punishment if they are to work adequately.
3. The average human being prefers to be directed, wishes to avoid responsibility, has relatively little ambition and wants security above all things, (in Bennis, 1970, p. 30)

Social research has shown, time and time again, that these assumptions are false. Overcontrol merely exacerbates tensions between management and workers (and between workers and clients), particularly in an "educated society". In some urban areas today, nearly half of all high-school graduates attend college (Bennis, p. 168). The average worker is better educated and more self-directing than his or her parents were, and will not accept X Theory treatment (as the automobile workers at Lordstown and other factories are proving).

In addition, advanced technology is bringing increasing numbers of professionals into businesses and government, professionals whose very expertise places them somewhat beyond the control of their superiors in the hierarchy. "Professionals," writes Warren Bennis, "are notoriously 'disloyal' to organisation demands" (1970, p. 177). Professionals tend to see their careers in terms of advancing in their field, not in the organisation. Their "most important incentive. . . is to 'make it' professionally," wherever they work. And increasing, professionals and experts are coming to dominate business and government as well as universities.

Looking to the future, Bennis forecasts major changes in the structure of organisations. Fixed departments and positions or offices will give way to temporary, problem-oriented systems, such as a task force created to attack a specific issue and dissolved when the job is done. Executives will become coordinators and diplomats whose main job will be "producing conditions where people and ideas and resources can be seeded, nurtured and integrated" (Bennis, p. 184). To supervise professionals and deploy brainpower effectively, executives will have to understand the system and how their own actions affect others. Finally, organisations will become more flexible and humanistic as they begin to recognise workers' desires for involvement, participation and autonomy on the job (Bennis, p. 12).

Underlying these changes are insights about human behaviour which McGregor called the Y Theory. It suggests that:

1. Work is a natural human activity.
2. [People] will work toward goals to which they are committed without coercion, and that commitment follows from the opportunity to realise their own potentialities.
3. Most [people] have a higher level of intellectual capacity than the usual conditions of modern industrial life reveal, (in Bennis, 1970, p. 30)

Many of the largest corporations - I.B.M., Exxon, Xerox, to name a few - are recognising these qualities and putting them into practice. The result is a different kind of organisation, one where executives are trained in several technical areas to gain wider knowledge, where the hierarchy is loose and decisions are made by group discussion, and where employee relations are more personal. These, of course, reverse the characteristics of the classic bureaucratic model we began with, which Max Weber described in the 1920s. Since then, social and economic changes, as well as an increased number of professionals in business and government, have called for revisions in bureaucratic structure to meet the needs both of modern managers and their employees.

11

COLLECTIVE BEHAVIOUR

COLLECTIVE BEHAVIOUR: AN OVERVIEW

Collective behaviour refers to the actions of relatively temporary, unstructured groups of people who are focused on and reacting to the same event information, person, group, or custom. This definition includes a wide range of collective activities: crowds, riots, panics, fashions, crazes, social movements and public opinion. What do these varied phenomena have in common? They develop more or less spontaneously and spread as if by contagion. Recall, for example, how "impeachment fever" broke out in early 1974 and how each new poll showed that more and more Americans had been "infected" with doubt regarding President Nixon. It is this susceptibility to behavioural contagion that makes rock audiences different from history classes, protest movements different from established political parties.

Preconditions of Collective Behaviour

Collective behaviour seems to defy explanations. Panics, such as the run on the banks that drove many to bankruptcy and precipitated the Great Depression in 1929, appear totally illogical and unpredictable. Fads, such as gold-fish swallowing in the 1920s or streaking in the 1970s, crop up spontaneously and spread of their own momentum. Or do they? Sociologists think not. Despite the impression of formlessness, there are patterns to collective behaviour. It does not simply erupt, any time, any place.

Some forms of collective behaviour develop around culturally significant symbols (such as wealth in a capitalist society, where money is a primary measure of self-worth, or the church and clergy in religious societies) and only under certain conditions. If a society encourages people to value things that may suddenly slip out of their hands, changes in the availability of those things is conducive to collective behaviour. A run on the banks, for example, will only happen in societies where money is highly valued. Obstacles to desired goals and to expressions of significant values may also generate collective behaviour. The 1960s riots in Watts and Detroit, for example, were in part expressions of frustration by blacks who were denied access to the "good life" in America. Unanticipated events, such as a terrorist attack or fire, may have the same effect. Although they do not always generate collective behaviour, one or more of these preconditions is always present when collective behaviour does occur. Below we will consider three preconditions for collective behaviour in greater depth.

Structural Conduciveness - The theory of structural conduciveness suggests that preconditions for collective behaviour are built into a society's social structure. For example, the possibility of financial panics is inherent in open, fluid money economies, where people are able to speculate and to acquire or dispose of assets on short notice, and where wealth is considered personally and socially important. Such panics cannot occur in traditional societies, where property is acquired only through inheritance and marriage. Thus, money economies are conducive to financial panics; traditional societies are not (Smelser, 1962, p. 15). Similarly, the concentration of minorities in urban ghettos, where unemployment is high and housing substandard so that people spend much of their time outdoors, is conducive to other forms of collective behaviour: social movements as well as "civic disorders". But the potential for collective behaviour alone does not explain its occurrence.

The Unanticipated Event–Sudden, unexpected events may create a state of *normlessness:* people do not know what they can or should do, and there are no cultural guidelines to direct them. For example, when a tornado struck Judsonia, Arkansas and surrounding towns in 1952, people had only a minute's warning. One moment the town was standing and people were heading home for dinner. The next moment 600 buildings had been levelled and 800 severely damaged; 46 people had been killed and more than 600 injured; electricity, telephone, and gas lines had been wiped out; and the nearest radio tower stopped broadcasting. The worst problem for police in the hours that followed was traffic: hundreds of cars poured into the area with people seeking relatives, offering help, or perhaps just "sightseeing," mindless of the fact that they were blocking roads needed for emergency vehicles (Barton, 1969, pp. 3 - 10).

When people are unexpectedly deprived of the world they take for granted, when catastrophic events such as a tornado throw their ability to cope into doubt, *doing* becomes more important than thinking and planning. There is a need to define the situation, to restructure the social world, to reaffirm one's sense of mastery - in action (Turner and Killian, 1972, pp. 72-73).

Unanticipated, unsettling incidents may precipitate mobs, riots, panics and social movements. The Free Speech Movement at Berkeley, forerunner of a decade of student activism, began when university officials suddenly announced that the strip of land outside the gates that students had traditionally used to raise funds and recruit members for political activities belonged to the university and was subject to its rules (Milgram and Toch, 1969, pp. 556-57). As often as not, however, the precipitating incident - the point of confrontation - is only the tip of the iceberg.

Frustrated Social Concerns - The Free Speech Movement of 1964 - a semester of sit-ins, strikes and rallies, some attracting as many as 7,000, during which time students occupied the central administration building and 200 police were moved onto the campus - clearly illustrates the role frustrated social concerns play in collective behaviour. Many of the Berkeley activists had participated in the Civil Rights Movement during the previous summer, working for the rights of black Americans in the deep South, only to return to a campus where they themselves were denied such basic rights as peaceful assembly and free speech. Students were not represented in the police-making councils of the university, so they could not register complaints there. Nor could they appeal to a higher authority, such as the law: a campus is private property, and the trustees had the legal right to say how the land could or could not be used. In short, there were no established, institutionalised channels through which students could express political concerns.

Frustrated social concerns, unanticipated events, and built-in sources of instability (structural conduciveness) do not automatically give rise to collective behaviour. Rather they create a sense of disorientation. Existing channels seem inadequate; consciously and unconsciously people seek to define their unrest, to determine what is happening, who or what is responsible, how they should act. This urge to act, in the absence of clear cultural guidelines, sets the stage for collective behaviour.

CROWDS

Crowds are temporary collections of people, gathered around a person or event, who are conscious of and influenced by one another's presence. The primary difference between crowds and other social groups is that crowds are ephemeral; they lack a past and future, and are relatively unstructured. For example, the people who collect around an accident will stop interacting as soon as they leave. In his classic essay "Collective Behaviour," first published in 1939, sociologist Herbert Blumer labelled such spontaneous congregations *casual crowds,* whose "members come and go, giving but temporary attention to the object which has awakened the interest of the crowed, and entering into only feeble association with one another" (p. 178). Blumer also identified three other types of crowds: conventional expressive, and acting crowds. Passengers on a plane, shoppers in a store, the audience at a concert are usually *conventional crowds.* These people are gathered for a specific purpose and behave according to established norms. For example, cheering and booing are expected at a football game, but would be considered extremely bad form at a concert of classical music or at a funeral. People shout "bravo" at appropriate moments at the opera; they applaud (but do not cheer) at tennis matches. There is relatively little interaction in a conventional crowd, where members individually pursue a common goal, a destination, a bargain, entertainment.

The people at rock festivals, revival meetings, and carnivals (such as those held in New Orleans and in South American cities) are *expressive crowds:* members may behave in ways they would not consider in other settings. The focus is on individual subjective experience, on people letting go. The crowd gives license to loss of self-control, but chaos need not result. The legendary Woodstock Music and Art Fair, held in New York's Catskill Mountains in August 1969, is an example of this type of crowd. An impressive array of rock stars drew over 300,000 young people to the farm where the festival was held. Mechanically, everything went wrong: traffic was stalled for miles; food and water were scarce; sanitation facilities were inadequate. There were "bad trips" on LSD, and hardly anyone got close enough to the stage to hear the music they had come for. Woodstock became a legend because of the peaceful, cooperative way the crowd behaved under these adverse circumstances. For most, being part of the "Woodstock nation" was an exhilarating communal experience. As one young woman told a reporter, "I just had the feeling that, wow, there are so many of us, we really have power. I'd always felt like such a minority. But I thought, wow, we're a majority - it felt like that. I felt, here's the answer to anyone who calls us deviates" (in Turner and Killian, 1972, p. 148). Woodstock would not have been the same if conventional norms had been strictly observed. It would not have been so peaceful if the promoters had attempted to bar people who had not bought tickets (the majority), or if police had made arrests for drugs, which were being hawked openly like hot dogs and beer at a ball game.

An *acting crowd* is an excited volatile collection of people who are focused on a controversial event that provokes their indignation, anger and desire to act - for example, a rape or an incident of police brutality, real or imagined. The difference between an expressive crowd and an acting crowd is that the latter is angry and purposeful. The difference between an acting crowd and a conventional crowd is that the members of an acting crowd are aroused to the point where established norms carry little weight.

> [The acting crowd] has no heritage or accumulation of tradition to guide its activity; it has no conventions, established expectations, or rules. It lacks other important marks of society such as an established social organisation, an established division of labour, a structure of established roles, a recognised leadership, a set of norms, a set of moral regulations, an awareness of its own identity, or a recognised "we-consciousness". Instead of acting, then, on the basis of established rule, it acts on the basis of aroused impulse. (Blumer, in Lee, 1951, p. 180)

Box 11.1

Panic

On November 28,1942, almost 500 people died in a fire that swept through a Boston night club - largely because the crowd panicked and jammed the revolving front door, which was one of only three exits for the audience of 1,000 or more, Panics occur when people believe that the only way to deal with an imminent threat (physical or psychological) is to flee and when communication breaks down so that people in the rear of the crowd do not see (or do not believe) that escape routes are blocked, and press forward. Thus, panic results from fear, entrapment and disorganisation: people become preoccupied with their own personal safety and behave in an individualistic way that actually endangers themselves and others.

Source: Ralph H. Turner and Lewis M. Killian, *Collective Behaviour,* 2nd ed. (Englewood Cliffs, N.J.: Prentice-Hall, 1972), pp. 121-22.

In many ways, these three types overlap. For example, expressive behaviour (jumping, snouting) is conventional at sporting events, and fans may throw things at the referees, becoming what Blumer would call an acting crowd. Nevertheless, as ideal types, Blumer's categories are useful in highlighting some of the characteristics of crowds that distinguish them from other social groups.

Mobs

A *mob* is a crowd whose members are emotionally aroused and are engaged in or are ready to engage in violence (Hoult, 1969, p. 206). In short, an acting crowd is a mob. For centuries people in power have had nightmares about the masses rising up in a destructive orgy. Mob action was common in eighteenth- and nineteenth-century Europe: in towns and country, throngs of armed men and women took over markets and warehouses, demanding rollbacks in prices and sometimes appropriating goods. In England angry bands of craftsmen burned factories and destroyed the machines that threatened their livelihood. On July 14, 1789, Parisians stormed the ancient Bastille in the most famous confrontation of the French Revolution. Violent, unruly crowds have also figured importantly in American history. The nineteenth century was marked by farmers' revolts, miners' rebellions, bloody battles between unions and police, lynchings, and urban riots. The Civil War Draft Riot of 1863, which raged for four days, was probably one of the worst riots in this country's history. Mobs of young New Yorkers roamed the city's streets, burning, looting, sniping and lynching, while police stood by. Most of the violence was directed against blacks, who came to symbolise a distant war that many urban Northerners did not want to fight. This outbreak became a prototype for urban riots in the first half of this century, which are best described as interracial wars, whites fighting blacks, as police did little. The civil disorders of the 1960s, however, were different. The following account of the Detroit riot of July 1967 is based on the *Report of the National Advisory Commission on Civil Disorders* appointed by President Johnson. Although the *Report* falls short of completely explaining the disorders, it does portray the dimensions of the Detroit uprising in concrete terms. For further explanations of the 1960s riots, see Box 11.2.

Riot in Detroit - In the summer of 1967, black ghettos in twenty-three cities exploded. Many white Americans who saw Detroit burn on their television screens were not only horrified, but baffled. Why were blacks rioting *after* Congress had passed the Civil Rights Acts? "What do they want?" The answer is that Civil Rights legislation had raised hopes but delivered little in the way of concrete improvements. Blacks, particularly in large northern cities, felt they had been cheated and misled. Continuing discrimination in a society that values equality generates rebellion and resentment. Equally important, the Civil Rights and Black Power movements had placed the blame for economic and social inequality squarely on the shoulders of the white institutions that created and maintained the ghetto and on the white society that had silently condoned it for generations.

Box 11.2

Urban Riots of the 1960s: What Researchers Found

By the time the urban riots of the 1960s were over "the ghettos were in shambles and white society was in shock" (Fogelson, 1970, p. 4). How and why did it happen? In the aftermath of the riots, several sociologists sought answers to this question.

Surely there is nothing new about ghetto resentment against police insensitivity. It has been expressed openly for decades (Yablonsky, 1962). Nor is there anything new about outbreaks of public disorder (Waskow, 1966). But there was something new about the riots of the 1960s: when looting took place during this decade, it was the looting of durable, material goods - the symbols of economic plenty that have been consistently out of the reach of most ghetto dwellers. When arson took place it was directed against visible, present oppressors (mostly white merchants who sold cheap goods at high prices) and not against symbols of vague, distant oppressors. In fact, as one summary article points out, the riots were far from acausal, they were "a means of achieving desired goals when more legitimate means were unavailable or had met with failure" (Allen, 1970, p. 3).

The aftermath of the riots would certainly support the notion that they were effective means of protest. They brought results that decades of peaceful protest had failed to bring. As one observer put it:

Box 11.2 - *(Contd.)*

"Reporters and cameramen rushed into ghettos elected and appointed officials followed behind; sociologists and other scholars arrived shortly after. The President established a riot commission; so did the governors" (Fogelson, 1970, p. 146).

To explain exactly why each riot occurred exactly when it did is beyond the capabilities of social science. But we do know something about the general features of the 1960s riots. They were not instigated or carried out by criminals; they were generally directed at property, not at people; their aim was to benefit from, not overthrow, the American social system (Allen, 1970). In short, they were "spontaneous protests against unjust social conditions" (Campbell and Schuman, 1968).

In trying to locate the causes and conditions of the 1960s riots, social scientists have taken several approaches. They have looked at the actual interactions between police and rioters to see how the violence escalated (Marx, 1970). They have carefully explored the characteristics of individual rioters (Sears and McConahay, 1969; Caplan, 1970) and for the most part they have found that "rioters did not differ from non-rioters in absolute income; rioters were not the hard-core unemployed; rioters were better integrated than non-rioters into the community, socially and politically; and rioters were not recent immigrants to the city" (Allen, 1970, p. 9). A third set of explorations has been concerned with the social and economic causes for the riots (Lieberson and Silverman, 1965; Fogelson, 1970). These studies have vividly documented the deprivation, hardships and injustice to which ghetto dwellers are subjected.

The National Advisory Commission on Civil Disorders found that 70 per cent of the rioters believed they deserved better jobs and blamed their problems on racism, not on lack of training, ability, or ambition. They were proud of their race, believing blacks to be superior to whites in some respects. They mistrusted both white politics and politicians, and they were extremely hostile toward whites in general and toward middle-class blacks who accommodated themselves to white society in particular. They hated the police. But they did not have organisations through which they might realise their ambitions (such as the political machines the Irish had established when they were trying to join the mainstream of American life).

Still, crowds do not become mobs unless they develop a generalised belief about who or what is responsible for their problems (Smelser, 1962). Anger must be focused; the energies and hostility of a crowd must be directed toward a target. In the ghetto, stores that tantalise with the goods America seems to promise, and police, who harrass and sometimes abuse residents but seem unable to protect them, are ever-present reminders of white dominance. Given the high visibility of police, the widespread anger and frustration, and the feeling that there was little to lose, Detroit was a time bomb that July. All that was needed was a spark to set it off. The police provided this spark.

On Saturday night, July 22, the Detroit vice squad conducted raids on five social clubs in the 12th Street area that were suspected of running gambling tables and selling liquor after hours. This mass arrest was the precipitating incident. A month earlier a prostitute on the block had been murdered by a member of the vice squad, or so neighbours believed, but another man was arrested. At about the same time, a gang of white youths shouting "Niggers keep out of Rough Park" had killed a twenty-seven-year-old black veteran, in the presence of his pregnant wife. Newspapers had not even reported the slaying. By the time police hauled the last of the party-goers away Sunday morning, July 23, a crowd of 200 had gathered on the street. A bottle hurled from the crowd crashed through the window of the last retreating patrol car. That was the beginning.

By 8 A.M., when police first tried to clear the area, the crowd on 12th Street had gown to 3,000. Outnumbered, police withdrew, trying only to keep the crowd within a six-block-square area. Emboldened by the police retreat, groups of two and three began breaking into liquor, appliance and grocery stores. Others followed, and for a few hours the street became a carnival. People were laughing, joking and generally enjoying themselves. When a black congressman tried to speak, he was met by hecklers: "Whose side are you on, man?" At about noon police reinforcements moved quietly into surrounding streets. Soon rumours were spreading: a black man, it was said, had been bayonetted just blocks away.

The crowd's mood shifted from revelry to anger; people began stoning police and setting fire to stores. Finally, at 4.30 Sunday afternoon, exhausted firemen abandoned the area. At this point, Mayor Cavanaugh proclaimed a 9 P.M. to 5 A.M. curfew and summoned the National Guard.

Although 800 state police and 1,200 National Guardsmen had moved into the neighbourhood by 2 A.M. Monday morning, July 24, scattered looting and fire bombing continued. At noon President Johnson authorised sending in federal troops. The number of soldiers in Detroit climbed to 5,000 by midnight. Many had travelled over 200 miles and gone without sleep for thirty hours; relatively few had been trained to handle riots. After hasty, on-the-spot instruction in mob control, troops were deployed in small groups. What they found, however, was dark, empty streets - not mobs.

As the number of fires and lootings declined, reports of snipers increased (reaching a peak of 534 reports on Wednesday, July 26), creating panic and confusion. Indeed, communication was so poor that an army officer's order for all troops to unload their weapons went unnoticed. The following incident was typical.

> A radio report of snipers brought several patrols of guardsmen and police to a dark intersection. In the confusion, a soldier accidentally fired his gun. Within seconds everyone rushed for cover. An officer yelled, "What's happening?" "Snipers." Without authorisation someone began firing at a building; a nearby tank drove in and sprayed the building with 50-caliber tracer bullets. When police finally searched the building, they found it empty.

By Wednesday police were breaking into homes on the slightest excuse and arresting anyone found to have a weapon. Although it would be exaggerating to say the police rioted in Detroit, they were not acting in a routine manner. There is nothing routine about a riot; both the rioters and the police were caught up in collective behaviour.

Before the end of the week, 7,200 people had been arrested. Some were held on buses for thirty hours or more; others spent days in an underground garage without toilets. Forty-three people had been killed, thirty or more by police and soldiers, two by store owners, two or possibly three by rioters. This number included on National Guardsman, one fireman, and one policeman (killed accidentally by a fellow officer). Thirty-three of the victims were black, ten white. Property damage was estimated at $ 22 million.

Explanations of Crowd Behaviour

Why did rioting break out in Detroit? Like many people, President Johnson believed in the "riff-raff theory"- that only criminal types (hoodlums, drifters, bums, drug addicts) would participate in riots. He and others suspected that a hard core of agitators had incited violence in Detroit and other cities, and that the vast majority of ghetto dwellers strongly disapproved. The Kerner Commission disproved this and other myths. The average rioter was better educated, better informed, and more involved in the community than the nonrioter, and he had a job (albeit one he thought beneath him). Nearly 40 per cent of ghetto residents in Detroit either participated in the riot or identified themselves as bystanders - hardly a deviant minority. The commission thus confirmed what sociologists have long believed: that the crowd itself generates a collective excitement that influences people's behaviour. There are several theories explaining how this comes about.

Emotional and Social Contagion - In a now classic work published in 1895 *(The Psychology of Crowds),* French sociologist Gustave Le Bon argued that the transformation of individuals into a crowd "puts them in possession of a collective mind" that makes people think, feel and act quite differently than they would if they were alone. Crowds give people a sense of invincible power: they "will undertake the accomplishment of certain acts with irresistible impetuosity," wrote Le Bon. The crowd gains control over the individual much as the hypnotist gains control over this subjects: individuals become highly suggestible; they are no longer conscious of their actions. Waves of emotion sweep through the crowd, infecting one person after another as though excitement were actually contagious. The thin veneer of civilisation falls away, allowing unconscious motivations and antisocial impulses to rise to the surface. "The age we are about to enter," Le Bon wrote, "will be in truth the *era of crowds*." He meant this as a warning.

Clearly, Le Bon believed an untamed, destructive creature lurked behind the social masks people ordinarily present to one another. Although his distaste for "the masses" is obvious, there is some truth of Le Bon's theory. The anonymity of a crowd does weaken conventional norms, by shifting moral responsibility from the individual to the group. And a large number of excited people in close proximity does create the impression of unanimity and "invincible power". Moreover, emotions and behaviour do seem to spread through crowds, as if they were contagious.

In his essay on collective behaviour, Herbert Blumer (1951) refined Le Bon's ideas. He traced contagion to an "exciting event" that creates unrest in a crowd. People begin milling about, "as if seeking to find or avoid something, but without knowing what it is they are trying to find or avoid." As people search for clues, excited behaviour or rhetoric catches their attention. Instead of interpreting and judging these actions, as they ordinarily would, people respond immediately and directly. Their reactions reinforce the original actors, making them still more excited (what Blumer calls the *circular reaction).* As excitement builds, people become more and more inclined to give immediate expression to their feelings, to act on impulse. This, in Blumer's view, explains "the relatively rapid, unwitting and nonrational dissemination of a mood, impulse or form of conduct" through a crowd. Like Le Bon, then, Blumer emphasises the irrational nature of collective behaviour and implies that people are not quite themselves in crowds.

Norms and Crowd Behaviour - More recently sociologists have questioned the idea that people behave in an unreflecting, irrational way in crowds (Turner and Killian, 1972). Wasn't looting a rational solution for ghetto residents who felt entitled to goods they could not afford and who saw the police caught momentarily off-guard? Weren't lynch mobs an effective method for keeping blacks in a subordinate position in the deep South? This does not suggest that these methods are desirable, but simply that the people who used them found them effective. Turner and Killian also question the implicit assumption that social pressure fails to operate in a crowd. Isn't it possible that crowd members act in deviant or unusual ways precisely because everyone around them is acting that way, and they feel pressured to join in? Moreover, if crowds influence the way people act, as both Le Bon and Blumer believed, individualistic, psychological explanations of crowd behaviour are incomplete at best.

The transformation of a crowd of bystanders (a casual crowd) into a mob (an acting crowd) can be explained by the development of new norms (this is called the *emergent norm theory).* In ambiguous, undefined situations, one or more "innovators" suggest a course of action - either verbally or by taking direct action (for example, throwing a bottle). Others follow. The crowd begins to define the situation, to develop a justification for acts that at first seemed questionable. (Thus, a radio announcer's slogan, "Burn, baby, burn" became the rallying cry in the Watts riot.) In this way a new set of norms emerges, and people who do not entirely share the crowd's mood are pressured into conformity or at least into suppressing contrary impulses.

The important point here is that crowds are neither normless nor totally lacking in organisation. In the riots of the 1960s, stores owned by blacks were usually spared, and violence was directed at property, not people. (Nearly all those who died in Detroit were killed by police or in accidents.) Nor are riots, panics, mass hysteria, and other types of collective behaviour accidental, unexplainable outbreaks. In Blumer's words, collective behaviour occurs when "impulses, desires, dispositions cannot be satisfied by existing forms of living."

SOCIAL MOVEMENTS

A *social movement* is an ongoing, collective effort to promote or resist social change. Social movements are more organised than crowds, and they are focused: goals, justifications and tactics are more clearly articulated. Like other forms of collective behaviour, social movements may also grow out of "structural conduciveness" and/or frustrated social concerns. Although they may include a number of formal organisations, as the Women's Liberation Movement does, for example, they are not as structured as political parties or interest groups. Their membership is shifting and indefinite; their leadership is determined more by popular acclaim than by formal procedures and is more symbolic than actual. (Martin Luther King, Jr., for example, never *controlled* the freedom marchers; rather, he inspired them.) In addition, movements use tactics that place them outside conventional channels of social action -marches and sit-ins, for example (Turner and Killian, 1972, pp. 246-47). The following passage describes the feelings of those who marched in 1965 with Martin Luther King, Jr., from Selma, Alabama, to the state capital:

> [T]he scene in Selma had been filmed on television and had been played again and again on the home screen in millions of living rooms.... Soon, from all over America, thousands of sympathisers, black and white, were bound for Selma - nuns, newsmen, debutantes, psychiatrists, banjo players, Senators' wives, stock clerks, sculptors, social workers - and for most of a month they lived in Selma's Negro quarter, shared the Negro's food and misery, sang his songs, and scorned his oppressors; helped inspire a new guilt, a new social conscience, a new voting bill in America; helped to instil in many illiterate and uninspired Negroes throughout the land a strange new hope that after Martin Luther King's marchers had crossed the little bridge and completed the fifty-mile journey down the road to the state capital, everything would somehow get better a kind of miracle would occur; it would be like Lourdes and the faithful might toss away their crutches. (Talese, 1970, p. 175)

In a word, social movements are crusades - crusades that inspire in people a new conception of themselves, or their rights and privileges, of the world they live in, and of a world they envision.

Women's Liberation: A History and an Explanation

Feminism, which gained strength as a social movement in the early 1970s, has a long and often overlooked history. As early as 1792 an English reminist named Mary Wollstonecraft was protesting women's frivolous existence and "slavish obedience" to men. She offered men "rational fellowship" and demanded legal rights and educational opportunities for women. In this country women not only fought for suffrage, but were in the front ranks of the abolitionist, labour and temperance movements in the late nineteenth and early twentieth centuries (Firestone, 1973). In the 1940s and 1950s, however, women as a group were silent about feminist issues - with the notable exception of Simone de Beauvoir, who explored history, biology, literature and philosophy to find why women were regarded as the second sex (the title of her book, published in 1953). Then in 1963, Betty Friedan's *The Feminine Mystique* was published, a book that helped to launch a decade of change in America. The private grievances of women whose careers had been thwarted, of isolated suburban matrons, of abandoned mothers with no means of supporting themselves or their children became a public outcry.

Three social forces contributed to the rise of the Women's Liberation Movement. First, the Civil Rights Movement stimulated protest in a wide variety of groups and provided a model for activism. Second, a growing number of women (including mothers and other married women) had begun participating in the labour force, some but not all out of necessity. Finally, dutiful suburban wives and mothers were finding their nest empty by mid-life. They had nothing substantial or socially useful to do (Dixon, in Adams and Briscoe, 1971, pp. 419 - 33).

These changes hit educated, economically secure, middle-class women the hardest. Trained from childhood not to be self-reliant, achievement-oriented, or autonomous, and having devoted their lives to serving others, many found themselves dependent, isolated, and beset by "problems, that had no name" (Friedan, 1963, pp. 281 - 95).

> The problem lay unburied, unspoken, for many years in the minds of American women. . . . For over fifteen years there was no word of this yearning in the millions of words written about women, for women,

> in all the columns, books and articles by experts telling women their role was to seek fulfilment as wives and mothers. Over and over women heard in voice of tradition and of Freudian sophistication that they could desire no greater destiny than to glory in their own femininity. . . . They were taught to pity the neurotic, unfeminine, unhappy women who wanted to be poets or physicists or presidents, (pp. 281,284)

Women's Liberation gave a name to the problems that faced conventional women whose children, successful husbands, and suburban dream houses had not saved them from feeling superfluous.

The movement also appealed to women who were not very happy with full-time domesticity and opted for careers in fields marked "for men only," or tried to combine home and work. Although not systematically discouraged from pursuing an education, women typically ran head on into "an invisible bar" of prejudice and discrimination when they left school.

> Girls who go to women's colleges sometimes crash unexpectedly on the Invisible Bar when they look for their first jobs. Men don't have to type and take dictation to earn a chance to begin learning!... Big companies give a Princeton senior who has majored in English an aptitude test to see where he might fit, but give a Vassar senior who has majored in English a typing test. (Bird, in Adams and Briscoe, 1971, pp. 361, 379)

Both of these groups fanned the demands for new patterns of earning, marriage and divorce laws, and opportunities for living and learning.

During 1963, commissions to investigate the status of women were organised in fifty states. These commissions not only brought large numbers of politically active women into contact with one another, they created a climate of expectations. Three years later, on June 29,1966, a small group of women attending the Third National Conference of Commissions on the Status of Women met in Betty Friedan's hotel room to discuss the possibility of founding a civil rights organisation for women. They decided to call themselves the National Organisation for Women, or NCW. With Friedan as president, NCW began to attract women in the professions, labour, government and the communications industry. However, it was not until 1969, when several national news stories on Women's Liberation were issaed, that NOW's membership reached into the thousands.

From its inception, NOW has concentrated on concrete, short-range goals, such as the Equal Rights Amendment to the Constitution, the repeal of abortion laws, and day care. Despite efforts to attract poor and minority women and career housewives, most of NOW's membership consists of working, upper-middle-class white women.

A second, more radical branch of Women's Liberation began to gather momentum in the same period. By 1966 thousands of young women under thirty were deeply involved in the Student Movement. Like their male counterparts they had "lived in an atmosphere of questioning, confrontation and change" ever since entering college. The movement had taught them to think of problems of "unfreedom" as political problems. They identified with the radical community and thought of themselves at movement people. More often than not, however, they found they were relegated to such traditional and unrewarding jobs as typing and cooking. They could not, after all, burn their draft cards, and in 1966 and 1967 draft resistance was the major issue in the movement. Many women found they had little to do.

In 1967 and 1968 a few small, independent groups attempted to introduce the subject of women's rights at various political meeting and conventions. They were met with laughter and derision (Firestone, 1973). Most radical feminist groups can be traced to political incidents that enraged a small group of women who were well versed in organising and then proceeded to apply their skills to their own cause. Rejecting formal structure and leadership of any kind, the radical branch of the Women's Liberation Movement has focused on changing the entire structure of human relations - not just on opening the system to women. The "rap session" was designed to change women's identities as well as their attitudes.

Jo Freeman argues that neither branch of the Women's Liberation Movement would have materialised without the communications networks developed through the commissions on the status of women and the btuaeiir[1] Movement. Women's opportunities in this country were as limited in 1945 or 1955 as they were in 1965. "What changed was the organisational situation. It was not until a communications network developed between like-minded people beyond local boundaries that the movement could emerge and develop past the point of occasional, spontaneous uprising" (1973, p. 804).

Box 11.3

The Student Movement: From the 1960s to the 1970s

From its inception as the Berkeley Free Speech Movement in 1964, the Student Movement grew through the 1960s to embrace a wide range of causes and styles - from demands for student representation on university councils to calls for world revolution, from the politics of confrontation to the "politics of experience" (including "be-ins," drug use, dropping out). But by 1974 campus radicalism had declined to the point where observers were suggesting that 1950s conservatism had returned to the campus. What had happened to the Student Movement?

Daniel Yankelovich attributes the present calm on campuses to the end of both the war in Vietnam and the draft, which had caused widespread disillusionment among young people with American society as a whole.

By 1974 concern over political morality had replaced anger over the war in Vietnam (Gallup, January, March 1974) - a concern students shared with other generations. Although rarely used, institutionalised procedures for unseating corrupt public officials do exist, and by 1973-1974 it was clear that the machinery for impeachment proceedings would be set into motion. As we have suggested, collective behaviour occurs when channels for expressing concern either do not exist or are blocked. This was not the case in 1974.

In some areas Yankelovich found moderate reversals in student attitudes. In 1973, 40 per cent of the college students polled thought most Americans shared their values, compared to 30 per cent in 1971; 60 per cent "anticipated no great difficulty in accepting the kind of life society had to offer," compared to 49 per cent just two years earlier; 66 per cent believed violence is morally wrong, even for a good cause,

Box 11.3 - *(Contd.)*

which was an increase of 10 per cent; and 66 per cent were "careerminded". Yankelovich concludes,

> We can now see, in retrospect, that both the generation gap and the campus radicalism of the 1960s were transitory phenomena. The radicalism was closely tied to the Vietnam War. And what seemed to be a generation gap was actually the leading edge of a new morality and quest for new self-fulfilling life styles that have now spilled over from the campus to influence all of American youth - and many of their parents as well.

In short, the Student Movement declined as the gap between its goals and those of the larger society began to narrow.

Source: Yaakelovich Youth Study © 1974 by the JDR 3rd Fund.

Equally important was the general ideological climate. The sixties was a period of turmoil and change, with numerous groups organising and demanding a hearing. The idea of a Women's Movement fit easily into already established patterns of thinking. Had the first groups of women who attempted to ride the Civil Rights bandwagon into legal equality been accommodated, however, the *idea* of a movement might never have been translated into *action*. Finally, the commissions and the Student Movement gave women experience in organising on a grass roots level. As Freeman indicates, "social movements do not simply occur"; they must be constructed (1973, p. 804).

To summarise, this example illustrates the origins and development of social movements. Structurally, they begin when people find that existing institutions are not answering a need. If enough people don't feel this need, the movement does not take hold. For a movement to become permanent it most continue to play a meaningful role in the lives to its members. Some movements, such as the temperance movement are short lived. Others, such as the Mormon religion and Christianity become institutionalised. Movements that succeed, for example, the Civil Rights Movement, leave a legacy of lasting social change.

COMMUNICATION AND COLLECTIVE BEHAVIOUR RUMOURS, PUBLIC OPINION AND PERSUASION

The invention of mass media must also be counted among the great revolutions of modern times and one that relates to the subject of this chapter. Newspapers (which became available in the nineteenth century), radio and television have created new forms of collective behaviour. When millions of people are frightened or angered by the same broadcast, they act very much like people in a crowd who have been ignited by an incident or speech. Even though each is in his or her own home, they are reacting to a common stimulus. And they carry their excitement to friends, relatives, and neighbours, setting off the circular reaction Blumer observed in crowds.

This was clearly what happened when Orson Welles's Mercury Theater broadcast *War of the Worlds* on October 30, 1938. The play began innocuously enough with a programme of music from New York's Park Plaza Hotel. Suddenly the music was interrupted for a bulletin about atmospheric disturbances. The radio station then took listeners to a laboratory in Princeton, New Jersey, for an interview with Professor Pierson, who assured the announcer that these disturbances could not possibly be the early stages of an invasion from Mars. The programme returned to the Park Plaze. Bulletins continued to interrupt the music, however and finally the station arranged for an eyewitness : eport of a strange meteorite.

> [ANNOUNCER ONE:] just a minute! Something's happening! Ladies and gentlemen, this is terrified. This end of the thing is beginning to flake off! The top is beginning to rotate like a screw! The thing must be hollow!
>
> [Murmuring from the crowd; the clanking sound of falling metal; shouts] Good heavens, something's wriggling out of the shadow like a grey snake. Now it's another one, and another. They look like tentacles to me. There, I can see the things body. It's large as a bear and it glistens like wet leather. But that face. It... it's indescribable. I can hardly force myself to keep looking at it. The eyes are black and gleam like a serpent. The mouth is V-shaped with saliva dropping from its rimless lips that seem to quiver and pulsate.... The crowd

> falls back. They've seen enough. This is the most extraordinary experience. I can't find words. . .. I'm pulling this microphone with me as fast as I talk. . . .
>
> [There is an interruption, cut back to the studio, then the broadcast from the farm continues, accompanied by shrieks and strange humming sounds.] A humped shape is rising out of the pit. I can make out a small beam of light against a mirror. What's that? There's a jet of flame springing from the mirror, and it leaps right at the advancing men.... Good Lord, they're turning into flame! Now the whole field's caught fire....
>
> [ANNOUNCER TWO:] Ladies and gentlemen, due to circumstances beyond our control, we are unable to continue the broadcast from Grovers Mill. Evidently there's some difficulty with our field transmission (quoted in Cantril, Gaudet and Herzog, 1947, pp. 15 -18). [The secretary of the interior begins advising listeners to put their faith in God.]

Of the 6 million or more people who listened to this broadcast, an estimated 1 million panicked. Telephone lines were jammed with calls to warn relatives and friends and to bid-loved ones farewell. Terrified parents bundled children into blankets and rushed to the streets for help; grown men and women hid in their cellars; excited crowds gathered in bars and other public places. Some people started driving, without much idea of where they were going, but they had to do *something*. Others remained glued to their radios in tears and prayer. After a few hours the confusion died down, but newspapers continued to print stories about the night of panic for a full week (Cantril, Gaudet and Herzog, 1947, pp. 47-55).

Some of this reaction can be attributed to the skill of the dramatist. All that fall regular radio programmes had been interrupted for bulletins concerning growing tensions in Europe. Listeners had begun to rely on their radios for news; they had learned to expect interruptions. *War of the Worlds* played on this familiar experience. At first both Professor Pierson and Announcer Phillips debunked reports of an invasion from Mars, giving expression to listeners' disbelief, sharing their incredulity and bewilderment. Once this rapport was established, however, the pace of bizarre happenings accelerated. "Ladies and gentlemen, *incredible as it may seem* ..." The use of "expert testimony" - the scientists, military officers, the secretary of the interior - gave credibility to increasingly terrifying descriptions. And although all of these characters were fictitious, the towns and highways mentioned were well known - particularly to the New Jersey-New York audience. How could so many people believe, however briefly, that slimy, luminous Martians were climbing out of a spaceship on a New Jersey farm? The study of rumours provides important clues.

Rumours

A *rumour* is an unverified story that circulates from person to person, most often by word of mouth, and is accepted as fact, although its sources may be vague or unknown. Rumours proliferate in tense and ambiguous situations, when people are unable to learn the facts or, for one reason or another, when they distrust the information they receive. When the Japanese bombed Pearl Harbour, for example, many Americans believed our entire fleet had been wiped out. There were rumours that the Japanese had occupied Hawaii. President Roosevelt's radio broadcast only partially dispelled these stories. Nearly half of the college students interviewed shortly afterward were convinced the president was covering up the true facts (Allport and Postman, 1947). Similarly, when President Kennedy was shot in Dallas hundreds of unconfirmed stories began to circulate by word of mouth: Vice-President Johnson had had a heart attack; eyewitnesses had seen more than one person in the book depository; Oswald was connected to the FBI, CIA, or a communist plot; Dallas police had paid Jack Ruby to silence Oswald.

A rumour may begin as an accurate report but become distorted and exaggerated in the process of transmission. After studying rumour transmission in the laboratory and in the field, Allport and Postman (1947) discovered a basic pattern. A person hears a story that strikes him as interesting. He repeats the story - that is, what he remembers - to a friend. This person talks to others: "Did you hear . . .?"

Gradually, the original story is reduced to a few essential details that are easy to tell. This is what Allport and Postman mean by *levelling:* "As a rumour travels, it tends to grow shorter, more concise, more easily grasped and told. In successive versions, fewer words are used and fewer details are mentioned" (p. *75).*

As a result of levelling, certain details gain in importance, and the rumour is *sharpened* - people remember and pass on only part of the original story. And, as a rumour circulates people tend to "correct" details so that the story seems more plausible and coherent. Thus, in a laboratory experiment on rumour transmission, subjects confused by a story of an ambulance carrying explosives changed explosives to medical supplies, which seemed more likely; in another rumour, a razor in a white man's hand moved (in the telling) to a black man's hand. Allport and Postman call this unconscious correcting of details *assimilation.* "... [w]e find assimilation in terms of deep-lying occupational needs. The rumour [in the lab] tends to fit into, and support, the occupational interests, class or racial memberships, or personal prejudices of the reporter" (p. 115). For example, during the riot in Detroit, residents believed reports of police brutality because they had come to expect the police to be brutal; police and Guardsmen believed rumours about snipers because they expected sniping during a riot. In short, rumours tend to confirm people's assumptions.

Rumours usually arise when people are anxious, when they feel something is wrong but are unable to focus or explain their tension. By exaggerating the destruction at Pearl Harbour, people justified the anxiety they felt, to themselves and others; by linking Lee Harvey Oswald to a communist conspiracy, they temporarily warded off the uncomfortable thought that a single person could penetrate the Secret Service guard and assassinate a president. Rumours "explained" the unthinkable. In confusing times any answer may seem better than no answer, and people are inclined to accept reports that confirm their suspicion. Rumours are a form of collective behaviour in that they are set off by precipitating incidents;

draw on a readiness for certain ideas and on communications networks; give problems a name and a reason; and draw people together around a common concern belief, or crisis.

Public Opinion

A *public* is a scattered group of people who share a common interest, concern, or focus of attention. (The Mercury Theater audience, environmentalists, and college students are all publics.) One of the effects of mass media is the creation and maintenance of publics. The formation of publics is greatly aided by the mass media because they can give frequent national exposure to an issue, product team, or politician. The media also influences the ebb and flow of *public opinion* - that is the prevailing interests (what people define as an issue), attitudes (predispositions to react positively or negatively toward certain people, groups, or events), and opinions (specific judgments of specific issues) of a public. Obviously, there have always been publics, and publics have always had opinions. But modern polling techniques have made it possible to collect these opinions, to bring the views of scattered individuals together into a new form of collective behaviour more powerful than a crowd or protest. For a shouting crowd may not represent general opinion, but a poll does. A simple table reflecting widespread opinion that the president should be impeached speaks louder than a demonstration in Washington.

When studying public opinion, the distinction between values, which tend to be stable, and opinions, which change more rapidly, is important. A comparison of the attitudes of Vietnam veterans about war in general and the Vietnam War in particular illustrates this point (Yankelovich, 1974). One out of four Vietnam veterans believes we lost that war, compared to one out of eleven among non-college youth as a whole, and only 7 per cent of veterans believe the war ended with honour (compared to 13 per cent overall). Yet 68 per cent of veterans believe we should go to war to counteract aggression (compared to 55 per cent overall), 54 per cent to contain communism (compared to 48 per cent overall), and 59 per cent to protect American allies (compared to 45 per cent overall). The fact that many veterans have negative opinions about the Vietnam War in particular has not changed their basic values about fighting wars in general.

Public opinion can fluctuate widely over a short time. In the fall of 1938, for example, most Americans did not believe war would break out in Europe. The public was evenly divided on the question of whether to sell war materials to Britain and France, the major issue at that time. Two weeks after war broke out, nearly half the American public favoured declaring war on Germany if Britain and France were defeated, but most considered this a remote possibility. When France fell in the spring of 1940, public attention shifted to our own defenses. The majority of Americans believed we should stay out of the war, not use our own ships to send food to Britain, and establish friendly relations with Germany if Britain fell. By that fall, however, neutrality was no longer an issue. Britain had shown she could fight back, and most Americans wanted to lend her food, money and planes. Polls conducted in the spring of 1941 indicated that two-thirds of the American public were committed to defeating Nazi Germany. More than 80 per cent believed we would eventually enter the war and that we could defeat both Germany and Japan. By the end of 1941 the question on most people's minds was not *if* we would enter the war, but *when* (Cantril in Turner and Killian, 1972, pp. 183 - 92).

One of the most dramatic shifts in public opinion in recent years was the swing from support to distrust of President Nixon by the American public. In January 1973, 68 per cent of the adults polled approved of the way Nixon was handling his job as president. By March 1974, after the Watergate revelations, only 25 per cent approved of the president's performance. Commenting on this rapid shift in public opinion, George Gallup remarked that Nixon's "approval rating has dropped faster, more precipitous[ly] than any one of the Presidents in [the last four decades]. The approval rating is really a confidence rating, and Nixon's clearly lost the confidence of the American people."

The Media and Public Opinion - The media not only report news, they *make* news. Not the Civil Rights Movement, the Student Movement, nor the Women's Liberation Movement would have had much impact on American society if journalists had not decided they were worth reporting. "News, if unreported, has no impact. It might as well have not happened at all. Thus, the journalist is the important ally of the ambitious, he is a lamplighter for stars... [E]ach day, unhaunted by history, plugged into the *instant,* journalists of every creed, quality and quirk report the news of the world as they see it, believe it, understand it. Then much of it is relayed through America, millions of words a minute" (Talese, 1970, pp. 1-2). In choosing to report and headline some stories instead of others, newspaper publishers and television news editors affect the flow of information.

In addition, the media carry considerable prestige: people tend to believe what they read in the papers or see on the evening news (Jarrell, 1961). This legitimating power of the media makes it hard to distinguish news from propaganda. For example, during the 1960s films on Vietnam from communist news sources were called "propaganda" by the network newscaster who emphasised how low-angle shots and other filming techniques were used to create a certain impression. However, when the networks used Pentagon-made films with the same techniques and using selected footage, they were treated as factual news, and their source was not given (Cirino, 1971, pp. 180-81).

But how much do the media influence opinion? To the extent that they are the only source of information, their influence is bound to be considerable. When researchers try to *change* people's opinions, however, the picture becomes more complex. Summarising the research on opinion change, Raymond Bauer states, "The audience selects what it will attend to. Since people generally listen to and read things they are interested in, these usually are topics on which they have a good deal of information and fixed opinion. Hence, the very people most likely to attend to a message are those most difficult to change; those who can be converted do not look or listen" (Bauer, in Wells, 1972, p. 235).

Moreover, the media work through the social networks that characterise everyday life. Studies by Elihu Katz and Paul F. Lazarsfeld (1955) indicate that mass media influence people *if* their social background predisposes them to accept a report as fact and a particular course of action as legitimate; *if* one viewpoint or another is associated with groups they consider significant (their reference groups); and *if* individuals whose opinion they respect (that is, opinion leaders) call their attention to the issue. Thus, social background, reference groups, and interpersonal influence seem to be the deciding factors in the creation of issues and formation of opinions. The media serve to amplify existing trends.

Polling and Public Opinion - In the last two decades public-opinion polling has become an industry in its own right. Political candidates depend on polls; so do business, labour, and a wide variety of lobbies and special interest groups (Roll and Cantril, 1972, p. 13). Gallup and other established pollsters regularly assess the American public's attitudes political views and behaviour. Hardly a week goes by without a report on public opinion appearing in the press.

These methods apply to measuring public opinion as well as to sociological research in other areas. But opinion polling is especially problematic. Suppose, for example, a pollster asks a person, "Do you trust the president?" and the respondent answers "No". This seems straightforward, but what does the answer really mean? Perhaps the person distrusts *all* politicians, not just the current president. Perhaps he or she voted for the president and is particularly bitter about his actions. Or suppose a pollster finds that a respondent thinks that the best way to stop crime is to increase the number of police. But is the respondent willing to pay higher taxes for this? To be valid, a poll should ask several questions to make interpretation more reliable.

Measuring the *strength* of an answer is also crucial in opinion polling since most people will try to answer questions, if only to be polite. Do respondents understand the question? A pollster may find that people answer "yes" when asked whether the president should be impeached, but "no" when asked if they think he should be indicted by the House and tried in the Senate. Finally, opinion pollsters must be wary of conventional responses. Few Americans would say they oppose free speech, but many think Communists, Nazis, black militants, and student radicals should be prevented from expressing their views openly. In short, a "poll is only as good as the question it asks" (Roll and Cantril, 1972, p. 103).

Manipulating Public Opinion

Lincoln once said, "You may fool all of the people some of the time, and some of the people all of the time, but you cannot fool all of the people all of the time." The wisdom of this oft-quoted epigram has not prevented many people from trying. Franklin D. Roosevelt, for example, supported American involvement in the war in Europe as early as 1938. He drew public opinion to his side by susceptitiously using American boats to send supplies to Europe. When these boats were attacked, the public began to get very emotional about protecting our men and property, and attitudes toward the war shifted. There are essentially two ways to "fool the people": by restricting the flow of information through censorship, or by presenting information in a way that is calculated to gain uncritical acceptance of a partisan point of view, that is, through propaganda and public relations.

Censorship - *Censorship* is the restriction of information from reaching its audience. Censorship is essentially a device for preventing collective behaviour that might foster social change. Popular American wisdom implies that censorship is something that foreign (especially communist) governments employ, but not our own. The fact that all governments, including our own, practice censorship is rarely mentioned.

During the early 1970s, however, two instances of government censorship in this country attracted the public's attention. In June 1971 the government went to court to prevent *The New York Times* and *The Washington Post* from publishing the Pentagon Papers, a secret 7,000-page report on the origins of the war in Vietnam, prepared within the Pentagon and leaked by Daniel Ellsberg. On July 1,1971, the

Supreme Court decided in favour of the publishers, but it was not the landmark decision journalists had hoped for. The decision was split (six to three), and three justices rejected the government's suit only because they did not feel it had proved that publication of the Pentagon Papers was a threat to national security. The government's right to censor the press was neither approved nor rejected. Public opinion on this issue was divided (see Table 11.1). Forty-one per cent of the people Louis Harris polled in August 1971 felt the newspapers had been "more right" than the government in this instance, and they supported the Supreme Court decision by nearly two to one. But although 54 per cent felt it was time the American public was told the truth about the war, and 47 per cent believed we would not learn the truth if newspapers

Table 11.1
Public Opinion and the Pentagon Papers

	More Nearly Right : Newspapers or Government?		
	News-papers Per cent	*Government Per cent*	*Not sure Per cent*
Nationwide	41	35	24
East	46	30	24
Midwest	46	34	20
Border States	29	41	30
Deep South	30	37	33
West	43	36	21
8th grade educated	34	31	35
High school	37	36	27
College	52	33	15

A cross section of 1,493 households was asked between July 10 and 16, the week after the Supreme Court decision [allowing newspapers to publish the Pentagon Papers]: "From what you know about the information in the Pentagon Papers published by newspapers and the government's attempt to stop its publication, who would you say was more nearly right - the newspapers which printed the secret documents about the war or the federal government which said printing such materials was harmful to the national interest?"

Source: Harris Poll, August 12,1971.

had to get permission to print inside information, 70 per cent agreed that "if there is any doubt about violating the national security in publishing documents such as the Pentagon Papers on Vietnam, then the documents should not be published" (Harris Poll, August 12,1971).

A second incident of censorship came to light in July 1973, when an Air Force major told a Senate committee that the government had conducted over 3,000 secret bombing missions into Cambodia and falsified reports to cover this up. At the time the government claimed publicly that it recognised Cambodia's neutrality and that we were "winding down" the war. Security around these missions was so tight that the secretary of the Air Force did not even know about the raids. In this case the government was clearly withholding information in order to maintain its peace-making image in the eyes of the American public and the world community. In other words, the government was manipulating public opinion.

Propaganda and Public Relations - Censorship is a way of manipulating collective behaviour; *propaganda* and *public relations* are methods for inspiring certain kinds of collective behaviour, such as voting for a particular candidate, buying bigger cars, demonstrating for or against a piece of legislation. Propaganda appeals mainly to people's emotions and prejudices, not to their critical abilities. This is the main difference between propaganda and simple persuasion through rational arguments. Name calling, the invocation of authorities ("Doctors recommend . . .") and sacred values, appeals to fear, and shows of strength (the bandwagon effect) are some of the more obvious tools of propaganda (Lee and Lee, 1939).

Adolf Hitler was a genius at mass propaganda. His rhetoric and symbols (the swastika, Nazi uniforms and salute), his storm troopers, who "protected" Nazi rallies and broke up opposition gatherings, all created the impression among followers that they belonged to an irresistible movement. Once in office Hitler created a superagency for "public enlightenment" that controlled the press, the arts, and education (Holborn, 1969, pp. 719; 738-39).

Political propaganda is also used widely in this country. Every election year political candidates are packaged by mass-persuasion experts and sold with posters, buttons, straw hats, television spots, articles planted in popular magazines, and "news items" about the candidate which reporters use because the story has already been written for them. During the 1968 presidential campaign, for example, Fred La Rue used music to advertise Richard Nixon in the South. It was, in his words, "a special ballad-type song in the current 'country and western' music style, by which nationally famous artists will 'sing' the message via the radio and television. The multi-stanza ballad will allow issues to be included or excluded *as the local situation indicates*" (italics added; McGinniss, 1969, pp. 120-21). The Republicans were not alone, of course, in using public relations techniques. McGovern's people wooed popular country singer Johnny Cash throughout the 1972 campaign and used television spots to project an image of their candidate.

Closely linked to propaganda is public relations, another means of manipulating public opinion. *Public relations* is a form of indirect advertising - including press releases (*The New York Times* receives some *5,000* press releases weekly from the business community); "briefings" for businesspeople, community leaders, and politicians; "junkets" (all-expenses-paid trips); gifts; and entertainment. The main purpose of public relations is to present a favourable image of the client to the public.

In 1974 Americans learned how public relations techniques had been used in the White House. Edited transcripts of eight presidential conversations with high-ranking aides, released in April 1974, include repeated references to public relations maneouvers as the White House staff struggled with a flood of damaging news reports about Watergate, campaign donations, and the like. "I can give a show - we can sell them, just like we were selling Wheaties on our position," White House lawyer John Dean told Richard Nixon. During a discussion of how to handle the Senate Watergate hearings, Dean warned the president against allowing White House staff members to testify. Nixon replied "Oh, no, no, no! I didn't mean to have everyone go up and testify. . . I mean put the story out, public relations people, here is the story, the true story about Watergate." Indeed, the very act of releasing edited transcripts of the tapes was, in part, a public relations tactic. Hopefully the public would conclude that if the president voluntarily made the transcripts public, he must be innocent. To be safe the White House issued an interpretation hours before it released the actual transcripts and gave newscasters little time to read the 1,300-odd pages before the evening news. (Excepts from the tapes, comparing public statements with private conversations, appear in the Box 11.4).

Box 11.4

In the News

Public Relations and Private Conversations: The White House Transcripts

In April 1974 President Nixon made public transcripts of conversations he had had with several of his closest White House aides. The transcripts were edited before Nixon made them public.

One of the most damaging revelations in the transcripts was that the president and his aides seemed to regard the "Watergate mess" as a tactical rather than a moral or substantive problem. The edited transcripts are sprinkled with discussions of how "to cut our losses"; considerations of different "scenarios"; talk of "How will it play in Peoria?" The transcripts exposed President Nixon as having been involved in planning a public relations campaign to "keep the cap on the bottle". In many cases the president's private conversations did not substantiate his public statements. Below, is a portion of the edited White House transcript of a meeting between President Nixon and his lawyer, John Dean. Above the excerpt is what the president told the public the night he released the transcripts.

Did the President Sanction the Payment of Hush Money and an Offer of Clemency to Hunt and his Coconspirators?

Public Statement

PRESIDENT NIXON: I then said that to pay clemency was wrong. In fact, I think I can quote it directly. I said: "It is wrong. That's for sure." .. . Now when individuals read the entire transcript of the

Box 11.4 - *(Contd.)*

21st meeting, or hear the entire tape where we discussed all these options, they may reach different interpretations. But I know what I meant, and I know also what I did.

Transcript

[From the meeting on March 21,1973]

PRESIDENT NIXON: How much money do you need?

DEAN: I would say these people are going to cost a million dollars over the next two years.

PRESIDENT NIXON: We could get that. On the money, if you need the money, you could get that. You could get a million dollars. You could get it in cash. I know where it could be gotten. It is not easy, but it could be done.

[President Nixon returned to this subject several times during the meeting]

PRESIDENT NIXON: Just looking at the immediate problem, don't you think you have to handle Hunt's financial situation damn soon?

DEAN: I am not sure that you'll be able to deliver on the clemency. It may be just too hot.

PRESIDENT NIXON: You can't do it politically until after the '74 elections. That's for sure. Your point is that even then you couldn't doit.

DEAN: That's right. It may further involve you in a way you should not be involved in this.

PRESIDENT NIXON: No. It is wrong. That's for sure. [That night, $ 75,000 in cash was delivered to Hunt's lawyer.]

One of the most fascinating public relations and advertising campaigns in recent years began during the oil crisis in 1973. For years the oil companies had done everything possible to sell more gasoline. They and the car manufacturers had made the automobile a symbol of personal freedom and power. By issuing credit cards, the major oil companies made it possible for their customers to cruise across the country without spending a dollar in cash. Statistics showed that people were driving millions of miles more every year. Then, in a sudden reversal, Mobil issued a public relations ad that said "Take the bus." The oil companies began attacking the American habit of driving alone in big, gasoline-guzzling V-8's (the bigger the better). They also attempted to persuade the public that the companies were not responsible for the impending oil crisis.

AMOCO, one of the nation's largest oil companies, outlined its arguments as follows. The crisis was due to unseasonably cold weather (which increased the demand for heating fuel), unexpectedly high demands for gasoline during the summer months, and an unusual number of operating problems. A 40 per cent decrease in drilling over the last decade left the industry unprepared for rising demands. ("Investors have found surer, more profitable investments than risking their money by drilling holes in the ground," the company claimed.) Pressure from environmentalists made the shortage even more severe: "Environmental Protection Agency regulations [that] prevent the burning of high-sulfur coal in most large metropolitan areas. . . . [are] the largest single cause of the tremendous surge in demand for petroleum in the nation" (AMOCO background memorandum, December 15,1972).

AMOCO's public relations office then translated these arguments into a campaign. First, they would explain the crisis to employees and outline steps to conserve energy within their plants, so that employees could intelligently respond to comments by their neighbours, friends and customers. A few ceremonies, such as dimming the AMOCO Torch and Oval sign, were planned. Advertising mats and tips on handling customers would be sent to the company's retailers. Second, every effort would be made to place spokesmen on television talk shows and to contact journalists and weathermen who might advise the public on the energy crisis. News releases would be issued "to keep before the public the fact that American Oil is working to fuel the nation." Regional vice presidents would visit governors and local leaders to brief them on the situation. Finally, they would "draft suggested form letters for use by the staffs of Congressmen to reply to constituents who write for information about the energy situation."

The campaign did not work. Market research indicated that four out of five motorists believed the oil companies - not consumers or environmentalists - were responsible for fuel shortages.

In recent years many large corporations have begun to broaden their view of public relations. AMOCO, for example, has sponsored conferences on minority problems pays the salaries of minority counsellors who work with youth in the inner city, and runs a Government Action Programme designed to encourage employees to become active in politics - all of which have nothing *directly* to do with selling oil. The idea behind such activities is both to improve AMOCO's image in the communities where its offices and plants are located, and also to improve these communities (which in turn will benefit AMOCO).

Public relations techniques are not used only by politicians and corporations. Many groups advocating social change, such as civil rights organisations and groups fighting discrimination due to sex and religion, have effectively used public relations campaigns to gain public support. The aim of these campaigns is generally to present information that the public would otherwise not be aware of. Persuasion through education is their goal.

BIBLIOGRAPHY

Adams, Don, "The Monkey and the Fish: Cultural pitfalls of an educational advisor," *International Development Review,* vol. 2 (1960): 22 - 24.

Allen, Vemon L., "Toward Understanding Riots: Some Perspectives," *Journal of Social Issues,* vol. 26, no. 1 (Winter 1970): 1 -18.

Allport, Gordon W. and Leo Postman, *The Psychology of Rumor,* New York: Holt, Rinehart and Winston, 1947.

Allport, Gordon W., *The Nature of Prejudice,* Reading, Mass.: Addison-Wesley, 1954.

Andreski, Stanislav, *Social Sciences as Sorcery,* New York: St. Martin, 1973.

Arensberg, Conrad M., and Arthur H. Niehoff, *Introducing Social Change,* Chicago: Aldine, 1964.

Aries, Philippe, *Centuries of Childhood: A Social History of Family Life,* New York: Vintage, 1962.

Aramoni, Aniceto, "Machismo," *Psychology Today,* vol. 5, no. 8 (January 1972): 69 - 72.

Asch, Solomon E, "Opinions and Social Pressure," *Scientific American, vol.* 193 (Nov. 1950): 408.

Ash, Roberta, *Social Movements in America,* Chicago: Markham, 1972.

Auden, W.H., *The Age of Anxiety,* New York: Random House, 1948.

Averech, Harvey, *et al.. How Effective is Schooling?* Princeton, N.J.: Princeton University Press, 1972.

Barnes, Harvey Elmer, *An Introductory History of Sociology,* Chicago: University of Chicago Press, 1948.

Barber, Bernard, *Science and Social Order,* New York: Collier, 1962.

Bauer, Raymond A., *Social Indicators,* Cambridge, Mass: MIT Press, 1966.

Baumrind, Diana, "Effects of Authoritative Parental Control on Child Behaviour, *Child Development,* vol. 37 (1966): 887 - 907.

Balswick, Jack O. and Charles W. Peek, "The Inexpressive Male: A Tragedy of American Society," *The Family Coordinator,* vol. 20 (October 1971): 363-68.

Bardwick, Judith M. and Elizabeth Douvan, "Ambivalence: the socialisation of women," in Vivian Gornick and Barbara K. Moran, eds., *Women in Sexist Society,* New York: Basic Books, 1971.

Barzini, Luigi, *The Italians,* New York: Atheneum, 1964.

Barton, Allen H., *Communities in Disaster,* New York: Doubleday, 1969.

Bauer, Raymond, "The Obstinate Audience," *American Psychologist* (May 1964): 319-28.

Becker, Howard S., *The Outsiders,* New York: Free Press, 1963.

Becker, Howard S., "Whose side are we on?" *Journal of Social Problems,* vol. 14, no. 3 (Winter 1967), 239 - 47.

Becker, Howard S., *et at., Boys in White: Student Culture in Medical School,* New York: Brown, 1961.

Becker, Howard S., *The Outsiders: Studies in the Sociology of Deviance,* New York: Free Press, 1963.

Bettleheim, Bruno, "The Problem of Generations," in Glen A. Newkirk, ed., *Contemporary Issues,* Glenview, 111.: Scott, Foresman, 1971.

Beauvoir, Simone de, *The Second Sex,* New York: Knopf, 1953.

Bernard, Jessie, *Women and the Public Interest: An Essay on Policy and Protest,* Chicago: Aldine, Atherton, 1971.

Bird, Caroline, "The Invisible Bar," in Elsie Adams and May Louise Briscoe, eds., *Up Against the wall, Mother....* Beverly Hills: Glencoe Press, 1971.

Bird, Caroline, with Sara Welles, *Born Female,* New York: McKay, 1968.

Bird, Carolyn, "The Invisible Bar," in Elsie Adams and Mary Louise Briscoe, eds., *Up Against the Wall, Mother.. ..* Beverly Hills: Glencoe, 1971.

Blau, Peter, "Dialectical Sociology: Comments," *Sociological Inquiry* (Spring 1972): 17-22.

Blau, Peter, and Marshall W. Meyer, *Bureaucracy in Modern Society,* New York: Random House, 1971.

Blythe, Ronald, *Akenfield: Portrait of an English Village,* New York: Pantheon, 1969.

Blumer, Herbert, "Collective Behaviour," in Affred McClung Lee, ed., *New Outline of the Principles of Sociology,* New York: Barnes and Noble, 1951.

Boroson, Warren, "In Defense of Adolescents," in Glen A. Newkirk, ed., *Contemporary Issues,* Glencoe, 111.: Scott, Foresman, 1971.

Bowlby, John, *Separation: Anxiety and Anger,* New York: Basic Books, 1973.

Bon, Gustave Le, *The Crowd: A Study of the Popular Mind* (1895), New York: Viking, 1960.

Brody, Jane £., "More than 100,000 Persons a Year Are Reported Seeking Sterilisation, As a Method of Contraception," *The New York Times* (March 22,1970), p. 22.

Burridge, Kenelm O.L., "A Tangu Game," *Man,* vol. 57 (1957): 88 - 89.

Cantril, Hadley, *The Psychology of Social Movements,* New York: Wiley, 1963.

Carroll, John B., *Language, Thought, and Reality: Selected Writings of Benjamin Lee Whorf,* Cambridge, Mass.: MIT Press, 1956.

Caplow, Theodore, *Two Against One: Coalition in Triads,* Englewood Cliffs, N.J.: Prentice-Hall, 1969.

Campbell, A. and H. Schuman, "Racial Attitudes in Fifteen American Cities," in *Supplementary Studies for the National Advisory Commission on Civil Disorders,* Washington, D.C.: Government Printing Office, 1968.

Cantril, Hadley, with Hazel Gaudet and Herta Herzog, *Invasion from Mars,* Princeton, N.J.: Princeton University Press, 1947.

Caplan, Nathan, "The New Ghetto Man: A Review of Recent Empirical Studies," *Journal of Social Issues,* vol. 26, no. 1 (1970): 59 - 73.

Chagnon, Napoleon A., *Yanomamö: The Fierce People,* New York: Holt, Rinehart and Winston, 1968.

Chesler, Phyllis, *Women and Madness,* New York: Doubleday, 1972.

Cirino, Robert, *Don't Blame the People,* Los Angeles: Diversity Press, 1971.

Clausen, John A., "The Organism and Socialisation," *Social Behaviour,* vol. 8 (1967): 243 - 52.

Coleman, James, *et al., Equality of Educational Opportunity,* Washington, D.C., U.S. Government Printing Office, 1972.

Comte, Auguste, *The Positive Philosophy,* trans, and ed-, Harriet Martineau, London: Bell, 1915.

Coleman, James S., *Abnormal Psychology and Modern Life,* Glenview, III.: Scott, Foresman, 1972.

Coleman, James S., *The Adolescent Society,* New York: Free Press, 1961.

Cooley, Charles Horton, *Human Nature and the Social Order,* New York: Schocken, 1964.

Cooley, Charles Horton, *Social Organisation: A Study of the Larger Mind,* Glencoe, III.: Free Press, 1956.

Coser, Lewis, *The Functions of Social Conflict,* New York: Free Press, 1956.

Cohen, Jerry and William S. Murphy, *Burn, Baby, Burn,* New York: Dutton, 1966.

Cook, Fred J., "Madison Avenue in Uniform," *The Warfare State,* New York: Macmillan, 1962.

Cutler, Stephen J., "The Availability of Personal Transportation, Residential Location, and Life Satisfaction Among the Aged," *journal of Gerontology,* vol. 27 (1972): 383 - 89.

Davis, Kingsley, *Human Society,* New York: Macmillan, 1937.

Davis, Kingsley, "The Sociology of Prostitution," *American Sociological Review,* vol. 2,1937: 744 - 755.

Davis, Kingsley, *Human Society,* New York: Macmillan, 1948.

Dixon, Marlene, "Why Women's Liberation?" in Elsie Adams and Mary Louise Briscoe, eds., *Up Against the Wall, Mother* .... Beverly Hills: Glencoe Press, 1971.

Dixon, Marlene, "Why Women's Liberation?" in Elsie Adams and Mary Louise Briscoe, eds.. *Up* Against *the Wall, Mother*.. . . Beverly Hills: Glencoe, 1971.

Dreitzel, Hans Peter, ed., *The Social Organisation of Health,* New York: Macmillan,1971.

Durkheim, Emile, *The Rules of Sociological Method,* Chicago: University of Chicago Press, 1938.

Durkheim, Emile, *Suicide* (1897), trans. J.A. Spaulding and G. Simpson, New York: Free Press, 1951.

Durkheim, Emile, *Suicide: A Study in Sociology* (1897). trans, by John A. Spaulding and G. Simpson, New York: Free Press, 1951.

Dundes, Alan, *Every Man His Way: Readings in Cultural Anthropology,* Englewood Cliffs, N.J.: Prentice-Hall, 1968.

Durkheim, Emile, *The Division of Labour in Society* (1893), trans., George Simpson, Glencoe, III.: Free Press, 1947.

Edmund Dahlström, "Analysis of the Debate on Sex Roles," in Edmund Dahlström, ed., *The Changing Roles of Men and Women,* Boston: Beacon Press, 1967.

Educational Broadcasting Corporation, *Bill Mayers' journal,* "A Question of Impeachment," 1974.

Ehrilich, Carol, "The Male's Socialisation Burden: The Place of Women in Marriage and Family Texts," *Journal of Marriage and the Family,* vol. 33, no. 3 (August 1971): 421 - 30.

Eisenstadt, S.N., "Archetypal Patterns of Youth," *Daedalus* (Winter 1962): 28 - 46.

Ember, Carol R., and Melvin Ember, *Anthropology,* New York: Appleton, 1973.

Erikson, Erik, *Childhood and Society,* New York: Norton, 1950.

Erikson, Erik, *Young Man Luther,* New York: Norton, 1958.

Erikson, Erik, *Identity: Youth and Crisis,* New York: Norton, 1968.

Etzioni, Amitai, "Policy Research," *American Sociologist,* vol. 16 (1971): 8 -12.

Farb, Peter, *Word Play,* New York: Knopf, 1973.

Farrell, Warren, "Guidelines for Consciousness Raising," *Ms.* (March 1972): 12-15, 116 - 117.

Fasteau, Marc, "Why aren't we talking?" *Ms.* (July 1972): 163.

Fennessey, James, "Some probabilities and possibilities in related research," *Social Science Research,* vol. 1, no. 4 (December 1972): 359 - 83.

Fesunger, L.A., Henry Riecken, and Stanley Schacter, *When Prophecy Fails,* Minneapolis: University of Minnesota Press, 1956.

Field, Mark G. and Karin I. Flynn, "Worker, Mother, Housewife: Soviet Women Today," in Georgene H. Seward and Robert C. Williamson, eds., *Sex Roles in Changing Society,* New York: Random House, 1970.

Firestone, Shulamith, "One American Feminism," in Peter I. Rose, ed., *The Study of Society* 3rd ed., New York: Random House, 1973.

Flacks, Richard, "The Liberated Generation: An Exploration of the Roots of Student Protest," *journal of Social Issues,* vol. 23, no. 3 (July 1967); 52 - 75.

Fox, Robin, "The Cultural Animal," *Encounters,* vol. 35 (July 1970): 31 -42.

Fogelson, Robert M., "Violence and Grievances: Reflections on the 1960sRiots," *Journal of Social Issues,* vol. 26, no. 1 (Winter 1970): 141 - 63

Freidson, Eliot, *Profession of Medicine: A Study of the Sociology of Applied Knowledge,* New York: Dodd, Mead, 1970.

Freud, Sigmund, *Civilisation and Its Discontents,* New York: Norton, 1961.

Friedan, Betty, *The Feminine Mystique,* New York: Dell, 1963.

Friedan, Betty, "The problem that has no name," in Elsie Adams and Mary Louise Briscoe, eds., *Up Against the Wall, Mother* .... Beverly Hills: Glencoe Press, 1971.

Fromm, Erich, *Escape from Freedom,* New York: Avon, 1941.

Freeman Jo, "The Origins of the Women's Liberation Movement," *American Journal of Sociology,* vol. 73, no. 4 (1973): 792 - 811.

Friedan, Betty, *The Feminine Mystique,* New York: Dell, 1963.

Furth, Hans G., *Piaget and Knowledge;* Englewood Cliffs, N.J.: Prentice-Hall, 1969.

Fulbright, J. William, *The Pentagon Propaganda Machine,* New York: Liveright, 1970.

Gans, Herbert J., *The Urban Villagers,* New York: Free Press, 1962.

George, Katherine, "The Civilised West Looks at Primitive Africa: 1400-1800, A Study in Ethnocentrism," Isis, vol. 49 (1958): 62 - 72. (Also in Dundes, 1968.)

Gergen, John A., "Physiological Aspects of Sexual Behaviour: Genetics, Hormones, and the Central Nervous System," in Clark E. Vincent, *ed., Human Sexuality in Medical Education and Practice,* Springfield, III.: Charles C. Thomas, 1968.

Goode William J. and Paul K. Hatte, *Methods in Social Research,* New York: McGraw-Hill, 1952.

Gouldner, Alvin W., "Anti-minotaur, the myth of a value-free sociology," *Journal of Social Problems,* vol. 9, no. 3 (1962): 199 - 213.

Goodman, Mary Ellen, *The Individual and Culture,* Homewood, III.: Dorsey Press, 1967.

Gove, Walter R. and Jeannette F. Tudor, "Adult Sex Roles and Mental Illness," in Huber, 1973.

Goodwin, John, *The Mating Trade,* New York: Doubleday, 1973.

Green, Richard, *Sexual Identity Conflict in Children and Adults,* New York: Basic Books, 1974.

Gutman, David, "The Hunger of Old Men," *Transaction* (November-December 1971).

Harold Finestone, "Cats, Kicks, and Colour" *Social Problems,* vol 5, no. 1 (1957): 3-13.

Hall, Edward T., *Vie Silent Language,* Garden City, N.Y.: Doubleday, 1959.

Hall, Edward T., *The Hidden Dimension,* Garden City. N.Y.: Doubleday, 1966.

Haring, Douglas, ed., *Personal Character and Cultural Milieu,* rev. ed., Syracuse, N.Y.: Syracuse University Press, 1949.

Hampton, John L., "Determinants of Psychosexual Orientation," in Frank A. Beacon, ed., *Sex and Behaviour,* New York: Wiley, 1965.

Harlow, Harry F. and R.Z. Zimmerman, "Affectional Responses in the Infant Monkey," *Science,* vol. 130 (1959): 421 - 32.

Harlow, Harry F. and Margaret Harlow, "The Effect of Rearing Conditions on Behaviour," in John Money, ed., *Sex Research, New Developments,* New York: Holt, Rinehart and Winston, 1965.

Hartely, Ruth, "A Developmental View of Sex Role Identifications," in Bruch J. Biddle and EJ. Thomas, eds., *Role Theory: Concepts and Research,* New York: Wiley, 1966.

Hare, A. Paul, *Handbook of Small Group Research,* New York: Free Press, 1962.

Hennessey, Bernard, *Public Opinion,* 2nd ed., Belmont, Calif.: Wadsworth, 1970.

Henry, Jules, *Culture Against Man,* New York: Vintage, 1965.

Henry, Jules, *Culture Against Man,* New York: Random House, 1963.

Hersh, Seymour, "My Lai 4," *Harpers,* vol. 240 (1970): 53ff.

Hecker, J.F.C., *The Epidemics of the Middle Ages,* London: Woodfall, 1844.

Hill, Reuben, *The Family: A Dramatic Interpretation,* New York: Holt, Rinehart Winston, 1938.

Hinds, William Alfred, *American Communities,* Secaucus, N.J.: Citadel, 1973.

Horowitz, Irving Louis, "The Life and Death of Project Camelot," *Transaction,* vol. 3 (November- December 1965): 3-7.

Hoult, Thomas Ford, *Dictionary of Modern Sociology,* Totowa, N.J.: Littlefield, Adams, 1969.

Holter, Harriet, *Sex Roles and Social Structure,* Oslo: Universitets Forlaget, 1970.

Horner, Matina S., "Fall: Bright Women," *Psychology Today,* vol- 3, no. 6 (November 1969): 36ff.

Horner, Matina S., "Toward an understanding of achievement related conflicts in women," *Journal of Social Issues,* vol. 28, no. 2 (1972): 157 -75.

Homans, George, *The Human Group,* New York: Harcourt Brace Jovanovich, 1950.

Hoover, Eleanor Links, "The Age of Encounter," *Human Behaviour* (January-February 1972): 8 - 15.

Holborn, Hajo, *A History of Modern Germany,* 1850 - 1945, New York: Knopf, 1969.

Hoult, Thomas Ford, *A Dictionary of Modern Sociology,* Totowa, N.J.: Littlefield, Adams, 1969.

Huber, Joan, ed., *Changing Women in a Changing Society,* Chicago: University of Chicago Press, 1973.

Huxley, Aldous, *The Devils of Loudur,* New York: Harper and Row, 1952. Jaco, E. Gartly, ed., *Patients, Physicians, and Illness,* 2nd ed., New York: Free Press, 1967.

Jarrell, Randall, "A Sad Heart at the Supermarket," in Norman Jacobs, ed., *Culture for the Millions,* Princeton, N.J.: Van Nostrand, 1961.

Joffe, Carol, "Sex Role Socialisation and the Nursery School: As the Twig is Bent," *Journal of Marriage and the Family,* vol. 33, no. 3 (August 1971): 467-75.

Kagan, Jerome, "Acquisition and Significance of Sex Typing and Sex Role Identity," in M. Hoffman and L.W. Hoffman, eds., *Review of Child Development Research,* vol. 1, New York: Russell Sage Foundation, 1964.

Kanter, Rosabeth M., "Commitment and social organisation: A Study of commitment mechanisms in Utopian communities," *American Sociological Review,* vol. 33, no. 4 (August 1968): 499 - 517.

Kanter, Rosabeth M., *Commitments and Community: Communes and Utopias in Sociological Perspective,* Cambridge, Mass.: Harvard University Press, 1972.

Katz, Elihu and Paul Lazarsfeld, *Personal influence,* New York, Free Press, 1955.

Keith, Jeff, "My Own Men's Liberation," *Win* (September 1,1971): 22 - 26.

Keller, Suzanne, "The Family in the Kibbutz: What Lessons for Us?" in Michael Curtis and Mordecai S. Chertoff, eds., *Israel - Social Structure and Change*, New Brunswick, N.J.: Transaction Books, 1973.

Keniston, Kenneth, "The Sources of Student Dissent," *Journal of Social Issues,* vol. 23, no. 3 (July 1967): 108 - 37.

Kinkade, Kathleen, *A Walden Two Experiment,* New York: Morrow, 1973.

Kluckhohn, Clyde, "Universal Categories of Culture," in Sol Tax, ed., *Anthropology Today Selections,* Chicago: University of Chicago Press, 1962.

Kohl, Herbert R., *The Open Classroom,* New York: Vintage, 1969.

Kohlberg, Lawrence, "Moral and Religious Education and the Public Schools: A Developmental View," In T. Sizer, ed., *Religion and Public Education,* Boston: Houghton Mifflin, 1967.

Kohlberg, Lawrence and Card Gilligan, "The Adolescent as a Philosopher: The Discovery of the Self in a Postconventional World," *Daedalus* (Fall 1971): 1051 - 86.

Kohn, Melvin L., "Social Class and Parent-Child Relations: An Interpretation," *American journal of Sociology,* vol. 68 (1963): 471 -80.

Komarovsky, Mirra, "Cultural Contradictions and Sex Roles: The Masculine Case," in Huber, 1973.

Komarovsky, Mirra, *Blue-Collar Marriage,* New York: Vintage, 1967.

Komarovsky, Mirra, *The Unemployed Man and His Family: The Effect of Unemployment upon the Status of the Man in Fifty-nine Families* (1940), New York: Arno Press, 1971.

Kuhn, Thomas S., *The Structure of Scientific Revolutions,* 2nd ed., Chicago: University of Chicago Press, 1970.

Labovitz, Sanford and Robert Hagedorn, *Introduction to Social Research,* New York: McGraw Hill, 1971.

Lawson, Donna, *Brothers and Sisters All over This Land,* New York; Praeger, 1972.

Labby, David, "Old Glory and the New," *Natural History* (June-July 1973): 26-37.

Lee, Dorothy, "Codification of Reality: Lineal and Nonlineal," *Psychosonatic Medicine,* vol. 12 (1950): 89 - 97.

Leavitt, Ruby R., "Women in Other Cultures," in Vivian Gornick and Barbara K. Morgan, eds., *Women in Sexist Society.* New York: New American Library, 1972.

Lederer, Wolfgang, *The Fear of Women,* New York: Harcourt Brace Jovanovich, 1968.

Lee, Alfred M., and Elizabeth Lee, *The Fine Art of Propaganda,* New York: Farrar, Strauss, 1939.

Linton, Ralph, *The Study of Man,* New York: Appleton, 1947.

Little, Roger W., "Buddy relations in combat performances," in Oscar Grusky and George A. Miller, eds., *The Sociology of Organisations,* New York: Free Press, 1970.

Lynd, Robert S., *Knowledge for What?* Princeton: Princeton University Press, 1939.

Lynd, Robert S., *Middletown in Transition: A Study in Cultural Conflicts,* New York: Harcourt Brace Jovanovich, 1937.

Lynd, Robert S. and Helen M. Lynd, *Middletown,* New York: Harcourt Brace Jovanovich, 1929.

Marx, Karl, *Capital,* ed., Friedrich Engels, New York: International, 1967.

Marx, Karl, and Friedrich Engels, *The Communist Manifesto,* ed., Samuel H. Beer, New York: Appleton, 1955.

Mathematica and the Institute for Research on Poverty, "Final Report of the New Jersey Graduated Work Incentive Experiment," Princeton, N.J. and Madison, Wis., unpublished report, June 1974.

McLuhan, Marshall, *Understanding Media: The Extensions of Man,* New York: Signet, 1964.

Melville, Keith, "A Measure of Contentment," *The Sciences* (December 1973): 12-15.

Melvill, Keith, "A measure of contentment," *The Sciences* (December 1973): 12 -15.

Merton, Robert K., *Social Theory and Social Structure,* New York: Free Press, 1957.

Merton, Robert K., *Social Theory and Social Structure,* New York: Free Press, 1968.

Mezzrow, Mezz and Bernard Wolfe, *Really the Blues,* New York: Random House, 1972.

Mead, George Herbert, *Mind, Self and Society,* Chicago: University of Chicago Press, 1934.

Mead, Margaret, *Sex and Temperament in Three Primitive Societies,* New York: Morrow, 1935.

Mead, Margaret, "A New Style of Aging," in *Christianity and Crisis* (November 15,1971): 240 - 43.

Merton, Robert K., *Social Theory and Social Structure,* New York: Free Press, 1968.

Michelson, William, "The reconciliation of 'subjective' and 'objective' data on physical environment in the community," 68th Annual Meeting of ASA, August 27 - 30, 1973.

Milgram, Stanley, "Some conditions of obedience and disobedience to authority," *Human Relations,* vol. 18 (1965): 57 - 76.

Milgram, Stanley, *Obedience to Authority: An Experimental View,* New York: Harper & Row, 1973.

Mosteller F., and Daniel P. Moynihan, eds., *On Equality of Educational Opportunity,* New York: Vintage, 1972.

Motwani, Kewal, *A Critique of Empiricism in Sociology,* New York: Allied, 1967.

Moore, Wilbert E., "Occupational Socialisation," in David A. Goslin, ed., *Handbook of Socialisation Theory and Research,* New York: Rand McNally, 1969.

Moskos, Charles C, Jr., *The American Enlisted Man,* New York: Russell Sage, 1970.

Murdock, George Peter, "The Common Denominator of Cultures," in Ralph Linton, ed., *The Science of Man in World Crisis,* New York: Columbia University Press, 1945.

Myrdal, Gunnar, "How scientific are the social sciences?" *Bulletin of Atomic Scientists* (January 1973).

Myrdal, Gunnar, *Objectivity in Social Research,* New York: Pantheon, 1969.

Myrdal, Gunnar, *An American Dilemma,* New York: Harper & Row, 1944.

Newcomb, T.M., *Personality and Social Change,* New York: Holt, Rinehart and Winston, 1943.

Newcomb, T.M., "Persistence and regression of changed attitudes: long-range studies," *Journal of Social Issues,* vol. 19 (1963): 3 - 14.

Neill, A.S., *Summerhill,* New York: Hart, 1960.

Newcomb, Theodore, "Attitude development as a function of reference groups: The Bennington Study," in G.E. Swanson, T.M. Newcomb and E.L. Hartley, eds., *Readings in Social Psychology,* New York: Holt, Rinehart and Winston, 1958.

Newcomb, Theodore, *et al., Persistence and Change: Bennington College and Its Students After 25 Years,* New York: Wiley, 1967.

Noyes and McAndrew, "Is This What Schools Are For?" *Saturday Review* (December 21,1968), in Silberman, 1971.

Parsons, Talcott, *The Social System,* New York: Free Press, 1951.

Parsons, Talcott, "The School Class as a Social System: Some of the Functions in American Society," *Harvard Educational Review,* vol. *29* (Fall 1969): 297 -318.

Phillips, J.L., Jr., *The Origins of the Intellect: Piaget's Theory,* San Francisco: Freeman, 1969.

Piaget, Jean and Barbara Inhelder, *The Psychology of the Child,* New York: Basic Books, 1969.

Rainwater, Lee, "The Lower Class: Health, Illness, and Medical Institutions," in Irving Deutscher and E. Thompson, *Among the Poor,* New York: Basic Books, 1968.

Reed, Piers Paul, *Alive: The Story of the Andes Survivors,* Boston: Lippincott, 1974.

Ritzer, George, *Issues, Debates and Controversies; An Introduction to Sociology,* Boston: Allyn & Bacon, 1972.

Riley, Matilda White and Anne Foner *et al. Aging and Society,* vol. 1, "An Inventory of Research Findings," New York: Russell Sage Foundation, 1968.

Riley, Beth Hess, and Marcia L. Toby, "Socialisation for the Middle and Later Years," in David A. Goslin, ed., *Handbook of Socialisation Theory and Research,* New York: Rand McNally, 1969.

Roethlisberger, F.J. and William Dickson, *Management and the Worker,* Cambridge, Mass.: Harvard University Press, 1939.

Rogers, Carl, *On Encounter Groups,* New York: Harper & Row, 1970.

Ruesch, Hans, *Top of the World,* New York: Harper & Row, 1951.

Saint-Simon, Henri de, *Social Organisation: The Science of Man,* trans. and ed., Felix Markham, New York: Harper & Row, 1964.

Scheff, Thomas J., *Being Mentally Ill,* Chicago: Aldine, 1966.

Scarf, Maggie, "He and She: The Sex Hormones and Behaviour," *The New York Times Magazine* (May 7,1972): 30 ff.

Schneider, Joseph W., and Sally H. Hacker, "Sex-Role Imagery and Use of the Generic 'Man', in Introductory Texts: A Case in the Sociology of Sociology," *The American Sociologist,* vol. 8, (1973): 12 - 18.

Shills, Edward, "The Calling of Sociefogy." In Talcott Parsons, *et al.,* eds., *Society,* New York: Free Press, 1961.

Shaw, Clifford R., *Jack-Roller: A Delinquent Boy's Own Story,* Chicago: University of Chicago Press, 1966.

Shils, Edward A., "Primary Groups in the American Army," in R.K. Merton and P.F. Lazarsfeld, *Continuities in Social Research,* New York: Free Press, 1950.

Shils, Edward A. and Morris Janowitz, "Cohesion and Disintegration in the Wehrmacht in World War II," *Public Opinion Quarterly* (Summer 1948): 280 -315.

Simon, Julian L., *Basic Research Methods in Social Science,* New York: Random House, 1969.

Silberman, Charles E., *Crisis in the Classroom,* New York: Random House, 1971.

Simmel, Georg, *The Sociology of Georg Simmel,* trans, and ed., Kurt H. Wolff, New York: Free Press, 1950.

Sjoberg, Gideon, ed., *Ethics, Politics, and Social Research,* Cambridge, Mass: Schenkman, 1967.

Slater, Philip, *The Pursuit of Loneliness: Ameritan Culture at the Breaking Point,* Boston: Beacon Press, 1970.

Snow, C.P., *The Search, New York:* Scribner, 1958. Herbert Spencer, *The Study of Society,* New York: Appleton, 1877.

Spencer, Herbert, *The Principles of Sociology,* New York: Appleton, 1898.

Spitz, R.A., "The Psychogenic Diseases of Infancy: An Attempt at Their Etiotogical Classification," *Psychoanalytic Study of the Child,* vol. 6 (1951): 255-75.

Stanton, Alfred H., and Morris S. Schwartz, *The Mental Hospital,* New York: Basic Books, 1954.

Stouffer, Samuel A., *Communities, Conformity and Civil Liberties,* New York: Doubleday, 1955.

Stone, L. Joseph and Joseph Church, *Childhood and Adolescence: A Psychology of the Growing Person,* New York: Random House, 1973.

Sumner, William Graham, *Folkways,* Boston: Ginn, 1906.

Töennies, Ferdinand, *Community and Society* (1887), trans. and ed., Charles A. Loomis, East, Lansing, Mich.: Michigan State University Press, 1957.

Ullman, L.P. and L. Krasner, *A Psychological Approach to Abnormal Behaviour,* Englewood Cliffs, N.J.: Prentice-Hall, 1969.

Walker, James in Alan Dundes, *Every Man His Way: Readings in Cultural Anthropology,* Englewood Cliffs, N.J.: Prentice-Hall, 1968.

Watson, John B., *Behaviourism* (1924), New York: Norton, 1970.

Weber, Max, *The Theory of Social and Economic Organisation,* trans., A.N. Henderson and Talcott Parsons, New York: Free Press, 1964.

Webb, Eugene, *et al., Unobtrusive Measures: Non-reactive Research in the Social Sciences,* Chicago: Rand McNally, 1966.

Weitzman, Lenore J., Deborah Eifler, Elizabeth Hokada, and Catherine Ross, "Sex Role Socialisation in Picture Books for Preschool Children," *American Journal of Sociology,* vol. 77 (May 1972): 1125 - 50.

Whyte, William Foote, *Street Corner Society: The Social Structure of an Italiati Slum,* rev. ed., Chicago: University of Chicago Press, 1955.

Whiting, J.W.M., "Effects of Climate on Certain Cultural Practices," in W.H. Goodenough, ed., *Explorations in Cultural Anthropology,* New York: McGraw-Hill, 1969.

Whyte, William H., Jr., *The Organisation Man,* New York: Anchor, 1957.

Wiiliams, Robin, *American Society,* 3rd ed., New York: Knopf, 1970.

Yankelovich, Daniel, *Yankelovich Youth Study,* copyright © 1973 by the JDR, 3rd Fund.

Yalom, Irvin D. and Morton A. Lieberman, "A Study of Encounter Group Casualties," *Archives of General Psychiatry,* vol. 25 (July 1971): 16 - 30.

Zablocki, Benjamin David, *The Joyful Community,* Baltimore, Md.: Penguin, 1971.

Zimbardo, Philip G., "Pathology of imprisonment," *Society,* vol. 9 (April 1972): 4-8.